DENISE

EDUCATION IS A HABITAT
FOR HEROES!

FOR

Rego

Praise for WHOLE

Many people talk about teacher burnout, but few have taken the time to really understand the problem and propose solutions. Rex and his team have. Highly recommended.
—**Tony Wagner**, best-selling author of *The Global Achievement Gap* and *Creating Innovators*

Growing up poor in Hell's Kitchen, New York, with a single mother who immigrated to the US at a young age, education was both critical and challenging. I knew it would be the most important factor in my ability to succeed in life. As the Chief Education Evangelist at Google, or any of the other organizations I am involved with, my mission is to give the millions of students who are growing up under similar conditions the opportunity to succeed. *WHOLE* is a bold book that successfully takes on the challenge students are facing today. It provides a roadmap for administrators and teachers to bolster teacher well-being and help students thrive.
—**Jaime Casap**, Chief Education Evangelist, Google

Too often technology becomes one more thing teachers must learn, which adds more work and stress. If applied properly, technology should instead reduce the load and free a teacher to engage more with each of their students in higher-quality interactions. I recommend reading *WHOLE* to think through ways to reduce teacher stress and improve their health and well-being. Less-stressed teachers are key to unlocking learning.
—**Michael B. Horn**, coauthor of *Choosing College* and *Blended* and cofounder of the Clayton Christensen Institute

In order to learn optimally, children need to feel safe and cared for. Teachers want to provide environments that give students what they need to thrive, but often find themselves so overworked and highly stressed, that they're unable to be the kinds of teachers they set out to be. *WHOLE* looks at the current challenges and obstacles our teachers and schools are facing, how they are impacting health, mental health, and the vitality for learning, and offers practical suggestions for bringing wholeness into our schools.
—**Tina Payne Bryson**, PhD, LCSW, co-author of *The Whole-Brain Child*, *No-Drama Discipline*, *The Yes Brain*, and *The Power of Showing Up*

Finally a book on conscious schools!! Schools have become places that demand our children to conform and perform. *WHOLE* does a wonderful job of exposing how this pressure is shutting down students and raising the stress on teachers. Neither can perform under these conditions. The stories and research *WHOLE* shares of schools that have broken out of this cycle provide hope and a path forward for your school and your classroom.
—**Dr. Shefali Tsabary**, acclaimed speaker, clinical psychologist, and author of *The Awakened Family*

Nothing is more important to me as a Superintendent than graduating students who are healthy, happy, and well-prepared for life. However, I'm concerned over the trend we are seeing with the levels of stress and anxiety our students and teachers increasingly experience. *WHOLE* has provided us with new insights into the problem and tools that have allowed us to launch a student-led, district-supported movement to reverse the trend. Every Superintendent and teacher needs to read *WHOLE*. It's the first book for educators to comprehensively tackle the mental health crisis we face and provide effective strategies and tools to make our schools safe havens for learning.

    —**David Tebo**, Superintendent, Hamilton Community Schools, Hamilton, Michigan

Traditional education prioritizes the transfer of information by teachers and the passive consumption of that information by students. It is grounded in uniformity and compliance. Yet, what students need to be successful in a rapidly changing world is creativity, curiosity, and adaptability. Our educational system is out of step with the needs of today's students. Schools are producing students who are dependent, passive, and disengaged. The lack of engagement, personalization, and human connection in many classrooms has negative impacts on both teachers and students. *WHOLE* examines how we are harming the mental and physical health of teachers and students with our current approach to education. *WHOLE* is a fascinating book that explores neuroscience, wellness, and the work-life balance to shine a light on what is possible in education if we are willing to question the status quo.

    —**Catlin Tucker**, Google Certified Innovator, best-selling author, international trainer, and keynote speaker

Once again Rex Miller has nudged and jolted us into understanding the complexities of teaching and health. Mixing stories with brain research and new understandings of how our bodies respond to stress, Rex offers insights and recommendations that will help teachers as they pursue their passion. Most importantly, as those teachers walk alongside their students, they will flourish together.

    —**Jonathan Eckert**, Professor of Education, Baylor University, and author of *Leading Together: Teachers and Administrators Improving Student Outcomes*

WHOLE artfully weaves together the science of the brain and nervous system, brave and inspiring stories from outliers, and plain old mindful common sense. The resulting "whole cloth" shows how better care for teachers is the most cost-effective strategy for improving their well-being and the health of our schools, resulting in healthier, happier, and better-educated children. This book is an infectious plea to restore passion and love in our schools, from authors whose own passion and love shine through.

    —**James Gimian**, Executive Director, Foundation for a Mindful Society

WHOLE recognizes and acknowledges the soulful (full of soul) work done by those who answer the call to teach. The unfortunate reality for many such people is that teaching as a profession is at odds with teaching as a calling. *WHOLE* honors, respects, and shows how to reunite the profession with the calling. If you're interested in the topic of education, and we all should be, this book serves as a beacon of hope, that taking care of our teachers is a critical part of taking care of our children and therefore taking care of our future.

    —**Andy Smallman**, Founding Director, Puget Sound Community School

Incorporating up-to-date scientific findings on stress, neuroscience, neuroimaging, and brain functioning, Rex Miller has launched an innovative path for schoolteachers and administrators to make a difference in students' lives. Written with a creative spirit and sharp analytical thinking, *WHOLE* offers educators a path for hope, optimism, and rejuvenation for the stress-ridden classroom setting.

—**Dr. Jay Faber**, Amen Clinic

School districts across the country are caught between improving academic outcomes and meeting the higher social and emotional needs of students. District 59 has been a pioneer in adopting social and emotional health (SEH) as an integrated part of learning. *WHOLE* is the first manual to capture these new social and emotional realities. *WHOLE* provides a science-based roadmap for us and others to continue meeting the growing needs of our students and community.

—**Art Fessler**, Ed.D, Superintendent, Community Consolidated School District 59, Elk Grove Village, CA

WHOLE

WHAT TEACHERS NEED TO HELP
STUDENTS THRIVE

WHOLE

WHAT TEACHERS NEED TO HELP
STUDENTS THRIVE

REX MILLER

BILL LATHAM

KEVIN BAIRD, AND

MICHELLE KINDER

JB JOSSEY-BASS™
A Wiley Brand

Published by Jossey-Bass
A Wiley Brand
111 River Street, Hoboken NJ 07030
www.josseybass.com

Jossey-Bass books and products are available through most bookstores. To contact Jossey-Bass directly call our Customer Care Department within the U.S. at 800-956-7739, outside the U.S. at 317-572-3986, or fax 317-572-4002.

Wiley also publishes its books in a variety of electronic formats and by print-on-demand. Some material included with standard print versions of this book may not be included in e-books or in print-on-demand. For more information about Wiley products, visit www.wiley.com.

Library of Congress Cataloging-in-Publication Data is available for this title

Hardback 9781119651031

Cover image: She creates such a happy classroom © STEEX/Getty Images
              Blank blackboard © kyoshino/Getty Images
Cover design: Michael Lagocki
Interior illustrations: Michael Lagocki

Printed in the United States of America

FIRST EDITION

Hb   V408061_021220

To Mrs. Stavoe, my first grade teacher; Mr. Roubidoux, my eighth grade teacher; Professor Clifford Christians; and my mom. These were the four guiding lights and inspirations throughout my education. It is because of them I maintain the belief we can and must do our very best to give every child a similar love for learning, throughout life.

CONTENTS

Foreword   *xiii*

Foreword   *xv*

Acknowledgments   *xvii*

About the Authors   *xxiii*

PART 1   **DYING TO TEACH**   **1**

Chapter 1 Dying to Teach   3

Chapter 2 Schools Are Killing More than Creativity   11

Chapter 3 Fear Is the Off Switch   24

Chapter 4 The Body Remembers   34

Chapter 5 Having the Stress Conversation in Your School   50

PART 2   **CHANGING THE STORY OF EDUCATION**   **65**

Chapter 6 To Change the Story   67

Chapter 7 The Early Childhood Challenge: Pay Me
               Now or Pay Me Later   80

Chapter 8 The Teacher Athlete   93

Chapter 9 Are Schools the New Field Hospitals?   103

Chapter 10 "Shots Fired"   116

Chapter 11 Do Healthy Buildings Improve
               Learning?   131

Chapter 12 The Heart-to-Head Connection:
Managing Emotions to Support the Brain   142

Chapter 13 Community Before Curriculum   153

PART 3   **PUTTING INTO PRACTICE**   **167**

Chapter 14 Waking the Dead: The Sleep Solution   169

Chapter 15 The Magic of Movement and Mini-Breaks   182

Chapter 16 Physical Education: The Gathering Storm   194

Chapter 17 How Small Changes Make Big Impacts   209

Chapter 18 Leading Change: From Compliance to
Ownership   225

Chapter 19 What Teachers Really Need to Help
Students Thrive   238

Appendix A: Contributors   *252*

Appendix B: Sleep Hygiene Tips   *263*

Works Cited and Further Reading   *265*

Index   *283*

FOREWORD

Many books have been written about how and why the industrial model of education fell out of step with the times. These books explain why education now kills creativity and creates growing inequities in the system. But *WHOLE* is the first book to examine the psychological damage to teachers and students in a system that no longer reflects society's demands upon it. And teachers are caught in the middle. On the one hand, they are expected to achieve higher standardized test scores. At the same time, they must also work with kids who are emotionally not ready to learn.

Yet, many school leaders just hope teachers and students will just somehow grit it through, that teachers will just figure out how to get kids to grade. That is a recipe for teacher burnout; it will assure more students get left behind. Schools that remain there will not achieve the excellence they can and must deliver if America's schools meet the realities of the twenty-first century.

The University of North Texas Dallas was specifically designed to address those new realities. More than 80% of the students we serve are classified as low-income. But the challenges are deeper than economic. Most are students of color, living in vulnerable neighborhoods, and characterized as under-resourced. Many are learning English as a second language. Children who live in these communities *experience some of the most turbulent, volatile, and traumatic experiences in life.*

That's why schools are becoming the new field hospitals—think M★A★S★H—in America. What kind of services and training and support would people need to work in a field hospital? Because *WHOLE* digs deep into that question, it gives us a field manual on how to prepare teachers for those conditions. This book tells us how to develop resilient teachers with a new sense of mission.

I was able to participate in the unique process that produced *WHOLE*. And I believe we all built a bridge enabling your school and community to lift the health and happiness of teachers and students. I believe we live in a golden moment; we *can* shift the social narrative and priorities.

But doing so means that schools need to re-mobilize around making sure the collective central nervous system of the team of adults in the building is being cared for. After all, these are human beings! They have brains and bodies. Our society must rise to preserve and protect the collective well-being of the humans charged with such a high calling. We must attend to them with urgency, genuine concern, and excellence of care for the WHOLE person.

Our future requires that.

—Dr. John Gasko,
Special Advisor to the President of UNT Dallas,
Dallas

FOREWORD

Whatever good things we build end up building us.

—Jim Rohn

Most of us know the pace of technological, social, and cultural change steamrolls many school districts and classrooms. But, you may not know teaching has become the fourth most stressful occupation in America. *WHOLE* captures the story of a revolution in education as schools respond to these new realities. Bottom line: We must take care of the whole teacher: body, mind, and soul in order to engage the whole student. That requires the courage to reimagine roles, skills, support, and new environments that will adapt to increasing demands.

Teaching is tough. Today, more than ever, educators must prepare learners for jobs and technologies that don't yet exist. The speed of change requires teachers to train students for a society that has not even arrived yet. That means educators must have spaces that are flexible, that can adapt to the tsunami racing below the surface toward our shorelines. That means those in my business must design and build the innovative spaces that inspire every stakeholder in the

Every kid is one caring adult away from being a success story.

—Josh Shipp

learning process—teachers, students, administrators, parents, legislators, and every member of the larger community.

The magic of learning requires meaningful connections between students and adults who care. But too many of today's parents are absent or overwhelmed. While we must try to reach and support them, we must also locate, train, and equip teachers who can step into that gap *now*. Shipp is right; one caring adult can make the difference between failure and success. We all know that; you and I can name the teacher who made that difference for us.

That's what makes the *WHOLE* story so exciting. The book provides examples of teachers and schools that dared to break out of outdated mindsets. But, the reader will also see the critical importance of the right type, size, and quality of learning space. As Rex Miller told us in a previous book, *Change Your Space: Change Your Culture*, designed space carries the power to build a culture that equips students to move competently and confidently into the rapidly approaching future. Welcoming spaces, open areas for relationship building, vibrant colors, and natural light are some of the elements that cultivate a trusting environment and a positive school atmosphere.

The greatest wealth is health.

—*Virgil*

Finally, this book addresses the holistic experience for all users. Designers are focusing more intentionally on the design of school spaces and schedules. For example, we know that casual interaction and cross-disciplinary activities improve the learning experience for everyone. Designs that provide designated spaces for reflection and relaxation, loud group activities, and individual quiet work, as well as brain breaks and movement, can alleviate increasing demands and stress levels.

Throughout my career with DLR Group, I've had the pleasure of meeting educators from around the world. I'm constantly in awe of their passion for nurturing young minds and for their devotion to the profession. *WHOLE* helps the design world to visualize how we can better support those educators, and those they teach, with space that allows the human spirit to soar!

—Jim French,
DLR Group Senior Principal,
Kansas

ACKNOWLEDGMENTS

WHOLE grew out of a cohort of educators and experts who were not ready to go home after finishing our earlier book, *Humanizing the Education Machine.*

Bill Latham was the catalyst for that book. He came to me because I had developed a process that resolved complex problems in large capital projects and corporate cultures. Bill and his team at MeTEOR Education persuaded me to use our MindShift process to help them in their quest to re-humanize the classroom. That book became the spark for change we all hoped it might be.

At our final gathering, we toasted one another, sang "So Long, Farewell," hugged, and went back to our respective fields in education, architecture, psychology, and various places in the corporate world. But, MeTEOR and the educators who came together continued their crusade. They operated much like a reserve army. They continued to meet, stay in shape, study new literature, share activities, stories, experiences, and new research on a virtual project site created for the Humanize project.

Although I didn't stay very active on the site, one day I posted some questions, "What if the problem isn't disengagement? What if it's deeper? What if fatigue and burnout look like disengagement?" A loud and emotional "YES!" quickly rippled through our network. Stories poured out; teachers told why they quit. Not because they didn't care, but they were worn out. Depleted. Running on empty.

Bill suggested we dig deeper. He brought Kevin Baird into our conversation. As the co-founder of the Global Center for College & Career Readiness and with his seminal work inside the education policy world, he understood the nature and scale of the new challenge. Kevin signed on as co-author; he also bridged our research to the complexity of a national conversation.

When Michelle Kinder served as the Executive Director for the Momentous Institute, she walked me through their work in Social and Emotional Health (SEH). That work became a compass for our new WHOLE work. I knew we needed her help, her resources, and her ability to communicate a still emerging mindset to educators and the public.

Our team was complete. Bill provided the passion and belief in the cause. Kevin brought his strategic overview of the stakeholders. Michelle understood the toll on teachers. And I was the war correspondent, doing my best to make the "fog of war" understandable for the folks back home.

We also had help. A lot of help. More than 120 educators, experts, parents, students, and leaders rallied to the cause; they engaged the good fight. Although we list our most active participants in Appendix A, I must thank those who made key contributions.

Thank You, Underwriters

Leaders win through logistics. Vision, sure. Strategy, yes. But when you go to war, you need to have both toilet paper and bullets at the right place at the right time. In other words, you must win through superior logistics.
—Tom Peters – Rule #3: Leadership Is Confusing As Hell,
Fast Company, March 2001

We held four summits in four cities over fifteen months. We visited dozens of schools, working with more than 200 people. We chased the stories, gained backstage access, and arranged food, transportation, and technology. We recorded the events, studied the research, and pulled clear signals from the noise.

None of that could have happened without the support, the networks, and the guidance of MeTEOR Education, the DLR Group, Carroll Daniel Construction, Paragon Furniture, Interior Concepts, the Mein Company, Tarkett, and In2 Architecture.

Each firm is a leader in the K–12 market. I want to extend a personal thank you to Jim French, Brian Daniel, Mark Hubbard, Remco Bergsma, Russ Nagel, Jonathan Stanley, and Irene Nigaglioni. Their willingness to support and assign some of their best talent to our work, share research, and open doors paved the way for many warm and welcoming site visits and interviews. Instead of coming in as strangers, we were received as friends of the family.

Thank You, Summit Hosts

I thank Matt Wunder, the CEO and one of the founders of DaVinci School in Los Angeles, and Carla Levenson, their Director of External Relations, for hosting our California summit. DaVinci is a distinctive ecosystem of five free public charter schools, serving 108 zip codes. They also coordinated our tour to RISE, an exceptional high school serving about 200 homeless students in South Central Los Angeles. DaVinci School provides an extraordinary model for innovative twenty-first-century learning—within the urban struggles faced by many students and their families. I get inspired each time I visit and hear the new stories of kids thriving. Matt represents the school administrator of the future. His entrepreneurial approach designed a solution fit for the school's demographic. To do that forced him to build a public-private partnership of support inside a traditional urban public school district and continue to walk the line between the competing agendas from all sides.

Matthew Haworth, the Chairman of Haworth, headquartered in Holland, Michigan, has been a friend for several decades. I reached out to Matthew when I read the story of Holland in James and Debra Fallows' book, *Our Towns*. I described our mission and desire to dig deeper into Holland's education and community story. He immediately offered to host our summit at their beautiful and inspiring headquarters. Matthew also made personal calls, opening doors to community and school leaders for us.

I also thank Dan Beerens, another longtime friend and a nationally recognized educator, who also lives in Holland. Dan served as our tour guide for the five schools, giving us the advantage of being accompanied by someone who knew everyone we met.

Dr. John Gasko hosted our final summit at the University of North Texas in Dallas. He took us deep into social emotional literacy. We learned how to process emotional and polarizing topics with the help of students from Cry Havoc Theater, led by Mara Richards Bim.

Will Richey, founder of Journeyman INK, introduced us to his tribe of artists, and ushered us into their world of transforming students who carry deep and painful wounds. Will took us into his Deep Ellum neighborhood in Dallas for a stirring evening at DaVerse Lounge. Dr. Jay Faber, a psychiatrist who specializes in neuroimaging, walked us through brain images ranging from healthy, to ADHD, to chronic stress, to the damage of trauma. We learned why the practices of social and emotional health restore much of this damage.

Thank You, Specialists

Good editors are like magicians. They bring the writer's intent to life. Ed Chinn is more than a good editor. He traveled to our summits, met and interviewed the participants, and joined the process. *WHOLE* was his fourth MindShift book project. When he received my manuscript, it was like a crisp handoff from a quarterback to a seasoned running back who knew the play and found the end zone. His experience and our relationship go beyond editing to collaborating. While I was in the weeds of writing, he often helped me see a clearer path or sharper angle.

Michael Lagocki, the illustrator for the book, designed the cover (his first for a MindShift book) and a companion comic book. He is more than an artist; he choreographs our summits. I build the theme and establish the goal, but Michael designs and manages the flow and rhythm. One of the main reasons our summits attract distinguished thought leaders is they have never experienced an event like what Michael designs. Many have told me they've never participated in enterprises that challenged, informed, inspired, and produced the level of collaborative work like MindShift. Thank you, Michael.

Richard Narramore has served as my Senior Editor at Wiley for four books. He has also coached me with great skill and finesse through each project. When I presented *WHOLE*, he validated our topic but felt it would be better stewarded in another division of Wiley. He generously introduced us to his counterpart at Jossey-Bass. Thank you, Richard, for your endorsement and preparation for this project.

Marilyn Dennison, a crucial part of the DLR Group team and a former assistant school superintendent, became an invaluable guide for our team. She helped us to better understand the needs of students and teachers. Marilyn also explained how her team leads a school district outside its comfort zone and into transformation.

Dr. Lynn Frickey has been one of our strongest supporters. Her career work with high-risk students helped us appreciate the very human side of our work. But, she also brought the academic rigor we needed to collaborate with educators.

There would be no *WHOLE* without Irene Nigaglioni, Chelsea Poulin, Ed Chinn, and Lisa Miller. As a team, they created a book cover using the Japanese art form of Kintsugi to convey the beauty of broken lives finding wholeness through education.

I invited Joe Tankersley, a longtime colleague, futurist, former Disney Imagineer, and master of storytelling to join our Holland summit. Joe went far beyond his workshop. He helped three students from Hamilton High School and their superintendent with the work and helped me integrate that work into the book.

Those three Holland High students—Colin, Haleigh, and Luke—developed a project and provided the material for one of our most important chapters, *Having the Stress Conversation in Your School.* Their superintendent, Dave Tebo, agreed to loan them to our project. He also secured approval to let them design the project for credit toward graduation. After learning the basics of designing and conducting surveys, they administered the survey, synthesized the data, and delivered the story of an American high school.

Chris Irwin, a former ISD Superintendent (and now part of Carroll Daniel's team supporting schools), received the call that administrators fear, an active shooter inside the school. He told me the timeline of events as if it happened the day before. His account was riveting and disturbing. Chris gave me a new appreciation for the ability of administrators to calmly navigate through chaos and later through the healing process. The next day I watched Chris and Brian Daniel guide a school's leadership through how to prepare for the worst.

I called Ron Burkhardt, the Managing Director of Newmark Knight, a commercial real estate brokerage, before our Los Angeles summit. I asked if he could produce a historical analysis of South Los Angeles to provide us a better understanding of the shifting demographics and the gentrification of the area. When he heard we were visiting RISE and researching the stressful condition of teachers and students, Ron asked his team to give us the reports they would produce for a potential client moving to the area. The excellence and detail of the report blew us away. Thank you, Ron.

I want to express my deep gratitude to my wife Lisa and our now-grown children. Lisa helped me sift through research on childhood development. She also took part in each of the summits. Our family became a laboratory for exploring new topics. They allowed me to share their school sagas. While they sometimes rolled their eyes when I described what I was doing, they support the mission. Thank you, Lisa, Michelle, Nathan, and Tyler.

The sheer expanse of the project—we left another big book on the editing floor—means I've almost certainly missed some people I should thank. I'm sorry.

This is the first book to tackle the vast terrain of mental health and well-being in education. I hope *WHOLE* becomes the catalyst for bringing more happiness and resilience to teachers and students and helps schools enter the twenty-first century. We are all stakeholders in that magnificent challenge. And those stakes are very high for every student, teacher, family, and neighborhood across the nation.

ABOUT THE AUTHORS

Rex Miller is a six-time Wiley author. *The Commercial Real Estate Revolution* and *Change Your Space, Change Your Culture* and *The Healthy Workplace Nudge* have won international awards for ground-breaking innovation. His book, *Humanizing the Education Machine*, has become a catalyst for rethinking education as a uniquely human and relational experience.

He is a respected futurist, frequent keynote speaker, and an elite leadership coach. His MindShift process applies a unique crowdsourced approach to tackling complex leadership challenges. Miller was named a Texas A&M Professional Fellow for his work combining leadership and scholarship to innovation. When organizations and industries are stuck, the MindShift approach to "wicked" problems has found breakthroughs by creating a uniquely human touch.

MindShift also guides organizations through the difficult change process of improving the project, team, and organizational culture. Recent clients include Google, Disney, Microsoft, GoDaddy, Intel, FAA, Delos, Haworth, Turner Construction, Balfour Beatty Construction, DPR Construction, MWH Constructors, MD Anderson Hospital, Universal Health Systems, Oregon Health Science University, University of Illinois, Texas A&M, University of Denver, and many others.

Miller is also a USPTA certified tennis professional, a member of the National Speaker's Association, and actively mentors young leaders. He believes leaders come from anywhere in an organization or community and hopes his work helps empower hidden leaders to step up and step forward to create positive change. He can be reached at www.rexmiller. com and on LinkedIn at linkedin.com/in/rexmiller

Bill Latham is a leader in a movement to design and implement High Impact Learning Environments in schools. He is a co-author of *Humanizing the Education Machine*, the *Thinking Guide for Educators*, MeTEOR Connect Courseware for High Impact Learning Environments, and *Cognitive Demand and High Impact Learning Environments*.

He is an Accredited Learning Environment Planner (ALEP) and today creates accreditation courses through the Association for Learning Environments for architects, educators, and consultants.

In October 2001, Latham acquired the assets of Contrax Furnishings with his business partner. Through his experience at Contrax, Latham was involved in some of the largest bond-funded school building initiatives in the United States. Those projects, funded by local communities and governmental programs, often had stated goals for school reforms which did not materialize.

Latham's observations of failed school reforms led him to create an approach now widely known as "Space Hacking"—the intentional use of disruptive school spaces to directly support the acceleration of high impact instruction and student inquiry. Latham contributed to an extension of the work of Dr. Karin Hess and Dr. Norman Webb in cognitive demand, creating a new model of immersive learning practice which leverages research-based learning environment design.

Latham spent his childhood moving from school to school as part of a military family. He earned a Bachelor of Science in Chemistry and later an MBA through the University of Florida. His early work at Clariant included the development of patents related to high purity alkoxytrimethylsilane3 and branched phenylsiloxane fluids (US5847179A; EP0855418B1).

Latham lives in Central Florida with his wife and three children. He is active in martial arts with his children and competes at both the national and international level.

Kevin Baird is a noted leader in global College & Career Readiness and an expert in accelerated human development. He is one of the world's first researchers to measure learner engagement through content immersion and psychological safety using real-time neuroscience technology. As well, he is part of the world's largest study of student engagement and classroom self-efficacy.

Baird has contributed to the development of the most widely used reading and language acceleration programs; designed K-12 artificial intelligence/predictive systems; and is the author of the National Implementation Pathway for College & Career Readiness. Kevin is also an Accredited Learning Environment Planner (ALEP). He reviews inquiry frameworks developed for high impact learning environments and consults on the development of new AI systems for classrooms.

Baird has trained administrators worldwide through his graduate-level College Career Readiness Black Belt Certification program, in partnership with the University of Southern California's Rossier School of Education. He is the co-creator of the ProSocial Paradigm for positive learning environments and is the principal designer of the Audible Learning Framework, Chairman & National Supervising Faculty of the non-profit Center for College & Career Readiness.

Outside of education, Baird is a patent-holding inventor in predictive analytics. He initiated the Huafeng partnership with the People's Republic of China, where his media has been viewed by a daily audience bigger than the Super Bowl.

Connecting classrooms with pragmatic, practical approaches which speed student learning is Baird's primary mission. He tweets regularly at @KevinEBaird.

Baird holds an MBA in Global Management, Bachelor's degrees in Sociology and Anthropology, has served as a member of the Secretary's Circle of Phi Beta Kappa, is a Beinecke National Scholar and a Wingspread Scholar, and supports global education efforts through EdLead: The Baird Fund for Education.

Michelle Kinder is a nationally recognized social emotional health expert. She is a keynote speaker, writer, and leadership coach and is the former Executive Director of the Momentous Institute. She has worked in executive leadership for over a decade, in children's mental health for more than two decades, and is a Licensed Professional Counselor. At Stagen Leadership Academy, she is the Director of the Social Change Leadership Programs. Michelle graduated from Baylor University with a Bachelor's degree in Theatre Arts and the University of Texas with a Master's degree in Educational Psychology.

Under Kinder's leadership, Momentous Institute was named one of the top 100 Best Workplaces for Women and one of the 50 Best Workplaces in Texas by *Fortune* magazine and Great Place to Work.

Kinder is a Public Voices Fellow and a Peer Coach with the OpEd Project and her articles have featured in more than a dozen publications, including *TIME*, the *Washington Post, Texas Tribune, Dallas Morning News, Mindful Magazine, Huffington Post,* and PBS' *Next Avenue*. In addition to her opinion pieces, Kinder is a published poet. She is a member of the Leadership Dallas Alumni Association and serves on a number of community boards and advisory councils. In 2015, Kinder was named CEO of the Year by CNM Connect. In 2018, she was recognized as one of the Faces of Hope by the Grant Haliburton Foundation and as Dallas-Fort Worth Teach for America's Honorary Alumni. Recently, Kinder was honored as Juliette Fowler's 2019 Visionary Woman and was selected by the Dallas Historical Society to receive an Award in Excellence in Education.

Kinder grew up in Guatemala and is fluent in Spanish. She lives in Dallas, Texas, with her husband, Patrick, and their two daughters, Maya and Sophia.

Part 1
Dying to Teach

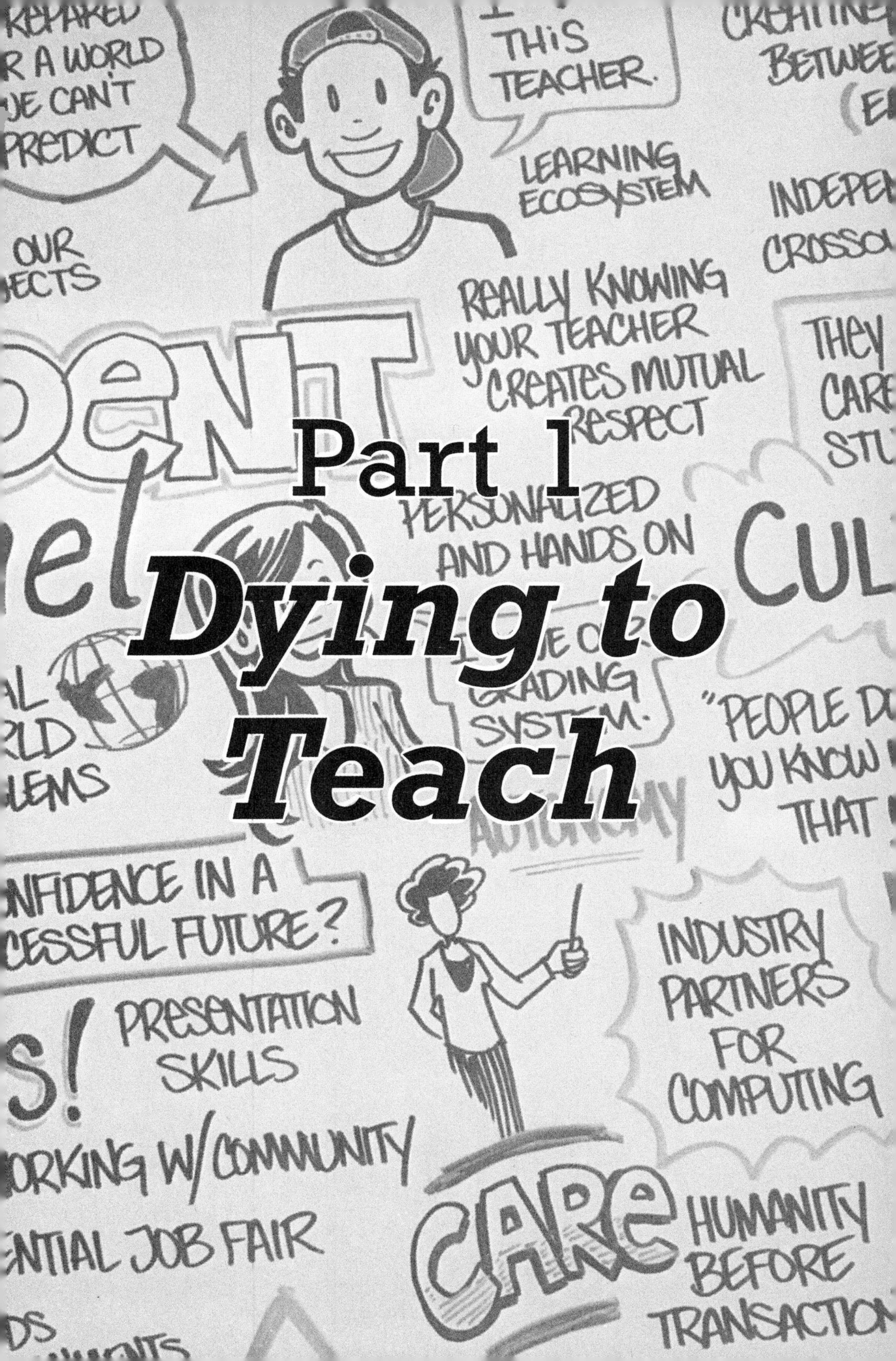

CHAPTER 1

Dying to Teach

*It is usually the imagination that is wounded first, rather than the heart;
it being much more sensitive.*

—Henry David Thoreau

Education is a habitat for heroes.

And, what else would we expect? Teaching tackles and fulfills one of the most foundational and primordial purposes of civilization. Teachers prepare children for adulthood and careers. More than that, they preserve the social order. That very milieu attracts those of heroic spirit.

That heroic dimension is why teaching provides an exceptional and recurrent focus for books and movies. Each generation of teachers can point to a printed or filmed story of heroes—*Up the Down Staircase, Stand and Deliver, Mr. Holland's Opus, Dead Poets Society, Goodbye, Mr. Chips*, etc. Each spoke to the hero's heart in millions of boys or girls, sitting in movie theaters or curled up in Dad's reading chair.

Our MindShift team also knows those heroes. They cared enough about the story of teachers to join our team. Lynn Frickey, Dan Bereens, Michelle Kinder, David Vroonland, Rachel Hucul, John Gasko, Denise Benavides, and other teachers (active or retired) knew the movies and books, and they knew the twenty-first-century educational machine that chewed teachers carefully and slowly before swallowing them up alive.

Another of those teachers, Dr. Marilyn Denison, was a long-time educator and administrator who specialized in launching new schools. She left education after two decades because of the stress. Six months into her new job with DLR Group she saw her doctor for her regular checkup. Her doctor had long been concerned about Marilyn's blood pressure. Soon after the checkup, her doctor called.

"Marilyn, what are you doing differently?"

Assuming a problem, Marilyn started to list several recent minor health issues when the doctor said, "No, that's not what I'm calling about. It's your blood work. You have NO stress markers at all. What changed?"

Marilyn told her the only thing that had changed was that she quit teaching and accepted a job she loved and a place where she was appreciated. Through subsequent conversations with her doctor, Marilyn clearly saw she had been dying to teach.

Who Cares?

The course of our work all over the country very naturally brought us into continuous interaction with the teachers on our team. As our work moved into stories of teacher and student trauma, as we talked to courageous and selfless educators, and walked through broken neighborhoods, we often saw our teachers suddenly look away, shake their heads, and wipe their eyes.

Sometimes it was like walking through old battlefields with the retired servicemen and women who once had fought there. In time, we all began to realize how much those old soldiers and sailors still care about those who remain in battle mode. Despite their own PTSD, some part of them wished they could return to the front.

Yet, even as we were surrounded with those genuinely intrepid teachers, we began encountering Gallup's reports that 70% of teachers have checked out and 20% are so indifferent that they poison the atmosphere. In fact, "teacher disengagement" sits at the center of the debate over school performance. So, there we were, working with teachers of generational, geographic, ethnic, and political diversity. But, they all cared. Every one of them. Deeply. And Gallup says 70% of teachers have disengaged?

What was going on?

The Next Jump

In January 2018, I attended a three-day leadership academy in New York City sponsored by Next Jump, the e-commerce company. As part of their passion for supporting educators, Next Jump's academy offers their unconventional philosophy, tools, and practices to teachers.

Next Jump's unorthodox approach grows out of their own unique history. After early success, they plunged to near bankruptcy during the dot-com crash. After surviving, Next Jump shifted its business platform from marketing to technology. That launched a period of rapid growth, an evolution that stripped away the culture which the founders built and cherished. As Charlie Kim, the driving founder, explained to our class, "We found ourselves with a small army of brilliant jerks." So, one Friday afternoon, Charlie and Meghan Messenger (another founder) fired 50% of their programmers. They started over, establishing the right culture and character, and then rebuilt the business on that new platform.

Next Jump now employs around 250 people, and those people generate $2.5 billion in annual revenue. That is $10 million of revenue per employee! To put this in perspective, Google makes about $1.63 million and Walmart about $230,000 per employee. Next Jump is clearly a cult, in the best sense of the word ("cult," as the root for culture).

The three-day academy felt like a group of little league baseball players showing up at Yankee Stadium for a day of training and workouts. It was a day of 90-mile-an-hour fastballs, magical curveballs, a lot of grins, and shaking our heads in awe of what we saw and did. The Next Jumpers were confident, transparent, genuine, and generous.

We watched young employees, just a few years out of college, quietly manifesting the poise and presence of seasoned executive leaders. That is part of their mystique and magic. Their transparency and willingness to go off script showed up the morning of our last day. Of course, that very genuine integrity and flexibility were a jolt to the group. But the whole Next Jump experience was an earthquake to my paradigm regarding employee and teacher engagement.

"I Just Got a View of Everything I Can't Do"

Charlie Kim kicked off the academy's final day by telling us, "The safest thing we can do is to follow our agenda. You'll have a great day, and at the end, we'll shower you with books and gifts, food, and a great send-off.

"But we think we might have screwed up the whole thing. We may have lost sight of the primary reason we held this academy. It is for educators, not for the VIP guests observing. You are very good people doing good work, but you are resource-starved, time-starved.

"I feel like we showcased our healthy food, exercise, and things you cannot imagine. We plopped you into how we run. That's why our team stepped back last night and asked, 'Are we actually helping them?'

"Is today going to end where you educators walk away, saying, 'Okay, that's cool, but I just got a view of everything I can't do.' That's why I reached out to Peter Chiarchiaro, our Director of Wellness, to provide a summary of the vitals we took from you yesterday. We take the same vitals with every academy. We've seen it for the CIA, the military, Fortune 500 companies, every group.

"Let me read Peter's summary:

This group's energy efficiency is bad, very bad. It sucks, to be blunt. Of the twenty people, sixteen are in a survival state, four are in varying states of alarm, and none are thriving. The four alarmed ones are very distressed. To have 20% of any group on hyper on-guard state is a really bad sign. These teachers and educators seem to be in a major fight-or-flight mode. This is a super-humble group. The takeaway? This group needs recovery program times 1000. These educators are the least energy-efficient of the groups we've seen. This is backed by blood pressure tests.

Then Charlie continued, "If that is true, we want to help you. So, could you somehow let us know what would help you?"

Then, as requested, the teachers began to talk.

From Jess: "My value priorities for my students are to foster nuance and inquiry; slow, deep, and thoughtful learning. But your tools and approach to feedback support a different value than what I'm trying to craft on a day-to-day basis. That's the part I'm struggling with the most."

Then Joe spoke, "You've been able to build a feedback culture from the bottom up. It works the way you want it to work. But, in a heavily routinized school system, where the feedback structure will not change, I am asking how Next Jump's approach can work in *my* world.

"I was really fascinated to hear how frankly ad hoc your system is. You can send an email, you can do this, you can do all these other things. In our environment, if someone sends a candid email, alarm bells will go off all the way up the ladder because it has. . . (pause) *implications.*"

"Hi, I'm Robert. I think we all recognize that schools run a different culture. So, there is naturally a lot of resistance to adding anything unless they have a high degree of confidence it will create value. I would be interested in going around the room and letting every person share one idea that you learned in this workshop that you think can realistically be used in your school. I'm starving for ideas to enhance what we're doing."

Then Charlie spoke up, "The two industries we have aligned ourselves with, and give most of our company resources to, are the military and education. Both recruit very good people in the line of service.

"But, it's like the flight attendant's announcement before takeoff, 'In case of an emergency the oxygen masks will drop down. First, place the oxygen mask on yourself and *then* help others.' Humans are wired to serve other humans, which is what you do in education. The same is true for the military. However, you can't help someone else if your cup is empty.

"But, people in education forget to take care of themselves. They forget that when you don't take care of yourself, you can't go far in helping others."

Wounded Warriors

When Charlie read the group's test results and interpreted the data, shoulders sagged, and heads dropped around the room. I heard long and slow exhales. We all saw that "survival," just barely getting by, had become the norm. No one could recall what normal felt like.

That pried the lid off; we began to hear stories from the front lines. One teacher told us, "I used to work in schools designated as turnaround schools, where the culture was very aggressive and chaotic. There was no trust. It was all upstream and taxing. I tried as best I could to build a loving and accepting culture. Now, I'm just tired. These schools have an 80% failure rate. Mine was 50%. How can I feel good about that?"

Most of the teachers were in a constant fight-or-flight mode, the autonomic nervous system's response to perceived danger. The report described the teachers as "barely hanging on."

When the academy finished, I immediately called Bill Latham. "Bill, what if disengagement isn't the problem? What if everyone has been working on the wrong problem for the last several decades? What if the real problem is battle fatigue that *looks like* disengagement? What if teachers are not *dis*engaged but *over*-engaged? What if they care too much?"

And Bill responded, "If that's true, we've built a multi-billion-dollar industry committed to solving the wrong problem!"

"A Thousand Invisible Betrayals of Purpose"

The educational-industrial complex thought it was grappling with teacher disengagement. But, they were wrong. The premise was flawed. So, they had leaned their ladder on the wrong wall. It was a good ladder; nothing wrong with it at all. Except that it was giving the specialists and their power tools access to the wrong work area.

Gallup's 2018 Teacher Wellbeing Index reports that 67% of teachers and 80% of administrators work under high stress. These demands interfere with home life for three-quarters of them. The same percentage have experienced a variety of physical and mental symptoms and one quarter received a medical diagnosis from their general practitioner.

And no schools and districts we saw have plans for tackling the problem. The approaches are reactive, too late, and ineffective. To compound the problem, many teachers feel that raising red flags about stress would hurt their careers.

The most common daily manifestations come in the form of insomnia, irritability, tearfulness, difficulty concentrating, forgetfulness, dizziness, and anxiety. This condition has made teaching the fourth most stressful job behind working parents, active military, and police officers.[1] And, most teachers are also working parents.

In fact, teachers have been absorbing the erosions of their physical energy, mental health, and souls. Dr. Jeff Jernigan, author and counselor, describes burnout as "A thousand invisible betrayals of purpose that go unnoticed until it is too late."[2]

All the signs show too many teachers have no buffer remaining. The cartilage is gone; they are bone-on-bone. And, because they are so exhausted and wounded, students with deep needs have no place to go. That condition places education on a collision course between the students who need care and the teachers who have nothing left to give.

Wrapping Up

- Education, by the nature of its call, becomes a gathering place for heroes.
- They serve society's highest needs and aspirations, preparing children for adulthood and careers. More than that, they preserve the social order.
- But, somewhere, our society got the idea that educators disengaged from that high calling. That judgment resulted from a misdiagnosis.
- Teachers care too much, not too little.

Practical Reflections

1. Think about the times you bought the disengagement story. Did anything about that ring false to you? Do you think exhaustion or battle fatigue might have been a better diagnosis or explanation?
2. If you are a teacher, and had been part of the Next Jump Academy, would your vital signs have told the same story?
3. If not, why not? How do you defy the odds?

Notes

1. Linda C. Brinson, "10 Most Stressful Jobs in America." HowStuffWorks, Oct. 12, 2010. www.money.howstuffworks.com/10-most-stressful-jobs-in-america7.htm
2. Dr. Jernigan's presentation to the WELCOA Summit, August 16, 2018.

CHAPTER 2

Schools Are Killing More than Creativity

> *. . . the student who is fully trained will become like the teacher.*
> —Luke 6:40[1]

A year before my mother passed away, each of her kids received a couple of footlockers of memorabilia. Mom saved everything. When mine arrived, I relived decades of my childhood . . . handicraft projects, childhood studio portraits, along with their receipts, and even all the paperwork from my birth, including the receipts. Mom seemed to mark our life events through receipts; receipts for tennis and music lessons, park passes, two accordions, and those I couldn't decipher without a call to my younger sister.

Then I hit another sedimentary layer: my report cards. Mom saved every single one, quarter by quarter from first grade through college. My first report cards were from Mrs. Stavoe, my first-grade teacher. Even in 1960, she was doing PBL (project-based learning). Our class raised chickens, studied our nation's space program, and created scrapbooks to chronicle that history. My scrapbook told the story of Enos, the space chimp.

Mrs. Stavoe made us stand in front of the whole class to present our work. That became my worst nightmare; I was so afraid I would forget the next line in my speech or, worse, just freeze. That fear stayed with me into my adult life. I could not read a speech, but if I thoroughly knew the information, I could talk my way through it. That counterbalance of conversing with a room rather than making a speech later became a strength, one that still serves me in my current work.

One line from Mrs. Stavoe, written in beautiful cursive on one of my report cards, was like discovering an ancient talisman in the footlocker; she wrote: "Rex has a wonderful imagination and loves to share his stories with the class. I hope he continues because he has a real gift." I didn't realize that my workaround for sticking to the script was to wrap what little I remembered into stories.

Mrs. Stavoe represents the deep and permanent influence teachers bring to every class and every student. She understood that superpower and, at least in my case, applied it intentionally and masterfully. In fact, after my first book was published in 2004, she and I resumed the relationship through correspondence. I sent her signed copies of my books, and she replied with handwritten notes of appreciation, encouragement, and affirmation. I was so very fortunate. When I was fully formed, I became my teacher. And I try also to devote a good bit of my professional work to helping others unlock their gifts.

Sadly, the opposite is also true. Gallup's engagement surveys tell us only 30% of teachers are functioning with the care and intentional influence of a Mrs. Stavoe. About 70% work with some degree of disengagement. But we also know that what might look like disengagement is likely the effects of chronic stress, fatigue, vicarious trauma, secondary trauma, depression, and burnout. We are now learning the mental and physical health of the teacher, along with the school

If you were to ask Gallup what are the most important elements for students to be successful in school, the research would tell you: having someone who cares about your development and having an opportunity to do what you do best every day.

—Gallup, Inc.[2]

culture, may have a greater effect on learning than the teaching gifts and skills. It is true; sometimes tragically, every child "who is fully trained will become like the teacher." How does that shape a student's ability to master life's many requirements and opportunities?

The Learning Flywheel

Picture a huge, heavy flywheel—a massive metal disk mounted horizontally on an axle, about 30 feet in diameter, 2 feet thick, and weighing about 5,000 pounds. Now imagine that your task is to get the flywheel rotating on the axle as fast and long as possible. Pushing with great effort, you get the flywheel to inch forward, moving almost imperceptibly at first.

Then, at some point—breakthrough! Each turn of the flywheel builds upon work done earlier, compounding your investment of effort. A thousand times faster, then ten thousand, then a hundred thousand. The huge heavy disk flies forward, with almost unstoppable momentum.

—Jim Collins[3]

Bill Latham described my experience with Mrs. Stavoe as "the Learning Flywheel." Her care and enthusiasm ignited my curiosity. A teacher who can move a student from boredom or naïveté to curiosity will spark questions that set the flywheel in motion. As the momentum builds, the wheel rotates through the increasing speeds of awareness, coherence, discovery, engagement, creativity, and finally into mastery. The flywheel builds motivation and momentum that remain for life.

In the classroom, secure attachments to teachers and other students optimize the ability to learn.

—*Lou Cozolino[4]*

The flywheel moves a student through the stutter steps of social relationships, then moves into the deeper waters of learning, and prepares them for academic rigor, complexity, team-based learning, and the future-ready disciplines needed to graduate into a VUCA (volatile, uncertain, complex, ambiguous) world. I was fortunate. Mrs. Stavoe helped me start my flywheel when I was 6.

Teachers and Students Relationships

Teachers are in the caring business. Caring for others is one of the prime motivating factors directing people into teaching as a profession. That

There is a cost to caring . . . Sometimes we feel we are losing our sense of self to [those] we serve.

—Deborah Boyle[5]

level of care also creates a willingness to sacrifice time, family, and health. But when the needs outstrip the design or capacity of the system, the extra acts of kindness within teaching can become an unhealthy servitude. That is when the reservoir of care dries up, even though the desire remains. Teachers, as humans, then try to refill it with guilt, shame, unhealthy coping behaviors, detachment, and hardness. Today, we mislabel that "disengagement."

Whether it is caring too much or no longer caring, the consequences for the child are the same. This is why performance psychologist Jim Loehr uses kindness as a leading indicator of health. To summarize the data, there is one Mrs. Stavoe for every three classrooms. The teachers in the other two classrooms have become emotionally detached. That kind of disconnection can become toxic. At that point, teachers project their pain onto the students. And that pain triggers the students' pain.

Most teachers don't start out as uncaring components of an educational apparatus. That comes through careful and heavy processing through the education "machine." And that's why our earlier book on K–12 education, *Humanizing the Education Machine,*[6] concluded that in order to improve schools, we must first restore the human qualities that make teachers the life-giving agents of learning. Part of that effort requires dismantling the mechanism that (1) strips away the training, agency, and common sense of teachers, and (2) self-corrects toward sterile conformity and compliance.

Why Mastery?

Mastery—one of the goals of many twenty-first-century learning efforts—springs from ancient roots: the relationship between the apprentice/student and the teacher. For example, consider mastery in martial arts, music, trades, and medicine. Bill Latham practices martial arts and competes at a national level. He says:

In martial arts, becoming like our teacher is the point, the goal. The journey to mastery involves extensive knowledge, precise technique, and a disciplined temperament. The entire process is a test. Over time it builds resiliency that turns into mastery. The external or visible side is the demonstration of proficiency. That is where many students and those outside the discipline misinterpret what is going on. They can only see or focus on the outcomes, the scores, and performance; they miss where the real competition or growth is taking place, inside.

If you follow martial arts and attend competitions, you will learn that the style of the competitor will telegraph where they were trained. Part of the training in martial arts is imitating the master's technique and philosophy until the student embodies it. That is the essence of mastery.

According to Bill,

They will move, fight, walk, and even breathe like their master. It's a great compliment to hear somebody say, "Hey, are you a student of master so-and-so?"

Take a moment and look back on your life. Who were the people who made lasting impressions on you? A piece of their character left its mark. It is a mysterious neurological duplication process.

But the education machine is more focused on outcomes, scores, and performance than the personal "neurological duplication process." That obsession with external metrics, and the enormous efforts to improve and double down on outcomes lead to many of our anxieties about education. We increase expectations and raise the stakes, which spikes anxiety. It feels like a death match between Ahab and the great white whale of test scores. We've become lashed to this monster; we can't break loose and return to the shore of sanity.

Times of historic disruption pull philosophers, artists, scholars, and other thinkers into revisiting and rethinking the ancient principles that birthed modern society. Mastery is one of those ancient principles that guided learning for millennia. The great wheel of civilization has brought mastery around to us again. We think it makes a serious contribution to a twenty-first-century education.

What Is Mastery by Default?

Can students also master *dis*engagement, self-interest, and lack of empathy? The data seems to tell us it is both possible and a new norm. What path does that new norm provide for students? How does mastery of the negative influence life, health, and the shaping of our nation?

For example, what happens to a student who spends 14,000 hours of his or her formative years with disengaged or toxic teachers? They will be like their teacher! Without care and inspiration, curiosity has no place to go.

Student disengagement doesn't happen overnight. Annual school surveys tell the story of the steady decline in engagement from first grade to twelfth grade. By their senior year, 60% have checked out.[7] What else would we expect? We systematically wipe out creativity, thinking, and the joy of learning.

The best way to learn a second language is to fall in love with someone who only speaks that language.

—John Schulman

When learning lacks the oxygen of a caring relationship, going to school becomes like a dental appointment; it's not learning, it's torture. Cognitive engagement comes after and grows with the relational engagement. That's because a good relationship with a teacher makes students psychologically ready to take academic risks. Only then can they tolerate the possibility of struggle or failure. Such a student becomes willing to stretch; she or he can navigate the cognitive dissonance of real learning.

If the teacher is stressed, the student will be stressed. If the student lives in a stressful home, they come to school with that anxiety and pass it along to others. Seeing what happens to the mind and body of those who live under stress clears away a lot of the noise in the debate for how to "reform" education. The map is simple; the road is hard. We need a compass pointed toward health and happiness.

We now believe Gallup's disengagement numbers reflect the fallout of stress and fatigue more than not caring. However, the effect on students may be the same or worse.

The Caregiver's Dilemma

In our research, we discovered the caregiver's dilemma as it applies to teachers. In short, they care so much that it leads to fatigue, burnout, and demoralization.

Great teachers are not entertainers who deliver marvelous content. Rather, they inspire students through their care. They are the ones who leave legacies, the ones who hear the kids, back from college or later in life, say, "You made such a difference in my life." That kind of commemoration comes, not because they did some great cognitive exercise, but because he or she cared, believed in, and invested time and attention in students.

If I'm going to choose a mentor, it's because they have mastered a skill or an art. But it's more; we must have a pivotal connection. Why do we go to the expense of travel, lodging, and time required to do job interviews? Why don't we just read resumés? We do it because we're looking for a good personal connection with a candidate. The entry point to engagement is a relationship.

A student asking a question marks the spot of engagement. That is the point at which the student takes a small piece of ownership for their pursuit. That is a vital part of the flywheel. If the student–teacher relationship remains healthy, we will see the unfurling process of another question, then a deeper question, then a muddled thought, followed by clearer and more profound thoughts. The flywheel spins faster; the student engages a little deeper. Over time, the flywheel takes students to more profound levels of learning.

When teachers begin asking questions bigger than one person can answer, the student moves beyond tactical conversations, the ones designed to find the "right" answers. That's when they must go higher, to become more discerning, integrated, strategic, and collaborative. Eventually, that leads to collective and creative reimagining to solve complex issues, the kind requiring the soft skills that companies demand. Sadly, many of those skills have been stripped out of the machine approach to learning.

The flywheel experience releases a hormone essential to motivation and learning: dopamine.[8] When the student experiences a caring connection, oxytocin is released, decreasing his or her heart rate and enabling the brain to embrace the discomfort of learning. It fosters the same trust a child feels when his or her parent invites him or her to jump to them in the deep end of the pool.[9] Positive attachment releases oxytocin, increasing the personal sense of safety. We will dive more deeply into the physiology of learning later.[10]

What about Students Who Disconnect?

The absence of a positive student–teacher relationship stimulates the survival triggers in the body. This releases cortisol, elevates breathing, places the brain in a defensive posture, and shuts down the pre-frontal cortex. That quickly translates into stress or anxiety.

Teachers set this hormone thermostat. When teachers are happy and connected to their students, their rooms display high levels of dopamine and oxytocin. Years of surveys reveal only 30% of classrooms receive that positive stimulation. Sadly, 70% show high levels of cortisol and exhibit stress-related behaviors and chronic anxiety. Biology surpasses curriculum.[11]

Gallup's engagement survey of fifth grade through twelfth grade students presents the data straight and clear: "Nearly three-quarters (74%) of all surveyed fifth-grade students are engaged, and only about one-third of surveyed students in 10th, 11th and 12th grades are engaged."[12]

That drop is not because kids are lazy, apathetic, or dependent. Curiosity, discovery, and mastering the world are intrinsic human drives. But the institutional nature inside every school creates a hostile climate for those drives. For various reasons, schools create apathetic, dependent, and stressed kids . . . by design. Good administrators equip and empower teachers to tame and re-humanize that beast, and they do that consistently. Sustaining a child-centered human scale school takes a village.

What about Students Who Connect with Reality?

Teachers know kids will take a chance if they have a relational safety net and an environment that rewards trying. The environment must allow falling and getting back up. For as long as it takes.

When our MindShift team visited the Outdoor Discovery Center's "Little Hawks Program" in Holland, Michigan, we joined the kids in play on the slides, logs, bridges, and wood and steel sound pipes. We also saw the tumbling, sliding, running, and jumping joy in the kids.

More than that, we saw kids discovering and cooperating with their own nature, rather than being forced into shapes and forms opposed to it. They were allowed to be themselves. No sitting in desks, in rows; no need to conform to rigid configurations. They were outdoors, connecting with what it means to be a human, learning social skills, and solving problems collaboratively.

The very exposure to *reality*—wildlife tracks in the sidewalks, surrounding woods, and water, harsh weather—tends to teach kids lessons about life. Yes, they "learned," but in a very intentional and integrated way.

Parental adjustments to that kind of learning reveal the chasm between the Gutenberg-era institutional form and this new and natural ecosystem of learning. The first time they see their child scamper across one of the large logs, many are afraid their child might fall. And they do. But they also get back up quite naturally, brush it off, and run off to the next activity that captures their interest. When some of the kids first fall, they might stay down and whimper a bit to get someone's attention. After a few moments, when no one comes to their rescue, they just get up, and that becomes the norm. Fall, get up.

Throughout our research and site visits for this book, we saw many expressions of Ken Robinson's great insight:

> *What we do know is, if you're not prepared to be wrong, you'll never come up with anything original. And by the time they get to be adults, most kids have lost that capacity. They have become frightened of being wrong. And we run our companies like this. We stigmatize mistakes. And we're now running national education systems where mistakes are the worst thing you can make. And the result is that we are educating people out of their creative capacities.* [13]

In *Humanizing the Education Machine*, we described how people go from engaged to toxic. We use an acronym to describe those at the toxic end: "C.A.V.E. dwellers; "Consistently, Virtually, Against, Everything." They make up about 20% of employees and teachers. Those unhappy people spread their unhappiness to those all around them. A Harvard Business School study established a 25-foot radius of negativity that surrounds each negative employee in the workplace. [14]

Organizations get their highest level of engagement in the first six months of an employee's work span. That's when some descend into the cave. It's the same journey for teachers or students. That's when a teacher loses the capacity to connect, stimulate learning, and empower kids. The work gets harder, and because it is harder, they cannot do their best. The vicious cycle continues: if teachers, students, employees, or others are not doing their best work, they won't receive positive feed-

> *Teachers are not interchangeable cogs in a factory machine that engage in the rapid repetition of specific behaviors. Teachers, like their students, are unique individuals, and it is the nature, quality, and uniqueness of teacher-student relationships that create possibilities for learning.*
>   —*Lou Cozolino*[15]

back. And that is demoralizing. It also marks the beginning of the serious energy drain, which creates chronic stress. Then, in order to cope, they begin unplugging or turning to unhealthy behaviors, or both. It is a dark and predictable road.

In the end, chronic stress and burnout are as much relational fractures as they are psychological and emotional drains. Teachers feel betrayed by those who allowed (or could have changed) those conditions. But, of course, the administrators are also cogs in a machine that eats administrators, teachers, students, and parents for breakfast.

Some 972,000 teachers, 27%, fall into the chronically absent category. They miss on average ten days of school per year. Cave dweller teachers further drain classrooms by their absence, requiring substitutes to fill 9,720,000 school days.[16]

Chapter 3 will dive into the traumatic and dangerous world that represents "home" for too many students. Sadly, that place of intended safety has become more battlefield than haven. And, teachers, fighting their own battles, make the environment even more hostile to students. We will also look at the hijacking of emotions that jerks students out of learning and into survival mode.

Wrapping Up

- Teachers are in the caring business.
- Caring creates the flywheel of learning for a student.
- The system exploits teachers to care too much.
- Stressed-out teachers elevate the stress in their students.

- Students mirror their teachers and over time master disengagement.
- Solid relationships provide the oxygen for learning.

Practical Reflections

1. What or who inspired you to become a teacher?
2. What did the flywheel of learning look like for you?
3. What are the key sources of stress you experience?
4. Who is a source of oxygen in your relationships and work?

Notes

1. Quoted from Holy Bible, New Living Translation, copyright © 1996, 2004, 2007 (Carol Stream, IL: Tyndale House Foundation, 2007). Used by permission of Tyndale House Publishers Inc., Carol Stream, Illinois 60188. All rights reserved.
2. Gallup, Inc. "Make a Difference. Show Students You Care." Gallup. com, Oct. 9, 2014. https://news.gallup.com/businessjournal/178118/ difference-show-students-care.aspx
3. Jim Collins, *Good to Great* (New York: HarperCollins, 2001).
4. Lou Cozolino, *Attachment-Based Teaching: Creating a Tribal Classroom* (New York: W.W. Norton, 2014).
5. Deborah Boyle, Advanced Oncology Nursing Resource. http:// ojin.nursingworld.org/MainMenuCategories/ANAMarketplace/ ANAPeriodicals/OJIN/TableofContents/Vol-16-2011/No1-Jan-2011/ Countering-Compassion-Fatigue.html
6. Rex M. Miller, et al., *Humanizing the Education Machine: How to Create Schools That Turn Disengaged Kids into Inspired Learners* (Hoboken, NJ: Wiley, 2017).
7. Francesca Duffy, "Gallup: Student Engagement Drops with Each Grade." *Education Week – Teaching Now*, Jan. 15, 2013. blogs.edweek.org/teachers/ teaching_now/2013/01/gallup_student_engagement_drops_with_each_ grade.html
8. Jeffrey Pettibone, et al., "The Role of Dopamine in Motivation and Learning." *Neuroscience News*, Nov. 24, 2015. https://neurosciencenews. com/dopamine-learning-reward-3157/
9. Katherine Wu, "Love, Actually: The Science behind Lust, Attraction, and Companionship." *Science in the News*, Feb. 14, 2017. https://sitn.hms. harvard.edu/flash/2017/love-actually-science-behind-lust-attraction-companionship/

10. Maria Cohut, "Serotonin Enhances Learning, Not Just Mood." *Medical News Today*, MediLexicon International, June 26, 2018. https://www. medicalnewstoday.com/articles/322263.php

11. Corey Allen, "Stress Contagion Possible amongst Students and Teachers: UBC Study." *UBC News*, Feb. 28, 2017. https://news.ubc.ca/ 2016/06/27/ubc-study-finds-stress-contagion-amongst-students-and-teachers/

12. Valerie J. Calderon and Daniela Yu, "Student Enthusiasm Falls as High School Graduation Nears." Gallup.com, June 1, 2017. https:// news.gallup.com/opinion/gallup/211631/student-enthusiasm-falls-high-school-graduation-nears.aspx?g_source=link_NEWSV9& g_medium=TOPIC&g_campaign=item_&g_content=Student% 2520Enthusiasm%2520Falls%2520as%2520High%2520School% 2520Graduation%2520Nears

13. Ken Robinson, "Do Schools Kill Creativity?" TED, 2006. https://www. ted.com/talks/ken_robinson_says_schools_kill_creativity?language=en

14. Michael Housman and Dylan Minor, "Workplace Design: The Good, the Bad, and the Productive." *Harvard Business Review*, 2016. https://www. hbs.edu/faculty/Publication%20Files/16-147_c672567d-9ba2-45c1-9d72-ea7fa58252ab.pdf

15. Lou Cozolino, *Attachment-Based Teaching*.

16. Alejandra Matos, "1 in 4 U.S. Teachers Are Chronically Absent, Missing More than 10 Days of School." *The Washington Post*, Oct. 26, 2016. https://www. washingtonpost.com/local/education/1-in-4-us-teachers-are-chronically-absent-missing-more-than-10-days-of-school/2016/10/26/2869925e-9186-11e6-a6a3-d50061aa9fae_story.html?utm_term=.83911df73c41

CHAPTER 3

Fear Is the Off Switch

After all, when a stone is dropped into a pond, the water continues quivering even after the stone has sunk to the bottom.
—Arthur Golden, *Memoirs of a Geisha*

Rats are playful. Play is part of their learning. But, what happens to that playfulness when they sense a threat? And, why am I telling you about rats?

Education, as a system, tends to create fear and insecurity.[1] Chapter 1 focused on why teaching is one of the most stressful occupations in America. Chapter 2 examined the damage that stressed-out teachers impose on students. This chapter connects the two. In Chapter 4, we will look at the effects of prolonged stress and trauma. We will look deeper into how stress is shortening the careers and lives of teachers, and harming too many students. That damage can remain for life.

At the University of North Texas at Dallas, Michelle Kinder introduced our MindShift gathering to an experiment with rats. Conducted by Canadian scientists and led by Hans Dringenberg, the analysis focused on how fear influenced the rats and their learning. Under normal conditions, rats initiate play an average of 10 times per minute over five minutes. After four days, Dringenberg's team placed a small tuft of cat fur into the rat's playground. No cat, just hair. Play stopped, and the rats sat frozen. The scientists only heard the sound of heavy breathing.

When the cat hair was removed, it took three days before the rats tried to play. Further, their level of play never reached above five times per minute, half of what it had been. That one traumatic experience reset their baseline for learning and memory.[2]

Of course, a cat is a terrifying presence to any mouse. But, there was no cat in sight. Do you think humans might react similarly to subtle indicators of malevolence?

Yes. The human autonomic nervous system (ANS), controlling the automatic functions of the body, triggers a similar survival response in humans.

Fight or Flight

The ANS is divided into two responses. The ever-vigilant sympathetic nervous system (SNS) provokes fight, flight, freeze, perform, and other non-voluntary actions in the human body. The parasympathetic nervous system (PNS) provides recovery; it allows the mind and body to recover and restore through rest and various forms of social interaction. Recovery only happens when the vigilance side turns off. Fear, worry, and anxiety keep the SNS on, regardless of whether a threat is real, present, or nowhere to be found. We humans carry a lot of cat hair in our imagination.

Cat Hair Contagion

The average classroom today is often an invisible battlefield. Teachers must be prepared for students who live with cat hair in their minds. Every morning, many come from traumatizing households. But, almost all student brains are fatigued by stress, worry, lack of sleep, and digital distraction when they arrive at school. They are a hair trigger away from an amygdala hijack.

According to teacher and journalist Jessica Lander, "Roughly half of American school children have experienced at least some form of trauma—from neglect to abuse, to violence. In response, educators often find themselves having to take on the role of counselors, supporting the emotional healing of their students, not just their academic growth."[3]

And, she refers to *all* school children. But, of course, urban and low socio-economic communities see a much higher percentage. Dr. John Gasko, former Dean of the School of Education for the University of North Texas at Dallas, told our MindShift gathering at UNTD that, "Given that the majority of students in large urban districts are from low-income households in vulnerable neighborhoods (e.g., 85–88% across Dallas ISD), the chances are that they have suffered direct exposure to trauma or vicarious exposure, which is often undetected and undiagnosed as part of their learning."

As we move deeper into that emotional minefield, school boards and administrators are responding by "hardening" the schools, in order to improve safety. But that strips away more of a school's soul, elevating every student's sense of fear and insecurity.

My contention is that the solutions to many of the problems of education are not technical but deeply human in nature. By relying on science, we have repeatedly underestimated the inherent wisdom in culture and human experience, which has been shaped over millions of years.

—Lou Cozolino[4]

An Amygdala Hijack

The amygdala is central to the brain's survival function, continually scanning sound, visual, and other sensory readings to identify and evaluate

Fear Is the Off Switch 27

threats.[5] Like America's Ballistic Missile Defense System, it vigilantly scans our environment determining:

- safety or danger
- friendly or hostile
- trustworthy or untrustworthy
- easy or hard
- fun or tedious
- interesting or boring
- like or dislike
- happy or sad
- in or out.

Each time you have lost your cool, flipped out, freaked out, acted out, sent an angry email, or otherwise reacted, blame your amygdala. Because it quickly identified a threat and fired a missile, it bypassed your thought processor, the prefrontal cortex. Your brain experienced a level of emotional load that shut down thought and switched to pure reaction. You cannot reason with anyone caught in an amygdala hijack. Trying to do so simply keeps their emotions amped up, creating an escalating feedback loop.

Jumping to Conclusions

A young girl came home in tears from her first day from Kindergarten. In fact, she cried before and after school for several days in a row. After she finally broke down and told it all to her parents, they hid an audio recorder in her hair; they had to know what was going on in school.[6] And they did; they heard the teacher yell, insult, and belittle the kids throughout the class. When they played the recording for school officials, the administration refused to address the teacher's behavior.

Look, I know these situations are difficult. Everyone walks across a minefield. My point is simply that our society reflects the tension between the sympathetic nervous system and the parasympathetic nervous system. Actions and reactions too often turn dangerous, even deadly. Our reactions to the various and myriad cat hair balls are stressing everyone, especially children. Both populations—teachers and students— arrive at school each morning with their Ballistic Missile Defense Systems scanning and screaming high-alert warnings.

Let's face it; what would have been the societal exception a generation ago has become a norm. Despite new training for teachers in social-emotional literacy and conflict de-escalation, many older administrators were trained in old practices and attitudes of control, classroom management, and discipline.[7] Because we now live in a new world, those old practices have the reverse effect. They raise the stakes and the pressure; in the end, everyone gets damaged.

A new social context has replaced the old lens of neighbors in community to one of combatants on a battlefield. As Robert Putnam documented in his book, *Our Kids: The American Dream in Crisis*,[8] we are losing the vital social airbags that once protected our kids and communities. That is a primary reason conflict among neighbors takes on a much different dynamic than conflict among strangers. Any one of us might just as easily react like the kindergarten teacher. We all experience sudden cognitive overload. My kids remember times when "dad flipped out." I regret those flashes. Most parents do. But, even in our most volatile moments, our relationships are strong enough to maintain continuing connections within our families and other social circles.

But, raw and visceral survival instincts kick in when someone gets "worked up" and begins to act out or get aggressive. Without the solid knitwork of interpersonal relationships or at least professional training, we can quickly find ourselves in escalating situations of triggers triggering triggers. The amygdala doesn't discriminate threats.

Hijack in the Hallways

James attends middle school just north of Fort Worth. The slender, active, and agile kid is a bit nerdy, enjoys a small nucleus of friends, and loves hunting with his dad.

One recent morning, James wore a T-shirt that seemed to communicate a political message. It didn't. He is not a political or even vocal kid; he didn't understand how others would react. He just liked the shirt. But that fateful decision would alter his life.

After the first period, three boys confronted James in the hallway. They shoved, slapped, and shouted insults at him. One grabbed his cell phone and shattered it on the ground. I was with John when he got the call from the school. I saw concern, fear, and anger settle around his shoulders. John's immediate instinct was to warn James's girlfriend and parents. It was too late; one of the boys found and assaulted her.

What happens in those situations? Damn little. When political perceptions are baked in, the system cannot find a path to resolution. The legal risks and fear of media attention are too great. So, all parties shrug, mutter some barbed comments, and slowly disperse, creating another source of simmering social tension.

Naturally, the students and teachers at James's school quickly heard a wide variety of versions of what happened. Those always take on a life of their own. The families bear anger and shame, feeling betrayed by a system that did its best to wash its hands of the situation. James is afraid to go to school. His parents are putting the home up for sale. It will remain an open wound.

We've all read the same script from other places, like inner-city school conflicts that escalate until gunfire flashes. We've seen the same story in confrontations between two cliques that explode into little wars, or the bullying of a vulnerable kid that goes unseen until something snaps. Schools work hard to contain those broken record narratives.

But, the real and larger story presents the unintended consequences that erode psychological safety. Where safety once prevailed, we now see misguided attempts to harden school security to convince parents their children's safety is a priority. These turn into proxy battles over school safety and futile and predictable debates over gun violence. When I interviewed Larry Rosenstock, Principal of High Tech High, I asked if they use metal detectors because of their tough neighborhood. He said, "We don't use them because we know our kids and their families." How did High Tech High find a third path while others remain stuck? We need a story that breaks the impasse, a third path that takes us down a road of restoration, growth, and learning.

A New Story for Schools?

Schools, once safe havens or at least buffers from rising incivility, are now actors in the theater of brokenness. Schools have become high-stakes, high-stress pressure cookers for administrators, teachers, and students. That has created a climate of fear, insecurity, and distrust. It becomes only a matter of time for the pain to expose the brokenness everyone works so hard to hide.

> *The human response to fear is hardwired. How can we go from schools that create fear in leaders, teachers, and kids to write a new script of safe, playful curiosity?*
>
> —*Kevin Baird*

What if we wrote a new script for schools? Instead of helpless victims in a regime of fear, could schools become places for healing and learning? Some leaders at World Vision, a non-profit humanitarian organization, gave me a few lines from their script for broken communities. Opening scene: The lands they explore are dry and impoverished terrains of broken relationships. Their mission: "Pulling up the roots of poverty and plant seeds of change." The plot follows these stages:

1. Build relationships.
2. Earn the right to be heard.
3. Plan and work alongside local leaders.
4. Find solutions to change the future for their kids and the next generation.[9]

Writing a new story will first require new thinking. The World Vision story is good, but it, or any other new narrative, will require new training in order to get to new thinking. For example, it seems clear to most educators that we must de-escalate tension and create true and firm safe zones.

How? Maybe it starts smaller and simpler than we think.

For example, consider how the Momentous Institute in Dallas has learned to calm the body, slow the heart rate, and turn the SNS off to allow the prefrontal cortex to resume control. They teach kids from 3 years old through fifth grade how to manage their brains. Because so many come out of stressful households, they know that too many kids walk into school with their brains already overloaded. Their cognitive load increases the moment they walk into the classroom to engage with other students. It further increases the moment they have to solve a math problem or read to the class. Those simple and normal activities may be tipping points that send a child into an amygdala hijack.

Mindful breathing is one of the tools Momentous uses to settle a student down. So simple, so wise, they use a simple glitter ball as a tool and name the practice, "Settle Your Glitter." When a child is acting out or showing signs of getting worked up, a teacher *or student* will hand that child a small glitter ball. The student takes the ball and sits in an area designed to calm the troubled heart. The student shakes the ball and breathes slowly to a count of four and then exhales as the glitter settles. After a few cycles of mindful breathing, the heart slows and stimulates the vagus nerve. At that point, the teacher can re-engage the child.

Schools should be natural environments for peace, embracing and encouraging social and emotional literacy. Yet educational institutions seem to have their own fight-or-flight trigger that prevents administrators from stepping back, reflecting, and then re-establishing what we know is necessary for learning—healthy and resilient teachers who care for their students as individuals and then communicate hope and possibility.

Wrapping Up

- Rats lose playfulness and learning in the presence of cat hair.
- Children come to school with similar fears stuck in their brains.
- The autonomic nervous system (ANS) controls our response to threat and fear.
- Almost all students' brains are fatigued by stress, worry, lack of sleep, and digital distraction.
- Classrooms can be a minefield of stressed brains waiting for a trigger.
- World Vision says poverty reflects the impoverished terrain of broken relationships.
- Reducing stress in school begins by rebuilding safe relationships.

Practical Reflections

1. Which activities stress some of your students much more than others?
2. How might you begin and end each day through building relational connections?
3. What kinds of situations trigger your fight-or-flight response?
4. Do you have a way to deal with triggered stress like meditation or mindful breathing?

Notes

1. Rex M. Miller, et al., *Humanizing the Education Machine: How to Create Schools That Turn Disengaged Kids into Inspired Learners* (Hoboken, NJ: John Wiley & Sons, Inc., 2017).
2. Hans C. Dringenberg, et al., "Predator (Cat Hair)-Induced Enhancement of Hippocampal Long-Term Potentiation in Rats: Involvement of Acetylcholine." *Learning & Memory*, vol. 15, no. 3, 2008, pp. 112–116, doi:10.1101/lm.778108.

3. Jessica Lander, "Secondary Traumatic Stress for Educators: Understanding and Mitigating the Effects." *KQED*, Oct. 8, 2018. www.kqed.org/mindshift/52281/secondary-traumatic-stress-for-educators-understanding-and-mitigating-the-effects

4. Lou Cozolino, *Attachment-Based Teaching: Creating a Tribal Classroom* (New York: W.W. Norton Company, 2014).

5. *Harvard Health*, "Understanding the Stress Response." May 1, 2018, www.health.harvard.edu/staying-healthy/understanding-the-stress-response

6. News, *ABC Action*. "Parents Accuse Teacher of Bullying." YouTube, www.youtube.com/watch?v=V2uMkMA5UZY

7. Seth Stoughton, "How Police Training Contributes to Avoidable Deaths." *The Atlantic*, Dec. 12, 2014. www.theatlantic.com/national/archive/2014/12/police-gun-shooting-training-ferguson/383681/

8. Robert Putnam, *Our Kids: The American Dream in Crisis* (New York: Simon & Schuster, 2015).

9. World Vision, "Our Work." www.worldvision.org/our-work

CHAPTER 4

The Body Remembers

*As long as you keep secrets and suppress information, you are funda-
mentally at war with yourself . . . The critical issue is allowing yourself
to know what you know. That takes an enormous amount of courage.*
                                                    —Bessel Van der Kolk[1]

I carry secrets. You do too. Sometimes we pretend to be just fine when
we're not. That's why we put on our game faces for the public. Nothing
weird or dysfunctional about that. It's called maturity; we suppress our
own needs and problems for the sake of social glue, assuring workplace
or other social group harmony and effectiveness.

Some secrets, however, need an outlet. Because of their destructive
power, they must be disclosed in order to break the grip they hold over
our minds and bodies. As Dr. Van der Kolk suggests in the quote above,
those secrets can create war zones within our minds and bodies.

Those who have healthy marriages and other close relationships
understand the very natural rhythms of exposing secrets and then releasing them. We say or hear things like:

Oh, honey, my boss really got to me today. I just wanted to scream.

*Karen, I'm frightened about Mom's health. I think her diabetes is
getting worse.*

Hey, guys, sorry I'm late. Our daughter Ashley had a car wreck last night. She's OK, but it was a long night in the ER.

But, what about those who have no such close-knit human connections? How do they dump the toxins?

PostSecret: The Power of Releasing Secrets

People send Frank Warren very personal, very private postcards about secrets. He has collected more than a half million. Here are some actual messages people sent to this stranger:

Inside this envelope is the ripped up remains of a suicide note I didn't use. I feel like the happiest person on earth! (now).

(From a U.S. Army nurse) Sometimes I look at pictures of my patients on Facebook to see how their lives were before they got hurt.

Planning my wedding has been a painful reminder I have NO friends.

In 2004, Warren launched an experiment. He printed 3000 self-addressed postcards and handed them out at random on the streets of Washington, DC. The cards carried simple instructions. He asked people to decorate the cards, sharing a secret they have never told anyone. Cards soon started pouring in. The idea spread and people began to create and send their own cards. They eventually arrived from cities around the world. As of this date, Warren has collected more than half a million. You can visit his website at www.postsecret.com.

What do these half a million cards represent? Why would so many people disclose things so private and painful? Might they be "core samples" of American psychological health? Is each postcard a sample of the "psychological soil" composition and sediment around the one who wrote and mailed the card? If so, they capture a certain view of the true scope of emotional damage and pain in our society.

A New Understanding of Emotional Hygiene for Teachers

To make it more specific, what happens when you are a teacher and put in a position of absorbing the pain and secrets of students? Dr. Gasko describes teachers who stand in those sociopsychological gaps as "human shields." Clearly, that kind of role is very dangerous; those conditions impose unbearable burdens on people. Something's gonna blow. That's why most human shields must inevitably leave those situations for new roles that are positive and life-giving and without pain and guilt. But, many will always look back through survivor's guilt: "I got out, but I had to leave others behind."

According to Dr. Gasko, "Rising classroom challenges rank third in the reasons why teachers leave. The lack of professional development for the more complex social and emotional needs students now bring with them is also a major contributor."[2] We have also seen that the lack of real-time support and care forces teachers to "suppress information and feelings," thereby compounding the stress levels.

Think about what happens when you receive one of *those calls*, "Mr. Miller, your son is here with us in the Baylor Hospital Emergency Room." You instantly get pulled into an alternate, slow-motion, reality. The drive to the hospital seems to unfurl within a blur. Your imagination

goes into negative scenario overdrive. When you walk through the ER doors, your adrenaline has you so amped up, you could knock anyone down who gets in your way.

But, once you see your child *alive* and healthy, you burst into tears of joy. Of course, depending on *how* he ended up in the ER, you may also shift into a burst of scolding. That's how the body releases the effects of cortisol and the emotional tension of fear and worry.

School administrators understand new teachers can feel overwhelmed as they adjust to the realities of a complex classroom emotional landscape. In our MindShift cohort of over one hundred research participants, more than half were or had been teachers. They all told stories about their first years of teaching. Not one felt like their education prepared them for the realities of the classroom. All felt overwhelmed and exhausted, like having a first baby. Several felt incompetent, like failures. Most eventually left because of those ongoing conditions. There seemed to be an unspoken acceptance of those first years as a form of initiation or toughening. You can find hundreds of comments on blogs or video confessions about the emotional toll. It's a recklessly under-attended topic in teacher training, and yet, simple daily "emotional hygiene" for teachers may significantly reduce the damage to teachers' mental health.

Juliette Low Elementary in District 59 in Arlington Heights, Illinois, is one of the most advanced practitioners of social and emotional literacy in the country. Under Principal Susan Emja's leadership, they go beyond a solid program and implementation. They weave their practices into the culture.

Juliette Low does two things to provide emotional support for teachers. First, they provide in-classroom coaches to help teachers plan and design their classroom engagement. Some coaches also give a margin of relief when a teacher feels overwhelmed. Second, stressed teachers can sit with Principal Emja or Assistant Principal Dominquez. Both of these caring professionals provide a safe place for the teacher. He or she can release the stress by talking through some of the pain they've absorbed that day.

Such practices grant a level of highly valuable and practical emotional hygiene. Teachers can drain the stress from their system with no stigma. They no longer have to carry it home. And we all know that when we carry work burdens home, our stress will often lead to unhealthy coping behaviors in our family.

Dr. Nadine Burke Harris is one of the pioneers in ACE (adverse childhood experiences) work. As a doctor in San Francisco, she saw first-hand the connection between bizarre health conditions in children and exposure to trauma and abuse. Her observations mirrored what Kaiser Permanente found in their landmark ACE study which began in the mid-1990s in which they identified ten kinds of abuse and a system for assessing a child's mental and health risks:

1. Physical abuse
2. Sexual abuse
3. Emotional abuse
4. Physical neglect
5. Emotional neglect
6. Exposure to domestic violence
7. Household substance abuse
8. Household mental illness
9. Parental separation or divorce
10. Incarcerated household member.[3]

Dr. Burke has successfully megaphoned this public health threat to the medical community and to educators. The ACE assessment simply looks at how many of the ten categories a child experiences before the age of 18. A score of four or more raises the risk significantly. When a child's brain development gets interrupted, the delay in learning, self-regulation, and social skills can send those children down a predictable path of failure. The stress and stigma often lead to higher risk behaviors, disabilities, social problems, and even early death.[4] One National Center for Biotechnology Information (NCBI) study found that people with six or more ACEs died nearly 20 years earlier on average than those without. The "Years of Life Lost" (YLL) is three times greater.[5]

According to Dr. Van der Kolk, "As the ACE study has shown, child abuse and neglect are the single most preventable cause of mental illness, the single most common cause of drug and alcohol abuse, and a significant contributor to leading causes of death such as diabetes, heart disease, cancer, stroke, and suicide."[6]

Trauma Is Now a Classroom Norm

When I spoke with Dr. Gasko, he provided a more graphic explanation of what was taking place on the front lines with teachers and students. "My time in Chicago started me on the path of a different kind of teacher training. I became really concerned when I found that a significant number of teachers across one of the largest school districts in America were using anti-anxiety and anti-depression medications—especially Clonazepam and Prozac—to cope with the stress and adversity of

Social and emotional learning (SEL) is the process through which children and adults understand and manage emotions, set and achieve positive goals, feel and show empathy for others, establish and maintain positive relationships, and make responsible decisions.

—*Casel*[7]

teaching. One of the most overlooked areas in adult-based 'Social and Emotional Learning' (SEL) training is the personal work. Teachers not only need to understand how meditation and mindfulness apply to the classroom, they need these practices and deep body work for themselves."

The Collaborative for Academic, Social, and Emotional Learning (CASEL) describes these practices as:

- *Self-awareness:* Know your strengths and limitations.
- *Self-management:* Manage stress, control impulses, and display self-motivation.
- *Social awareness:* Understand and appreciate the perspectives of others.
- *Relationship skills:* Listen, communicate effectively, cooperate, resist negative social pressure, engage in positive conflict, stay connected, and be supportive.
- *Responsible decision-making:* Make principle-based decisions that respect others and reflect the Golden Rule.

Dr. Gasko told us, "Our shift is focusing on emotional and body-based work. There is no route to emotional healing and well-being outside the body. Engaging the body is one of the most overlooked facets of well-being work. If we don't take the body's role in healing into account, it is only 'neck up' work and not going to get teachers to a baseline level of wellness.

"During my training with Bessel Van der Kolk,[8] we found that memory is stored from toes to crown. In fact, traumatic memory gets equally stored in our body's tissues, just as it is in the brain. How do we unlock trauma? You have to engage the body as much as you engage the brain and the mind, which is the conceptual apparatus on top of your brain."

How many mental health problems, from drug addiction to self-injurious behavior, start as attempts to cope with the unbearable physical pain of our emotions? If Darwin was right, the solution requires finding ways to help people alter the inner sensory landscape of their bodies. Until recently, this bidirectional communication between body and mind was largely ignored by Western science, even as it had long been central to traditional healing practices in many other parts of the world, notably in India and China. Today it is transforming our understanding of trauma and recovery.

—Bessel Van der Kolk[9]

"Oh, Daddy, I Can't See. What's Happening?"

I got that call from our daughter Michelle while she was in class as a high school sophomore. Through the fog of my pounding heart, dry mouth, and jumbled thoughts, Lisa and I were able to get Michelle home right away. Dr. Hu, an ophthalmologist and a friend cleared his appointments for us.

He diagnosed Michelle with optic neuritis, inflammation of the optic nerve. It collapses peripheral vision by 70% and more. If not immediately treated with steroids, the inflammation leaves permanent damage. Following fast treatment, the swelling subsided and her vision returned. But Michelle's life continues to be governed by this new invader.

During the next seven years, Michelle experienced seven similar flare-ups. Finally, after a couple of years of examinations and tests by various specialists, Michelle was "diagnosed" with multiple sclerosis. But, that diagnosis isn't conclusive; sometimes doctors use certain descriptions to explain what they can't explain.

Michelle is now among the 160 million people in the U.S.—half the U.S. population[10]—that carry some form of chronic disease. And that means a lifetime of managing symptoms. That includes an estimated 1.8 million teachers. My friend Phil Williams describes it as "sicker sooner, living longer."

The diagnosis of MS happened just as Michelle entered the job market. Eight months into her first job, she started to receive push back and criticism for taking time for doctor's appointments. Even though she had disclosed her MS diagnosis during interviews, they soon eliminated her job. Her second job started and ended in the same pattern. I've worked and consulted for enough companies to understand the uphill challenge Michelle will always face when employers have to accommodate a young person managing a chronic disease. Most young adults who manifest strange symptoms that get labeled as some form of chronic disease will have to struggle, pretend, live in insecurity, and face the dehumanizing wilderness of our health-care system.

Most who suffer with chronic disease manage it well. They see good days and bad days and learn how to present an "I'm good" public image.

Like many parents, spouses, and other loved ones who serve as caregivers, we travel a journey to find answers. Today it's pain relief with injections of gabapentin; tomorrow we'll explore mitochondria support. Next month, we may try the Wall Diet to reduce inflammation and then on to hyperbaric oxygen treatment. If those trials don't yield answers, we'll try something else. That's the journey.

Last summer I gave the commencement address to the National University for Health Sciences. I took advantage of the opportunity, searching out some of their top experts in autoimmune diseases. I met with Dr. Robert Humphreys, recipient of the Lifetime Achievement Award from the International Association of Functional Neurology. After telling him Michelle's story, he asked me to recap her history beginning with the optic neuritis. After carefully listening, he explained that MS would be a rare diagnosis for a teenager. He suggested trauma as a more likely explanation of how a 17-year-old might experience these symptoms. That took us to the next piece in this puzzle.

Unraveling Michelle's Mystery

Michelle was an outgoing and unusual child during elementary school. That's when we learned she fell on the autism spectrum. According to the National Institute of Neurological Disorders and Stroke, the overlap between Asperger's Syndrome and high-functioning autism is unclear. The ASD classification is to some extent an artifact of how autism was discovered, and may not reflect the true nature of the spectrum.[11]

Michelle was also diagnosed as high-functioning and hyperlexic. In other words, her verbal skills hid her struggle to understand and navigate social nuance. She did wonderfully during elementary school. The only comments of concern we received from teachers were about recess. Through them, we saw that Michelle gravitated toward playing with younger kids, hung out with teachers, or preferred to be alone in her classroom.

Middle School was different. She started getting harassed and teased. Other students made fun of her. She had a harder time with standardized tests even though she could verbally answer all the questions. Although it was hard on Michelle, she was still resilient and determined to fit in. Lisa and I did not see how those social challenges created a firestorm in Michelle's brain. Without a fully functioning prefrontal cortex to buffer and process social complexities, her sympathetic nervous system (SNS) was always *on*. Our outgoing little girl did not fight, she just retreated into her mind and imagination.

One day, when Michelle was in high school, two upper-class students, a boy and his girlfriend played a "prank" on Michelle. The girlfriend turned her chair to face Michelle and placed her hands on Michelle's knees. Then her boyfriend came up to Michelle from behind, draped his arms across her torso, and threatened various sexual acts against her. They also threatened her if she told anyone. It took a year before we found out. During that year, Lisa and I saw dramatic changes in her moods and behaviors. Her anxiety levels jumped, she even jerked and became rigid when hugged. Then we saw cut marks on her wrists. We soon discovered she was cutting herself almost nightly. We sought help, we were confused. Was such behavior a reflection of Michelle's Asperger's? Was it related to the fact she was adopted? We desperately reached for any explanation. We had to find a lost key to our lovely daughter's pain.

Michelle eventually told us about the assault. After our tornado of sadness, hurt, and anger, we took the matter to the school. The young man and his girlfriend admitted their prank. He received a minor suspension, but the damage was done. That very next year was Michelle's first flare-up of optic neuritis. When I shared the story with Dr. Gasko, he explained, "Michelle's experience is connected to a pattern that neuroscientists call the brain's 'Default Mode Network' or DMN. This network usually runs too much. The default mode locks you into the cycle of rumination. Rumination usually locks in on negative things, creating narrative loops reinforcing the experience and imminent threat."

Dr. Daniel Amen is a neuroscientist, psychiatrist, best-selling author, and founder of the Amen Clinics. He is famous for pioneering SPECT brain scans. After meeting him at a wellness conference in 2017, he connected us to Dr. John "Jay" Faber in the Los Angeles Amen Clinic. Dr. Faber showed me examples of healthy brains and brains with ADHD, with concussions from sports, abuse and trauma, autism, chronic stress, and brains that have taken different kinds of medication.

So, I asked my family if they would like to go to Los Angeles for our summer vacation. They love going there for the beach, museums, and the food. Then I said, "What would you think if we all got our brains scanned?" Once we walked through it, they were all onboard. Nathan was fascinated by the technology, Michelle was okay as long as we went to Umami Burger, and Tyler wanted to return to the Getty Museum.

After our scans, Dr. Faber reviewed our results one-on-one, and I recorded each session. He pointed out three areas in Michelle's scans— the basal ganglia, the anterior cingulate, and the thalamus—that displayed higher than normal levels of blood flow. Those areas of the brain, all connected to one another, present a clear diamond pattern on the scan. All three lighting up gives evidence of past emotional trauma. It is a visual view of Dr. Gasko's default mode network explanation.

Michelle's trauma may explain how her brain developed this pattern and DMN; it's her cat hair. Seeing it on a screen was a big step for Michelle too. Those on the autism spectrum can often relate better to images and patterns than to verbal explanation or recommendations.

Michelle has begun her journey to breaking the past vicious cycle. For the first time the scans provided a step on a ladder she could understand and begin climbing. She started with recommendations to change her diet to remove foods that contribute to inflammation that affect her brain and body. We have new language about what's happening inside when stressful situations trigger her DMN. She can now better put her mind on pause and regroup. She has built a strong network of friends over the past five years from her involvement in the Renaissance Festival in Waxahachie, Texas. They have become a close-knit extended family. She is attending college majoring in graphic arts. Finally, during this year's Renaissance Festival, her boyfriend proposed and gave her a beautiful ring he made. Lisa and I will probably never forget the pain and struggle Michelle walked through and wonder, what if? But we would not trade that what if for what she has become, the strength and compassion she has developed, and promise ahead of her. Our family understands, perhaps better than most, how our issues get stored in our tissues and the journey to restoration.

Let's Start by Washing Our Hands

Consider these simple aphorisms that have long endured as foundation stones for a way of life:

> *Early to bed, early to rise makes a person healthy, wealthy, and wise.*
> *An apple a day keeps the doctor away.*
> *A penny saved is a penny earned.*
> *Don't let the sun go down on your anger.*
> *Never ruin an apology with an excuse.*

Whether from Ben Franklin, the Bible, or anonymous sources, they capture elemental wisdom that once formed a cultural consensus.

Simple habits often prove to carry great impact over time.

In the same way, during the mid-1800s, Austrian doctor Ignaz Semmelweis observed maternal mortality rates were significantly lower in one hospital where doctors washed their hands between procedures. "Following the implementation of [his] measure[s], the mortality rate fell dramatically to 3% in the clinic most affected and remained low thereafter."[12]

Dr. Gasko says, "I equate our work to what happened when we learned how to wash our hands. That simple act eradicated 85% of known diseases in America. What if the psychological and emotional equivalent is taking the extra step to focus on very simple things around the holistic wellness of educators, where we attach real interventions and resources?

"Singapore does this really well. When I was there last year, I saw them do a couple of things that are anathema in the U.S. One, they never let a teacher office in isolation. They've created a space called the *Pulse* (labeled the same in every school). It functions like a hive where everybody offices in a community setting. They design it for interaction.

"In every school, on the opposite side of the building, they have space called the Living Room. It is a teacher decompression chamber, designed by the teachers. We are working with schools across America helping to redesign teacher spaces in schools to support this notion of a decompression chamber."

Removing the Stigma

During our last MindShift project, which tackled workplace health and well-being, a series of personal tragedies hit me within a relatively brief period. I lost my mom because of medical neglect. Three months later my younger brother died suddenly. Then my mother-in-law suffered a massive cerebral aneurysm and passed away. Within that same time, our daughter Michelle was diagnosed with multiple sclerosis.

Although I didn't publicize those events to our team, my absences and the need to shift some of the load must have signaled something. To my surprise, members of our team began to speak up and reach out. The first was from Charlie, a Harvard Ph.D., Vietnam vet, and a long-time colleague. I've known Charlie fifteen years, but until he reached out to me, I had not known he has struggled with PTSD since the war. Another colleague confided she just learned her husband had early-stage dementia. Her job required a lot of travel and she wasn't sure what she would do. More stories and perspectives continued to flow toward me.

Through it all, I saw that because my life was so intertwined with the research team, my struggles—the issues in my tissues—made it safe for others to express encouragement and reveal their pains. Everyone has a story of deep pain. But, without the safety of genuine relationships, those stories can remain hidden.

But, we all need the treasure buried in those around us. That's why we should do all we can to wash the stigmas away. Just as the simple act of washing hands eradicated most of the known diseases in nineteenth-century America, the relational cleansing we receive from one another is also important. The healing balm of care and compassion should flow freely to every member of society.

Wrapping Up

- Some secrets are stored in the body and will do harm if they are not worked out of our systems.
- Teachers become human shields, absorbing the pain and trauma of their students.
- Schools need to provide help for teachers so they can process the vicarious trauma they absorb from students.

- Some children have a high level of ACEs (adverse childhood experiences) that puts them at high risk of falling behind, dropping out, and a life of emotional pain and sickness.
- Trauma is now a norm in many classrooms.
- Social Emotional Literacy is becoming part of a teacher's basic tool kit.
- Schools must practice simple emotional hygiene to provide care and recovery for teachers on the front lines.
- Removing the stigma of needing help is the first step in emotional hygiene.

Practical Reflections

1. Can you think of something that compromised you and added to your stress because you didn't have a safe place in which you could share it?
2. Have you learned to flush things from your system by using the mind and the body?
3. What do you wish could happen in your school—like the Pulse and Living Room areas in Singapore schools—that could help you move stress out of your body and increase your sense of well-being?
4. How would removing the stigma of judgment free you and others in your school?

Notes

1. Bessel Van der Kolk, *The Body Keeps the Score: Brain, Mind and Body in the Healing of Trauma* (New York: Penguin Books, 2015).
2. Presentation by Dr. Gasko to a gathering of educators working to develop the University of North Texas as Dallas's Third Place teaching lab.
3. "Got Your ACE Score?" *ACEs Too High*, Feb. 27, 2019. www.acestoohigh.com/got-your-ace-score/
4. Centers for Disease Control and Prevention, "About the CDC-Kaiser ACE Study for Violence Prevention and Injury." www.cdc.gov/violenceprevention/childabuseandneglect/acestudy/about.html

5. David W. Brown, et al., "Adverse Childhood Experiences and the Risk of Premature Mortality." *American Journal of Preventive Medicine*, Nov. 2009. www.ncbi.nlm.nih.gov/pubmed/19840693

6. Van der Kolk, *The Body Keeps the Score*.

7. Casel (Collaborative for Academic, Social, and Emotional Learning), "What Is SEL?" www.casel.org/what–is–sel/

8. https://besselvanderkolk.net/index.html

9. Van der Kolk, *The Body Keeps the Score*.

10. Rex M. Miller, et al., *The Healthy Workplace Nudge: How Healthy People, Cultures, and Buildings Lead to High Performance* (Hoboken, NJ: John Wiley & Sons, Inc., 2018).

11. https://www.ninds.nih.gov/Disorders/Patient-Caregiver-Education/ Fact-Sheets/Autism-Spectrum-Disorder-Fact-Sheet

12. "Historical Perspective on Hand Hygiene in Health Care." *WHO Guidelines on Hand Hygiene in Health Care: First Global Patient Safety Challenge, Clean Care Is Safer Care.*, U.S. National Library of Medicine, Jan. 1, 1970. www.ncbi.nlm.nih.gov/books/NBK144018/

CHAPTER 5

Having the Stress Conversation in Your School

We feel we are having conversations <u>about</u> our school that we should have <u>in</u> our school.

—Colin, Haleigh, and Luke

That was the closing line of the presentation by three high school students to forty national experts in education. We had worked side-by-side with them for two days in our Holland, Michigan "Book Barn Raising," the culmination of our research and writing gatherings across the country. The seasoned leaders all looked at each other like we had missed a turnoff somewhere back down the road. Colin in ninth grade and Haleigh and Luke in eleventh had gently reminded us that this was their conversation too. We flew in and would fly out; they lived with the issues every day.

MindShift's process for books includes a Book Barn Raising as the culmination of each project. We invite our veterans to come together to rapid-prototype our book. We provide all the tools, weeks of preparations, a mini-boot camp, and a coach to help our designated teams create a model for the book.

We did not design it to be competitive, but it is. Think of the cooking shows, *Hell's Kitchen* or *Chopped*; people dashing around the "kitchen," working under hard deadlines, bumping into each other, spilling work on the floor. Our participants have to come up with a full course "meal:" a book title and subtitle, the cover art, a movie trailer, a full table of contents, stories, and a review of each chapter. You can see, the stakes are high.

Then, just like in the movies, three kids in the middle of forty national experts end up stealing the show.

Five schools joined our Holland Summit. But one, Hamilton High, is located 11 miles from Holland. That's because Holland is landlocked. Housing prices have climbed during the town's comeback. So, if a family wants a larger home on a 3-acre wooded lot, they have to go outside Holland. So, 15 minutes southeast on Highway 40, Hamilton has become a natural magnet for those searching for more affordable housing.

Hamilton is farming country. The deep dark soil reveals why Western Michigan has some of the best "muck farming" in the country. Muck farms are drained swamps, ideal for onions, carrots, celery, and potatoes. Hamilton High just rises from the muck. No subdivisions ring the school. And, there is no town, no hint of a Main Street. Hamilton Community Schools Superintendent Dave Tebo explained, "People move out here for the school and to get a bigger house and land for far less than in Holland or Zeeland. The high school *is* the community and that makes a diverse and interesting demographic.

"We have kids who live in mobile homes, and we help some families with propane during the winter. We have other families that are certainly among top income earners and drive their kids to school in BMWs."

Colin, Haleigh, and Luke attend Hamilton High School. Luke was the self-described nerd and deep thinker in the group. Colin considered all the angles. Haleigh was the passionate "go with your gut" spokesperson.

The student team came out the chute with an idea that captured our imagination. They called their book, "The Passion Code." Imagine *The Matrix* meets *Pleasantville*. Haleigh, the passion crusader, kicked it off, "When a teacher who is passionate about the subject connects with a student who is curious, passions collide."

The room resonated. The educators looked at each other: *That's right. Yes.*

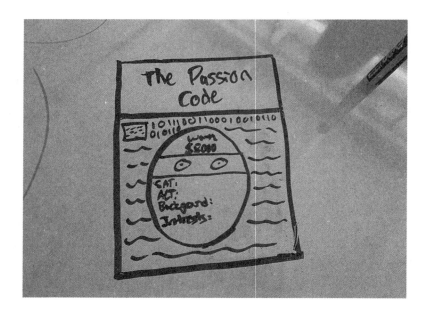

The Art of Story Telling

Over our two years of research for our books, we at MindShift collected and collated hundreds of stories, articles, academic research, statistics, infographics, and big ideas. I use Evernote to store and tag everything for easy access. The content falls into three main buckets: current state (positive and negative), OMG shockers, and positive deviants as signposts for hope and the future.

As much as I need, use, and love technology, I've also found a low-tech approach allows the human factor to lead the process. So, before the Book Barn Raising, I sift through my Evernote files and pick the most memorable items to transfer onto 6" x 8" grid-formatted index cards, using multicolored markers. I end with a stack of about 200 cards, sorted by color. A nineteenth-century writer could have done it the same way.

We use the cards to create a table of contents. They also serve as prompts. Teams use many or few; some toss them and create their own cards. We use our whole wall space to create storyboards for each team. By the time the chapter headings are laid out and the 6 x 8 cards for each chapter placed under them, each storyboard spans about 8' in height and more than 25' wide.

I knew we could use help to convert all those cards into stories. So, I turned to Joe Tankersley, a futurist, author, and storyteller. As a former Walt Disney "Imagineer" and producer for theme parks, the stories he created shaped the experiences for billion-dollar park attractions all the way down to talking trash bins. I invited Joe to walk us through a storytelling boot camp and then coach the teams during the exercises.

His first words were, "Story is one of the most powerful tools that we have to create change." Then, Joe walked us through ten keys to telling stories well:

1. *Embrace your voice.* Readers want to hear your unique perspective. We all need those who can help us make sense of the avalanche of data out there.
2. *Ask four questions.* Why are you writing this? What is your purpose? What is the promise? Why would someone spend time reading it?
3. *What is your hook,* the central idea that anchors your work? In a theme park, we always made sure that there was one central icon—think of Cinderella's castle—that could orient our visitors. Books need the same clear beacon.

4. *Consider the waders, paddlers, and divers,* three distinct audiences with different attention spans. Waders scan the cover, table of contents, and flip through the pictures. Paddlers scan the chapter headings, perhaps the first and last paragraph in each chapter. Divers read everything. How will you satisfy all three?

5. *Keep it simple.* Every chapter must start with a clear idea and premise. It should be long enough to cover the subject and short enough to be interesting.

6. *Imagine you are in a conversation with the reader.* Don't try to convince them you're right, but give them space to consider your point of view and respond with their own.

7. *Help them feel it.* Create emotion, tension, and make it personal.

8. *Everyone wants to be the hero.* When they read your story, can they imagine themselves doing all that?

9. *Start in the middle of the story,* that is where the action gets interesting.

10. *End at the beginning.*

After Joe's presentation, each team found a comfortable area to spread out and work on their project for the next full day:

- Step 1: Start with a big idea.
- Step 2: Translate the big idea into a full book cover.
- Step 3: Create a movie trailer from the cover.
- Step 4: Build a table of contents from the trailer and card deck.
- Step 5: Tape the chapter headings along a horizontal row.
- Step 6: Use the cards to organize and build subheadings for each chapter.
- Step 7: Write your story using Joe's guidelines.
- Step 8: Present your story to the room.

The Truth About Stress

Colin, Haleigh, and Luke took the summit experience deeper and further than we even hoped. After the summit, I huddled with them and Superintendent Tebo in a video call. They dug deep into what stress looks like in the daily life of all the students. They started the process with a survey of all the students. The questions examined the joys, disappointments, stresses, and drama of the students' everyday lives. They

examined sleep patterns, nutrition, social media, screens, and approaches to the future.

They sent out 768 surveys; 275 came back (a very good response). From those, they chose 38 students for in-depth interviews.

From all the data, they compiled riveting details:

- Some students also work a job after school.
- As a result of jobs, sports, and other demands, some students don't get home till 9:30 p.m. or later.
- And, many must get up at 5:30 a.m. in order to make the bus and be in class by the 7:30 start.
- Because of that, school administrators are considering a rollback of the start time.
- Including their jobs, some students "work" an 80-hour week.
- Many students must prioritize sleep over class attendance and home work.
- About half the students don't take time for breakfast. Convenience foods fill the gap.
- Students need teachers to build better relationships and safe space.

Joe and I met to review the surveys and interviews. As we talked, we were both drawn to Emily's story (told later in this chapter). Her decision to be a teacher drove her into stress. Yet, as Joe observed, "It wasn't more than 20, 30 years ago, if a student wanted to be a teacher, we'd say, 'Wow; what a great choice.' So, for her to exist in a world where that's not validated—even by her family—ties back into the bigger story; teaching has become a thankless and dangerous job."

The interviews revealed that most students live in high stress. If the three project leaders were unaware that everyone felt stress like they did, it's reasonable to assume that most of the student body didn't know that either. Luke probably spoke for all students when he told us it helped him to know he wasn't the only one, that stress was a common factor for the students. It helps just knowing they were all in it together.

It seemed that the stress factor boiled down to the students' perceptions that everyone was expected to be the perfect student. Perhaps the kids with learning differences saw the stress most clearly. They were continually reminded of it by the fact that people treat them disparately because they are "different." The environment makes them feel like they don't fit or belong.

Joe noticed, "The interviews reveal just how far the system is designed against learning. If you go to school, study, take a test, and get graded on it, then that's not learning. The learning process is iterative. You try something, you get some of it right, you fail some of it, and go learn more about it.

"I was struck by how these students are terrified of 'failure.' And their definition of failing means to get a bad grade. But that's not *failure*; that's an inability to regurgitate facts. These students feel like they are in an education arms race. The system tells them, 'Hey, guess what? You're competing against everybody else in the room, and we're going to judge you on how well you do.' The natural reaction of playing it safe and avoiding risk seems contrary to the whole concept of learning."

The students in general did not clearly understand how stress affected them, or even how to talk about it. They lumped everything into a generic stress bucket, "I have too much to do or not enough time to do it." They didn't seem to know how to ask for help. They say, "I'm stressed," or "it's a drama" as catch-all phrases. The word "drama" showed up a lot in the interviews. That probably hides a lot of stuff that's potentially serious, stuff that needs attention. We saw that building awareness of how stress hurts everyone, but in different ways, could help students to objectify it, and thereby reduce it. Developing language to help distinguish different kinds of stress could help.

These students could also use help to explore some of the bigger questions, like "Why are we killing ourselves for grades? What is the purpose behind it all?"

Emily's Story

Although names and details have been changed to protect privacy, Emily's story is based on a true story. At 17, her burning curiosity told everyone that she had a plan. The light in her eyes danced; details and questions seemed to try to break out. But, what looked like a plan was a passionate search for something to be passionate about.

One day she signed up for Mrs. Lowe's AP English literature class. Emily quickly learned that she taught with passion. With a Master's in history and a minor in theater, Mrs. Lowe taught in a theatrical panache, bringing characters alive with clothes, artifacts, and dramatic voices. A couple of weeks later, Emily told her mom, "English is my oxygen for the day." Her mom listened silently.

Over the dinner conversation that evening, she told her parents she wanted to be a teacher. After an awkward silence, her dad cleared his throat. "You know, Em, you need to really think about this. I'm afraid you'll be poor and unhappy." Her mother nodded agreement, and said, "Oh, honey, I know you're excited by Mrs. L's class, but you live in a different time, a different economy. You'll be sorry if you end up unable to live, drive, and wear what you want. We just think you can do better."

After crying herself to sleep that night, she closed the door to the dream and locked her code away. But, secretly she held onto her dream to become a great teacher someday. Like Mrs. Lowe.

One day, Mrs. Lowe gave Emily a glimpse of her secret. "When you see passion in someone, let the passions collide. If you let the passions grow together, that fusion will open your code up again."

Emily continued to love and live for Mrs. Lowe's English Lit class. But, she kept noticing some students came out beaming, while others seemed to just sleepwalk out the door. One day Emily got the courage to ask Mrs. L, "Why do some kids stumble out of your class like zombies?"

"Oh, Emily. That's the hard part about being a teacher. Some kids, like you, find their passion code. Others have been raised to fear passion. They don't even know they have a code. Others know it but are afraid to unlock it. They don't want it stolen or damaged."

A few days later, when Emily slowly cracked the door of her heart to Mrs. Lowe, all her fears and stress "monsters" just tumbled out onto the floor. In the end, a tearful Mrs. Lowe patted Emily on the shoulder and said, "Yes, I've seen the monsters." Then she took her student's hand; "Emily, I can help you," she almost pleaded. "Dream stealers are the first villains to attack. Others will follow. But, you have it within you to be a great teacher. If you go down this path, I will be your guide; I will work as hard with you as someone once did for me."

Emily loved how one solitary woman brought so many characters into the classroom. Emily was enraptured as the class worked through *Les Misérables* for five weeks. And, then the day of the final lesson came. Emily wondered what living characters would step from *Les Misérables* into the classroom today. She seemed to float to class on a magic carpet of anticipation.

But, when she stepped into the room, she shut her eyes and dropped her head. *No. No.* Instead of Mrs. L, she saw a substitute teacher standing at the front of the room. She knew by looking, the woman could not fill Mrs. Lowe's shoes. Surely, the whole four weeks had been a waste. But, then the substitute introduced herself to the class and pulled out a letter from Mrs. Lowe. She read out:

Class, I am so sorry I can't be here. There is no place I'd rather be than with you. However, sometimes life just gets in the way. But don't worry. You have a great teacher until I get back, someone who will make these characters come alive. I know how well prepared she is and I have confidence Emily will do great and you will give her great support.

Emily had to sit down; she looked up at the substitute who smiled and said, "Yes, Emily, you're the teacher for this final lesson. I'll be here to help if you need me."

The next hour exhilarated Emily, and terrified her. At first, she was so nervous standing in front of the class that she could feel herself shaking. She couldn't replicate the skills of Mrs. Lowe, but her passion for the subject kept rising to the surface. Soon the entire class joined the collaborative moment of true learning. She got her first taste of what teaching means. Because of that moment, that day, Emily knew, "I want to be a teacher."

Over the summer Emily worked at the Tutoring Center. Teaching kids who needed help was hard, much harder than she expected. But Emily learned she had a gift of helping others discover a passion for learning. Most never knew it was there. But it opened like a large red parachute against a bright blue sky. One day a young girl, Isabel, came to the center. She had recently moved to the area. Isabel was far behind because her parents moved so often looking for work. But, she had a hunger to learn.

When Mrs. Lowe's words about passions growing together came back to Emily, her passion flared again. She came in early and stayed late to help Isabel. By the end of the summer, Isabel was heading well-prepared for fifth grade math. Isabel's parents were so proud. Emily had given their daughter a new superpower: confidence! That was the first year she felt buoyant about starting at a new school. Isabel adopted Emily's joy in learning; she also hugged her when she arrived and left. At the end of the summer, the Tutoring Center director said, "Emily, you've got the gift. I'd love to have you come back next year!"

Emily had coffee with Mrs. Lowe throughout the summer. They both shared war stories from the front lines of teaching. They also mapped a plan for Emily's senior year and looked ahead to the challenges of picking a college, figuring out the finances, and rebuilding Emily's family support.

Finally, Mrs. L told her, "Emily, you learned this summer teaching can be hard, rewarding, frustrating, and joyful. Remember, joy is the spark that ignites passion in a student. Protect it. Don't let anything or anyone steal your joy or your passion."

Emily is an actual student at Hamilton High. She has a dream to teach, and her dream stealers are real. The tension between the dream and its thieves creates deep stress. That's why Emily doesn't get enough sleep. As part of the Advanced Placement group, she pushes herself hard. But, sometimes, she doesn't know why she strives so hard.

Many teachers like Mrs. Lowe can be found out there; they're doing all they can to help students find their passions. The students of Hamilton High helped us see those teachers need our help. Everyone in the community can become part of the conversation about passion, the monsters, the dream stealers, and helping one another to reach higher.

Colin, Haleigh, and Luke's book idea, "The Passion Code," follows what stress looks like in a day in the life of five student personas (Emily is one of the stories). They explore how the five student character types navigate (and try to overcome) a system designed to kill their passion. Each student represents a different group at Hamilton High:

- The AP Students
- Sports and Clubs
- Fine Arts (band, theater, choir, and art)
- Learning Differences
- Family Differences

The first phase of the project built a deeper awareness among students, teachers, and the administration. They plan to share their discoveries with the school board. They hope the data and stories will pull the board into a larger process of addressing the stress students and teachers carry every day.

Colin, Haleigh, and Luke created the way to have that crucial school-wide conversation about stress. Dave Tebo, their superintendent, who supports their effort, knows it will be uncomfortable and will likely lead to difficult conversations and trade-offs. But Dave concluded, "We all know it; now we have a way to get our arms around it."

The steps in Hamilton High's project may be helpful for starting the conversation in other schools:

1. Recruit a team of students from different grades and groups.
2. Enlist one or two adult guides.
3. Define, "Why we are doing this and what do we hope to learn?"
4. Identify the different student groups, from which to create personas.
5. Create a list of survey questions relevant to your school and community.
6. Find a tool to deliver the survey (they used SurveyMonkey).
7. Collate the data based on persona groups. Identify the common and outlier attributes.

8. Identify and interview five to six individuals out of each persona.
9. Create a composite individual who represents each persona group.
10. Build a story.

Joe Tankersley's steps for building the story could also be helpful. He reminded us of the classic approach to building stories. If you're looking for an outline for your story, the Hero's Journey is a great place to start.

1. Who is your protagonist (hero or heroine)? Describe him or her. What does your hero hope or dream for?
2. What is his or her average day like?
3. Identify and describe the external villain or villains (people or circumstances) that stand in the way of your hero's or heroine's dream.
4. Who is the enemy inside that holds the hero back?
5. Why would it be tragic if either the external or internal villain wins?
6. Who is the guide who shows up, understands what they face, and knows how to overcome?

7. What are some trials your hero must overcome?
8. How did the journey change the protagonist?
9. How will they take their lessons and newfound magic back to help others?

What Happens in Holland Stays in Holland

When the summit concluded, when the last of our team members left Holland, I looked back over what happened in that place. Forty educational leaders gathered in Western Michigan to examine the details of life within a specific community. Like those on safari, we gazed through our own lenses at native life, including schools, businesses, and social capital.

But, for the first time, we invited high school students to become part of our summit. I don't think we realized that they didn't know the attitude and behavior patterns of the sophisticated adults in these sessions. They just jumped in. They brought the realities they live with every day. As a result, they expanded our view of stakeholders. In all our site visits, conversations, and sessions, we probably interacted with a couple of hundred students. Their participation was not academic. When they spoke of classrooms, teachers, students, stress, damaged sleep patterns, students holding down jobs while still in high school, they carried pictures in their minds we could not see. We saw abstract types; they saw their friends.

I'm sure they hoped we would find the magic, the elixir that could change lives and schools all over the country. Oh, and, ladies and gentlemen, don't forget Holland.

I keep thinking of Joe Tankersley's comment about how the educational system is designed "against learning." He saw the learning process as a generic and multifaced function of civilization. It's often haphazard, meandering, more organic than organized. Joe called it "Iterative." It becomes successively better as you do it. As Joe said, "You try something, you get some of it right, you fail some of it, and go learn more about it." That is a classic and often spontaneous way of learning. Learning should be fun, creative, and the result of great curiosity. Learning should be a joyous venture.

Instead, learning is often somewhat like iatrogenic medicine; besides it being of great benefit, it also injures. So, we have a student survey revealing inordinate pressure from schools and parents, drama, stress, lack of sleep, and fear of failure.

Perhaps the most helpful development of our work in Holland, and across America, would be if we could help teachers and students cross back over the big divide into the sheer joy of learning.

Then, watch them share that joy with their families and communities.

Wrapping Up

- Students want to have conversations about their complex lives.
- The interviews revealed most students live with high stress.
- To know you are not the only one who feels stress reduces stress.
- The system is designed against learning.
- Taking a test is not the same as learning.
- Most students are terrified of failure.
- Most students do not clearly understand how stress affects them.

Practical Reflections

1. Does your school have a way to openly talk about and process what life as a student is like?
2. What do you think are the three major drivers of stress for your students, in your school, and for you?
3. If you were to launch a school-wide conversation, what topic would you like to talk about?
4. How do you distinguish the different kinds of stress in your life and in what you observe among students?

Part 2

Changing the Story of Education

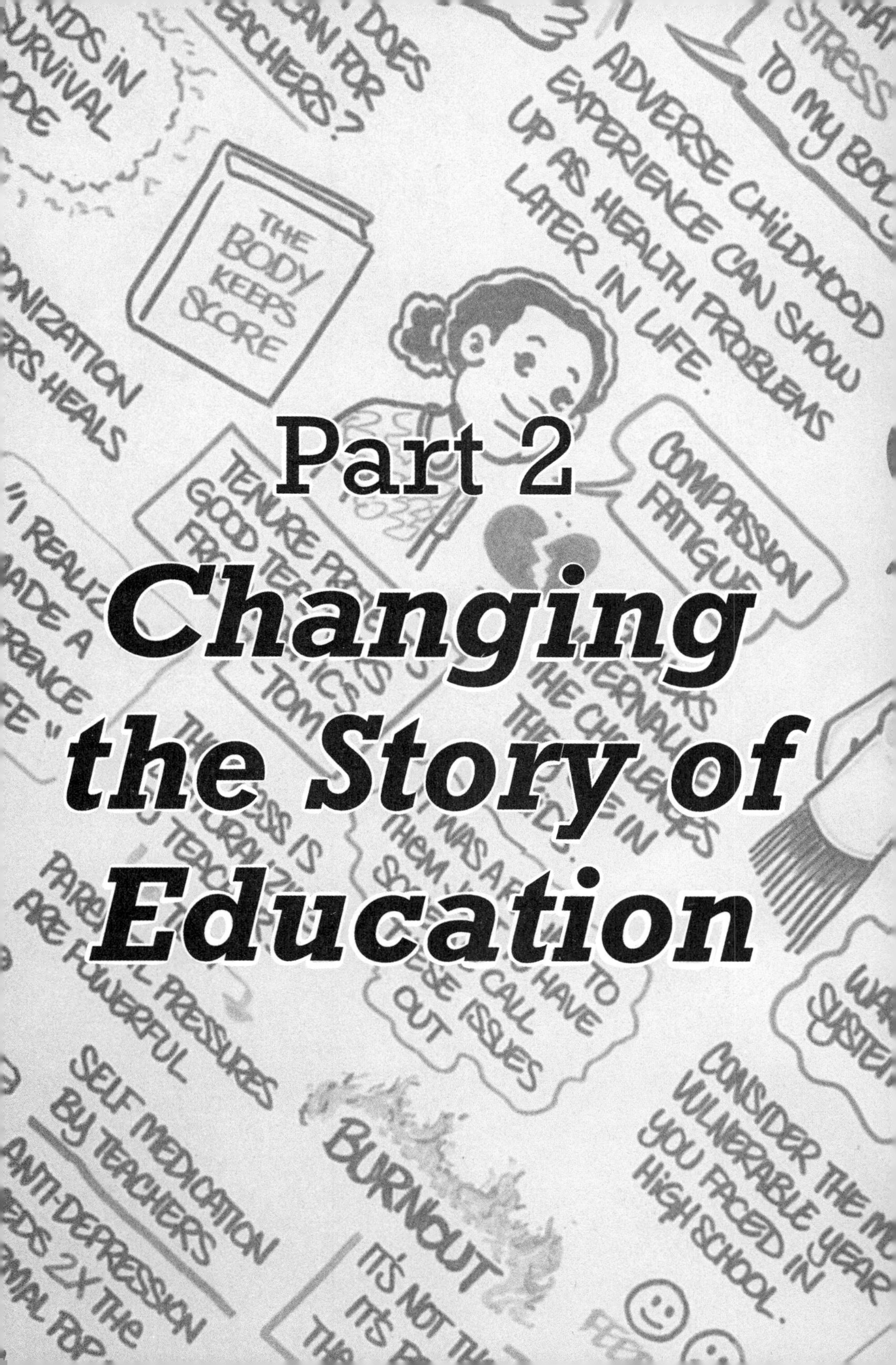

CHAPTER 6

To Change the Story

Katie Reilly wrote stories of thirteen teachers for a September 2018 *TIME Magazine* cover story. Each of the several teacher photos depicted sadness, hopelessness, or anger through cold blank expressions. The headline statements for each teacher reflect despair and outrage:

> *My child and I share a bed in a small apartment, I spend $1,000 on supplies, and I've been laid off three times due to budget cuts. I'm a teacher in America.*
>
> *I have a master's degree, 16 years of experience, work two extra jobs and donate blood plasma to pay the bills. I'm a teacher in America.*
>
> *I have 20 years of experience, but I can't afford to fix my car, see a doctor for headaches or save for my child's future. I'm a teacher in America.*[1]

That story matters. I understand the challenge and struggle that teachers face. But, how we tell the story matters more. Is teacher pay the grand narrative? Does that viewpoint shape an effective message for restoring teaching to a rightful place of honor and appreciation in society? I'm sure the author would say that's not her job. But the stories we tell produce the results we get.

The Power of Story

The Momentous Institute in Dallas understands the power of a story. Many of their kids, aged 3–11 years old, live in poverty and chronic stress; many know trauma. But, the students also know about power and influence. Despite their circumstances, they learn about how their brains work, that they are the masters of their brains, and they can control their responses to situations. Teachers provide tools, coaching, and modeling. All of those strands become woven into a tapestry of mastery and resilience.

The school challenges students to *imagine* their future. They help them to visualize high school graduation, where they want to go to college, and to prepare for a career. They also meet former students, people like themselves, who have graduated from Momentous and college. That kind of dopamine hit goes straight to the pre-frontal cortex and inspires. Each student makes a self-portrait. Along with a sketch of their dreams, the portrait gets posted in a hall corridor. That wall—I call it the "Hall of the Future"—is inspiring and effective as a story builder.

The Institute's website proudly announces:

When our students leave us after fifth grade, they go on to any number of middle schools and high schools in the city. And we track them. Seven years after leaving us, 98% of our students graduate from high school. 82% then enroll in higher education. We believe that social emotional health makes all the difference.[2]

Over recent years, I have seen future-focused walls in more schools, usually high schools serving high-risk communities. Circumstances will create one narrative, and many will become trapped in that one. However, the Momentous Institute (and other schools) help the students create their own inspiring story of defying the odds. They have learned to resist the forces that try to push them into a different story. And, their resistance turns to resilience.

The same stories and strategies work for teachers too. The *TIME Magazine* covers present one story. That narrative is valid; it breaks our hearts. But, it's not the only story. Teachers who adopt social emotional learning (SEL), trauma-informed care, movement, and agency create a positive vision for the future.

Reclaiming the Narrative: Teachers Speak

Dr. Gasko voiced concerns about the *TIME* cover story; "Who wants to send their kids to a school full of stressed-out and beleaguered teachers? Who in their right mind would even think about going to college to become a teacher?"

So, he partnered with Karen Blessen—the first graphic artist to win the Pulitzer Prize—and her organization, 29 Pieces. Together they identified over one hundred strong, resilient, and inspiring teachers with the Dallas ISD.

Dr. Gasko knew that unless the narrative shifted away from teachers as victims, it would be more difficult to fill the projected teacher shortages in the Dallas ISD over the next several years. If that story prevailed, schools could forget about portraying teachers as resilient and inspiring change agents.

He saw a clear mission: "We wanted to depict them in ways that the community is not used to seeing teachers portrayed, so imagine seeing teachers . . . being portrayed as on a cover of *Vogue* Magazine. What would that likely invoke in the community? What would that invoke in kids . . . when they see their teachers depicted in this way?"[3]

Blessen and her team took portraits using iPhones and iPads and used them to create high fashion-style magazine covers, enlarged to poster size for a Dallas exhibition, *Dallas Teachers Speak*.

The project included interviews with 160 teachers speaking about their work and the challenges they faced and had overcome as teachers. The covers reveal strength and personal and intriguing details about each teacher. The interviews were then organized into two statements for the cover copy: "Why do I teach?" and "What do I need?"

You can see all 160 posters at http://29pieces.org/dallas-teachers-speak/

That high-concept campaign of teacher recognition contributed to a DISD turnaround and transformation. That cultural moment grew from Dr. Gasko's concern for the teachers fighting in the trenches. It was not a question of whether the *TIME* story was right or wrong, but rather what was the best unifying and empowering story for education at that moment.

As he explained in an interview, "A dimension of teaching that's elegant and beautiful sometimes gets lost in these larger grand narratives around pay and . . . performance."[4]

The Superhero Story

At the beginning of our University of North Texas at Dallas (UNTD) Summit, Dr. Gasko handed out the first edition of a comic the university had produced, *Jovi, La Justiciera*. He told us:

"Jovanna (Jovi for short, and *justiciera*, which in Spanish means the one who fights for justice) is a dreamer from Honduras who is a product of Dallas ISD schools. She is modeled on a real student who moved from Honduras to Dallas, spent her days in Dallas ISD schools, then came to the Emerging Teacher Institute at UNTD to polish her bilingual superpowers and become a teacher in Dallas. The student has returned to South Dallas as a teacher of record by day with an alter ego, 'Justice.'[5]

"Superheroes have always been a part of the imagination of young people. In fact, the interest is accelerating in the U.S. and globally. For example, the largest consumers worldwide of anime and manga are Latinos.

"We also have different ethnicities, different parts of the population all converging on a symbolic universe that provides a lens for them to see themselves and the world around them in ways they are not finding in school, at home, or in our communities. What have been the largest grossing movies over the last few years? Films based on Marvel and DC comics.

"Jovi is comparable to Ms. Marvel, who is a Pakistani immigrant, and one of the few female superheroes in comics.

"We draw a large percentage of students into the Emerging Teacher Institute who consume comic books. Because of that, we imagined a superhero who had powers born out of trauma and refined along her journey. Power out of trauma is a recurring theme for superhero characters. Batman, for example, saw his parents murdered. This is one of those themes for our times. How do we accept our wounds and brokenness and then embrace and develop it as a source of strength?

"I have talked to a lot of high schoolers about going into teaching. But, they can only imagine what they have experienced, and for the most part, that story is not inspiring . . . If imagination is a superpower . . . there is a lot of kryptonite in the system that kills student imaginations.

"Our first challenge is reaching those high school students and letting them see teaching as a heroic adventure, one they can relate to. Once they enroll, it allows us to pick up on the interest and deepen the dialogue around the kinds of the teacher archetypes that inspire them to become superhero change agents."

From What's Wrong to What's Strong: The Atlanta Story

When Dr. Meria Carstarphen ("Dr. C") became the superintendent of Atlanta Public Schools in 2014, she inherited a demoralized, discredited, and disgraced school system and culture. APS had been battered by a system-wide cheating scandal that sent teachers and administrators to prison.

Carstarphen, however, brought a superpower to the job; she can see through deficiencies and recognize the strengths that can be built upon. She developed her new lens and skills as superintendent of the Austin, Texas, ISD. There she adopted a strengths-based model for teachers and students in a partnership with Gallup. They used the Clifton Strengthsfinder Assessment and began by identifying the top natural talents for each employee. It shifted the focus from what's wrong to what's strong, from punishing shortcomings and mistakes to building on strengths. That attitude brought with it a transforming effect.

Austin ISD went from good to great. But, APS was an altogether different story. As Angela Smith, APS' Chief Engagement Officer, recounted to me, "I remember Dr. C asking a room full of teachers and principals, 'Do you guys know the little bird on your emblem logo? It's a phoenix! Y'all need to rise out of the ashes. It's time to stop with the burning . . . Atlanta, we are moving from what's wrong to what's strong."[6]

She came in with the belief and confidence that a good culture can overcome a bad system. Dr. C's grand narrative can be summarized, "Strong Students, Strong Schools, Strong Staff, Strong System."

DaVerse Lounge: Rewriting the ACE Stories

Death has that sort of ink on your clean white shirt stained effect on the brain. This thing, like acid, eats away at the nerve endings which translates feeling, leaving only apathy. Anger was our resistance to apathy. . .
—Darius Frasure[7]

Approximately four million children will be born in the U.S. this year. By the time they reach 18, nearly a million will suffer trauma through abuse or neglect. Not one of those children chose or scripted their story. It was branded into their souls, rewiring their brains, altering biology, affecting their deepest emotions, and stealing hope.[8]

These castaways become part of a secret society, those with adverse childhood experiences (ACEs). Without some kind of intervention, those thrown into that club live predictably tragic lives. If a child experiences four or more types of trauma, they grow up more likely to drink, smoke, use drugs, be depressed, receive a sexually transmitted infection, break the law, drop out, or end up in jail. Even if they escape from their neighborhoods and make it to adulthood, the "issues in the tissues" will reduce their life by twenty years.[9]

Will Richey, the founder of DaVerse Lounge,[10] carries a gift of restoring connection for kids and families locked away by pain. DaVerse Lounge provides a stage for students to speak their truth and share their light in spoken word poetry. We watch teenagers from middle school through high school step up to the mike; they may be shaking, emotional, dramatic, humble, bold, or frozen. But each one delivers, and with each story, the audience's embrace seems to baptize them into a community of new hope.

The DaVerse process begins in an after-school club. Kids somehow find their way, often as a last chance stop. Darius Frasure hosted the first DaVerse Lounge club when he taught at Carter High School from 2005 to 2010. The success showed that unlocking the creative voice can stop despair and defeat. Several of the kids in Darius' club made complete turnarounds, graduating with honors. Darius' own story follows the common DaVerse script: poverty, abuse, gangs, violence, and then escape, finding hope, and eventually reclaiming and rewriting his own story.

Will explained to me that middle school is the crucial time when he sees teenagers coming from these conditions going from naïve to numb: "It is the start of coming to terms with their situation. Numb quickly turns to anger, shame, and survival. If they can open up and talk about the hard things, the process of embracing and telling their story begins the healing. But we can't start with the story or go into hard topics. We have to make it safe, connect, be interested, and most of all, listen. These kids will be transparent if you prove you will listen and respect. There are no gimmicks. We don't treat them as children and sugar-coat their reality. We see and treat them as humans deserving of respect."

The process is elegant and it is easy to miss the depth of design and mastery of social emotional skills. Will and his partner Alejandro Perez,

Jr. ("AP") embody what they teach. In fact, I have invited Will and AP to lead some of my business workshops. The first time I wondered how a group of buttoned-up professionals would respond. I had no cause for concern; Will and AP use the same process with everyone; connection before content, and moving from experience to understanding to trust. Will explains the process: "We don't look at children as children. We look at children as human beings and that means we take the same humanizing approach with them that we take with adults." I think he speaks for everyone on the planet. Respect must be given; it cannot be contingent on understanding. But, true respect will lead to greater understanding.

Serenity Harris was a spunky seventh-grader when she joined the spoken word club at Comstock Middle School in Dallas. Outspoken and kinetic, Serenity braided her infectious joy with her strands of hidden trauma. Sharing with the small group gave her classmates a different view of Serenity; they encouraged her to read that same piece on the big stage at DaVerse Lounge in front of an audience of over 300.

And she did. That night, when Will encouraged her to take a deep breath, Serenity found the courage to speak:

I just thought you should know I come from Shreveport, Louisiana.
And the chemical soil that left my head half-bald.
From movin' to Dallas from Shreveport and going back and forth for the holidays.
I just thought you should know I'm a different kind of person,
Who spends a lot of time thinking and drawing.
That I come from the days as a child when I locked my mom outside and burnt the skin off my chest.
I just thought you should know I come from lots of trips and falls
That I don't feel angry because of you talking trash,
And that time I fussed with you was really big deal.
I just thought you should know I miss the way you used to talk to me,
That I won't ever hate you, just can't worry about you anymore.
I just thought you should know I also come from grandma's baked beans,
From Mom's Frito pies and crying when I couldn't see my father.
I'm so lucky to come from a warm family filled with love.
I just thought you should know.

After a rousing ovation, Serenity beamed. Will invited her to join him in engaging the audience with the call and response, "When I share my joy, I multiply my happiness. When I share my pain, I divide my sadness. And when I embrace the two, I become whole . . . we become whole!"

The teacher, administrator, and student voices reveal how they reclaimed and reframed their stories. They prove that people can rewrite the future by changing the trajectory of those stories. They all seem to recognize the need to clarify their story if they hope to penetrate the wall of noise that surrounds them.

Time to Stand and Deliver

"Good morning, ladies and gentlemen. Welcome to *BrandSpankinGood*! Is your brand old, tired, and beat up? OK, yes, lady, I see you. Just come on up here; you came to the right place. We can help. So, tell me your story."

"I'm not sure where to start. I'm a teacher. I guess you could say our brand has fallen on hard times. Teachers used to be appreciated, even loved. Students brought us nice red apples, thank you notes, and gift cards to Starbucks. They loved it when we challenged them to do better. But, now we get angry calls from their parents screaming, 'Why did my Clifford get a B instead of the A he deserves?'

"You know, that *Time* article was devastating, the last straw. It showed pictures of miserable-looking teachers and told stories of how pathetic it is to be a teacher in America. Since that article, I even hate going to the store because if one of my students' mom recognizes me, she will ask if I need help paying for my groceries or if I drive Uber part-time."

"Ouch. But, we've seen this before. You've become what we in the trade call the 'Scapegoat Brand.' It happens more than you think. Do you remember Sears? They were the Amazon of their day. But, they didn't change with the times; they quit offering what people wanted. Soon, people forgot what once made them special. Sadly, they forgot it too.

"But, hey, everyone gets knocked down at some point. At that moment, you can either give up and let others tell your story or you can write your own.

"Now, let me tell you about one of my favorite philosophers, Rocky Balboa. He said, 'Let me tell you something you already know. The world ain't all sunshine and rainbows. It's a very mean and nasty place and I don't care how tough you are, it will beat you to your knees and keep you there permanently if you let it. You, me, or nobody is gonna hit as hard as life. But it ain't about how hard ya hit. It's about how hard you can get hit and keep moving forward. How much you can take and keep moving forward. That's how winning is done!'[11]

"So, what's it gonna be? You gonna let some reporter out there tell the world you're pitiful? Look, you've got a brand problem. So do many others. Well, grab a pad and write some things down if you want to fix it.

1. "Go and see the outliers, those people and places creating their own story and ignoring what others say. You know, go see the Atlanta Public Schools; Jennings, Missouri; Columbus, Indiana; El Paso, Texas; Holland, Michigan, places that got beat down but fought like tigers to rise again.
2. Listen to their journey. Skip the happy ending part. Start at the beginning. Someone helped; someone became their guide. Find out who; get the details on what they did. Each story passed through a dark night. Sure, they thought it was the end. Sometimes, it was; they had to come back from the dead. You need to hear those stories so you can be prepared for your dark night.
3. You also have outliers in your own school and community. Dig out their story. Those are the stories you will build on.
4. Bring people together, champions who believe you can overcome the challenges and change your story. Imagine what a better future could actually look like.
5. Now write your story. Make it a doozy, an epic journey. Paint a portrait that will make grown men cry. Don't ask permission, don't hang onto your old story, don't cling to your old identity. Wake up in a brand-new day. Walk into your market like you own the damn place.

"Apple fell so far by 1985, they fired their founder, Steve Jobs. That was his dark night of the soul. You think he quit? Gave up? Hell, no. When he rose again, when he walked back in the front door, he carried more than a good story. He saw what Apple could and must be. The journey will force you to let go of the old. You can't rise to a new and inspiring story until you let go of what others say about teaching.

"Harley Davidson is another example of lost and found identity. They fell on hard times in the 1980s and became just another motorcycle manufacturer. But, they took the journey I just outlined for you; they talked to the customers who were still loyal fans. They came back with a new story—they would make motorcycles for their fanatics. And so, they did.

"According to John Russell, former European managing director for Harley-Davidson, 'Harley-Davidson sells to 43-year-old accountants the ability to dress in leather, ride through small towns and have people be afraid of them.'[12]

"Brand stories that are powerful deliver on the promise. Harley-Davidson is so powerful that customers tattoo their logo on their bodies.

"OK, now, get back to your classroom. Never forget that you have a choice; you can let someone else tell your story or you can tell your story. I hope I've helped you to know how."

Wrapping Up

- Who tells and shapes the story for education matters.
- The Momentous Institute helps students craft their story of the future at an early age. DaVerse Lounges helps students recraft a story from tragedy to hope.
- There is an elegant and beautiful dimension to teaching we should not lose to the larger grand narratives.
- Superheroes reflect themes of our times that appeal to students.
- Power out of trauma is a recurring theme for superhero characters.
- One out of four children will experience trauma through abuse or neglect by time they reach 18.
- Middle school is a crucial time for kids coming out of abusive conditions.
- When education reaches out to recruit high school teachers, help them see the heroic adventure side of teaching.

Practical Reflections

1. How are we elevating student voices? How can you create a DaVerse experience?
2. Where can you share why you teach and what you need?

3. Do you have the superpower of seeing through deficiencies to recognize the strength your students, class, or school can build upon?
4. Does your school or district have a story that is moving from what is wrong to what is strong?
5. Are you crafting and telling your school's story well?

Notes

1. Katie Reilly, "Exactly How Teachers Came to Be So Underpaid in America." *Time,* Sept. 13, 2018. www.time.com/longform/teaching-in-america

2. "A Peek Inside Momentous School," www.https://momentousinstitute.org/blog/a-peek-inside-momentous-school

3. UNT Dallas, "Dallas Teachers Speak." YouTube, www.youtube.com/watch?v=XqG07z4yflQ

4. UNT Dallas, "The Innovative Dr. Gasko Does It Again with Launch of Dallas Teachers Speak." *News,* Oct. 17, 2018. www.news.untdallas.edu/innovative-dr-gasko-does-it-again-launch-dallas-teachers-speak

5. Jovi's comic style was created by Hector Rodriguez, who is a bilingual teacher in McKinney and owner of Rio Bravo Comics.

6. Rex M. Miller, et al., *Humanizing the Education Machine: How to Create Schools That Turn Disengaged Kids into Inspired Learners* (Hoboken, NJ: John Wiley & Sons, Inc., 2017), p. 223.

7. Nicole Stewart, "What Is Oral Fixation?" YouTube, Oral Fixation, youtu.be/QE5P14Xv86I.

8. Jane Ellen Stevens, "Nearly 35 Million U.S. Children Have Experienced One or More Types of Childhood Trauma." ACEs Too High, Apr. 25, 2017. www.acestoohigh.com/2013/05/13/nearly-35-million-u-s-children-have-experienced-one-or-more-types-of-childhood-trauma/

9. Carina Storrs, "Is Life Expectancy Reduced by a Traumatic Childhood?" *Scientific American,* Oct. 7, 2009. www.scientificamerican.com/article/childhood-adverse-event-life-expectancy-abuse-mortality/

10. A partnership between Big Thought and Journeyman Ink.

11. Sylvester Stallone, *Rocky Balboa,* 2006, MGM, Columbia, and Revolution Studios.

12. http://www.dukece.com/insights/how-harley-davidson-brought-biker-brand-india/

CHAPTER 7

The Early Childhood Challenge: Pay Me Now or Pay Me Later

The highest rate of return in early childhood development comes from investing as early as possible, from birth through age five, in disadvantaged families.

—James J. Heckman[1]

Joan Maltese founded the Childhood Development Institute (CDI) twenty-five years ago. From the beginning, she wanted to provide early childhood support to under-served communities. Although CDI operates two comprehensive Early Intervention Centers and two Early Learning Centers and serves over 500 people a day, it feels more organic than organizational. Joan has maintained a local and human touch even while reaching thousands with its services. That is very unusual. CDI is a private nonprofit organization, with its Early Learning Centers sustained by community partnerships and volunteerism and private philanthropic gifts. They keep a fiercely protected independence in order to serve the real needs of their families. CDI has avoided the trap of just feeding a system or bureaucracy.

As Joan recalls the birth of CDI, you hear the heart of a maverick: "When I look back I realize I was always meant to be here. I did not know it at the time. One of my first jobs in college was working in residential care for infants six and under. It was an actual house. This was in the 70s. I was a 17-year-old, taking care of six babies with no oversight.

"My job was simply to feed, give medicine, change diapers, and keep them in their cribs. I come from a large family. So, on weekends, I packed them into my VW Bug and took them home to play with my little sisters. By the time I finished community college, I was hooked. I went to San Diego State and created my own major. You know, it was the 70s. No one in my family went to college, so I didn't have any real idea of the rules. I'm just out there making my stuff up.

"I took baby classes, and then psychology because that seemed important. San Diego State's psychology program happened to focus on brain science. After that, I took special education. By my senior year, the school asked, 'What is this? It's not a major.' That led to a short stint of teaching in special education. I was still at an impasse with the college, but I managed to sidestep that hurdle and went to graduate school studying neuroscience.

"Neuroscience and personal therapy opened a new door; I became a clinical psychologist. So, who do you think came into my practice? Lots of families with kids with special needs. I did not advertise. I didn't tell anybody. But that's who came.

"Working with these families—most were low income—I started to look for more organized resources to help. I thought it couldn't be just me. There had to be a system of support available. And there was; unfortunately, it was often dehumanizing. Instead of developing a child's capacity and building up families, that system relegated kids to a discard bin. The families felt shame and left on their own. That was a turning point. I brought together people in a study group and said, 'Let's think about this differently. And what could we do?' That's when and how and why I started our Child Development Institute.

"We started a nonprofit for families being kicked out of everything. We sent 250 letters to preschools offering to come for free. We sent psychologists and marriage and family therapists to their schools. With all of that work, no school responded, not one. We were really mavericks because no one was talking about early childhood mental health."

CDI's Director of Clinical Programs, Tessa Graham, joined our conversation: "We realized that we needed to bring these services to the community. And that was the birth of the Early Learning Center. We deliberately chose Canoga Park because they had a high under-five population. Not one child from the zip code was getting services. How do you get zero? We started hanging out in this neighborhood, we started coming to the fairs and talking to parents. It's really a wonderful community. Very family-oriented and tight-knit.

"One of the virtues we found is they tend to rely on family support to help their children. So, they're very accepting of special needs. Getting and giving help were natural. However, they were unlikely to use a government source to get help. So, they were not visible to all the places where the system might have identified a community need, not until they got to school. By then the child was too far behind and sent into special education, which was essentially a throwaway solution."

A Day at the Early Learning Center

We found our best role was creating community and tying things together. We're just finding and making space. And when people have that opportunity to be human with hands-on involvement, it's amazing to see what pours out.

—Joan Maltese

CDI's Early Learning Center is housed in a former public library built in 1959, a classic low-profile, mid-century modern structure. The CDI partnered with the city in 2007 to convert it into their first Early Learning Center. When I arrived one morning, the facility was bustling; the inside flow pulled mothers and children through different learning zones to explore and play together. I asked Joan about the large tree/playhouse sitting in the center.

She explained, "We are a Nature Explore Center, helping children to connect to nature. We don't have technology here, everything is natural. We celebrate all the seasons and everything we do has a nature theme to it." I hear that natural theme as Joan talks about the social environment.

"We let parents know how vital they are to their child's development. Everything we do creates opportunities for parents and children to play together so that we reduce social isolation. Lots of families tell us that one of the best things that happens here is they met their best friend."

When Joan and I walked out the back door of the facility, she told me we were walking on the former library's old parking lot. "As you can see, it is a place for playing in the sand and making music with some of the sculptures. We hold gardening classes every week. This is a gathering place; I love to watch parents sitting around speaking five different languages to one another, or seeing the expressions of children who see and touch a ladybug for the first time."

Deep Design

If you look at the wide ranges of services, support, and activities on their website, www.cdikids.org, it feels like a comprehensively designed community service organization. But there was no masterplan. CDI didn't grow out of design, not the way you and I think of it. It was a deeper architecture. Joan and her team really care about, and concentrated on, relationships, trust, and partnering with the community. The services they provide did not emerge as the results of products of professionals coming to the community, prescribing or imposing what was good for them. Everything they do for their children is homegrown. Nothing is parachuted in.

When I see projects that work, positive outliers, I always want to know how the magic can be scaled. But, before I asked Joan, I realized that wasn't the right question. To scale something, you have to become efficient, standardized; in short, a machine. The real question is, "How do you plant more seeds like this?"

That same issue speaks of funding. An old civil rights leader told a friend of mine, "In my day, we looked for problems that were solvable; today, we look for what is fundable." For a quarter-century, Joan and her team have remained above that snare. She speaks about that:

"The nice thing is that nobody owns us. If we don't like our environment, it's up to us to recognize that and figure it out. We do the heavy lifting upfront. We cover all the capital costs and that frees us up to function with far fewer overhead expenses. It also forces creativity. We have what we've got and we use what we have.

"We're not beholden to anybody. We are not willing to sell out to anyone. We have a reputation of sticking up for parents. To some, that labels us as mavericks. We never want to be in a position where a funder, for example, says, 'We don't want you to give the reports to a parent.' 'That's never going to happen.' We participated in the neighborhood before we opened our doors. We went to the farmers' market, street fairs, art shows, all kinds of things. We were just *present*.

"This approach has built bridges and grown support for local partnerships. These are vital. Our local university, for example, now provides over a hundred service learning students every year. The university has also started a program called Neighborhood Partners in Action. They have created a network with police, the schools, nonprofits, businesses, and the health systems. So, if we discover someone homeless camping in our parking lot, rather than getting rid of them or calling the police to remove them, we ask the police to help us find better accommodations. And they do; they're very thoughtful about it."

Later, Joan and Tessa talked to me about the kids who go into the schools. Are these kids really ready for school? How much have their childhood experiences preconditioned them to start and stay behind?

Joan framed the issue very succinctly: "When we're born with our nearly 100 billion neurons, we're waiting for the experience of figuring out what world am I in. How do I organize this world in order to adapt? Because of what we know about plasticity, we know kids who have had a lot of negative experiences, some traumatic, can be reconditioned.

"The system disregards the educational needs of children who are developmentally behind. They are simply set aside, put into special programs. Too often, those children and families are completely discounted. It's as if they are not human. Our challenge is to develop support in a strength-based way, removing the stigma on the front end so they don't fall out or get tossed out. The system is not aligned or prepared to nurture and grow those children to their full capacity. It is designed to make them comply and keep them out of the mainstream so they don't bother anybody."

Pay Now or Pay More Later

Dr. Tom Backer, Senior Research Fellow and Executive Director for the Valley Nonprofit Resources, serves as a partner with CDI. From his experience, he articulates a clear perspective on why the work with children is so vital: "… you either fund and deliver services early in life or you pay for them later on. Kids who don't get services early on wind up in therapy longer or have other issues and may even end up in the juvenile system."[2]

University of Chicago Professor of Economics and Nobel Laureate, James J. Heckman agrees. Much of his work supports investing in disadvantaged children very early in life. According to Dr. Heckman, "Gaps in knowledge and ability between disadvantaged children and their more advantaged peers open up long before kindergarten, tend to persist throughout life, and are difficult and costly to close. Taking a proactive approach to cognitive and social skill development through investments in quality early childhood programs is more effective and economically efficient than trying to close the gap later on."[3]

I often tell our MindShift leaders, researchers, and other specialists, "Look, I'm the least knowledgeable person in the room. That's why I ask so many questions." And that's true. My background is working with commercial and industrial architecture and construction. From that perspective, I can see the principles for successful capital projects are the same for building children into strong adults. The time and dollars spent early make the smallest and best investment. The strength of the foundation for a building or in a child is the single leading indicator for their future.

After more than a hundred interviews with teachers, I'm sure I heard this phrase more than any other: "*Children are not showing up ready to learn.*" I understand it; children from low-income families are usually not ready to learn on the first day. The realities of life push school to the bottom of the priorities. As Dr. Heckman says, "… disadvantaged families are strained to the limit. They have fewer resources to invest in effective early development."[4]

Just as in commercial construction, if we can spend early, those dollars will be the best investment we can make. For comparison, if you have invested in a moderately aggressive 401K program, it is probably earning between a 5–8% return on your investment (ROI).[5] Professor Heckman and his colleagues calculate the social ROI for comprehensive, high-quality, birth-to-5 early education at 13%, more than double.[6] Every 5.5 years a community's investment doubles in value through better outcomes in education, health, sociability, economic productivity, stable families, and reduced crime."[7] Communities who make this kind of investment in children "can break the cycle of poverty across generations" for those families.

The brain science explains the "why" of Heckman's economic projections. The central nervous system (CNS) controls a child's capacity to handle the load of structured learning. That precious window for building a healthy CNS in a child is from birth to about five or six years of age. It is not a coincidence that both CDI and the Momentous Institute start their work in the same early childhood window. Both focus on health, social learning, and parent and family support.

Yet, municipalities seem to look anywhere and everywhere *except* making that kind of investment. Schools run a frantic race to find something, *anything* that works. Consider the number of programs and interventions from outside organizations that get sold to school districts. I asked my research team to list as many intervention programs as they knew. I stopped counting after fifty. Who can keep up with that?

Each school also realizes these programs will rotate in and out, depending on funding or the new principal in charge. In other words, schools have no continuity and no strategy, just desperate efforts and a lot of wasted costs. And, the fact that this vast menu of auxiliary services exists and is growing tells us the need is great. That they are aimed at one thing—bridging the social emotional gap in the very young—should tell us to make the solid, thoughtful, strategic investments in early childhood development.

Every community leader, educator, and concerned citizen should take a close look at early learning through an economic development lens. Total what your community spends on reacting and repairing. Be sure to include the demand on physical and mental healthcare services and the judicial and social systems. Recognize that every dollar spent to repair and restore is like buying a lottery ticket. Then ask how the same dollars might act as an investment if shifted to early childhood efforts.

That is simple financial planning. After a hard financial season left me in debt many years ago, I hired a financial planner who explained the formula to dig out. Set a goal, create a budget that supports the goal, grind down the debt, and don't borrow on the future. After six years, it worked. Dollars that were once going down a black hole did their magic as compounded interest for the future. The very same strategy works in education investments.

Heckman tracked when this latency effect begins to make a difference. By age 21, these children are twice as likely to enroll in higher education and three times as likely to stay through four years. They secure skilled jobs at double the rate. Other indicators, such as teen pregnancy and criminal behavior, also show great improvement.

By age 30, these children continue to do well. They are four times more likely to graduate from a four-year college. They have kept consistent employment at double the rate. Fewer than 20% use public assistance compared to those who did not receive early childhood learning.

A Centers for Disease Control (CDC) report compared the return on investment at three levels for just one factor: earnings gains.[8] State and district-run programs show the highest return on investment. One dollar spent returns $3.00–5.00 as a combination of increased taxes on earnings or social costs. Federal Head Start programs return $1.58–2.51 for every dollar spent. Innovative private models create a return of $1.75–4.39.

The return on investment was much higher when all the benefit components, including earnings gains were considered.[9] These benefits include: Self-control, openness, the ability to engage with others, to plan, and to persist—these are the attributes that get people in the door and on the job, and lead to productive lives.

The Kindergarten Effect on Earnings

Raj Chetty was born in New Delhi, India, in 1979. His family migrated to America in 1988. After graduating from Harvard, he earned a Ph.D. in economics from Harvard. Today, he is considered one of the world's top economists. After teaching at UC-Berkeley and Stanford, he joined the faculty at Harvard. In addition to teaching, Chetty is known for many awards and honors, research papers, public speeches, and lecture videos.

His research examines many themes, including race, intergenerational mobility, education, taxation, and upward mobility, the core of the American Dream. That dream has vanished, and especially for children born in low-income neighborhoods. Similar to Heckman, Chetty sees early education as the linchpin.

But, the real reason Chetty's research is important and new is that evaluating the success of early childhood education has usually focused on how a child would do with test scores. But these programs, even the good ones, don't move that needle much. Therefore, many have assumed that early childhood investment is unnecessary. However, the real return comes as an adult. We now see a latency effect attributed to the development of soft skills. Tests don't measure them, but bosses do, clients do, and parents do. And, children do.

Chetty understands, "… what's going on is that the teacher is not teaching you skills that end up showing up on later tests. It's not so much that they're teaching you how to do math better, or teaching

you trigonometry or something in later grades. Rather, it's that they are teaching you things like discipline and social skills and other things that are valued in the labor market directly."[10] These kinds of skills, unlike cognitive learning, stick with students through life.

The Momentous Institute: Getting Beyond Sucking Up, Giving Up, or Blowing Up

The Momentous Institute, like CDI, provides brain science-based early childhood and family support. In addition, Momentous offers a lab school beginning at age 3 through fifth grade.

I joined Michelle Kinder, the former Executive Director, and other Momentous leaders to dive into their philosophy and process. The conversation included Sandy Nobles, Director of Education, Rhonda Vincent, Director of Educational Training, and Tina Robertson, Director of Clinical Training.

Tina observed that too many schools "ignore the science of the body, how it operates, how it learns, and they keep doing the same things over and over, thinking we'll get a different outcome."

Rhonda agreed, adding, "Because so few teachers are trained in SEL of stressed-out kids, those with deficits of social and emotional skills bubble up as bad behavior. So, they end up labeled as bad kids."

After a break, Rhonda continued, "If nobody feels safe, they also don't feel a sense of control. One thing we do intentionally is giving teachers a voice and respect as a professional. Many systems have this sense of fear. 'I have to be accountable to my executive director, or my superintendent.' Superintendents have a sense of fear. It's their Board of Education. It all goes up, but it also trickles down.

"If you've got the superintendent controlling the executive directors, the executive directors controlling the principals, the principals controlling teachers, teachers control kids. Then you've got the kids, and there is nobody down line that the kids can push to. In my mind, they do three things. They either suck up, give up, or blow up!"

Sandy jumped into the conversation: "I work with teachers exactly the same way I want them to work with kids."

Knowing that healthy children develop through progressive stages, Momentous begins with safe relationships. Teachers work to make students feel safe, valued, confident, and optimistic. They visit student homes to establish an early partnership with the family. It also allows the teacher to understand the child's living environment. Momentous also strips away external forms of motivation.

They design classes to have a predictable daily ritual at the beginning and end. Knowing that some children come out of stressful homes or neighborhoods, they create relational connection, develop social skills, and reduce anxiety. Any morning a child may arrive in a heightened state of stress and agitation. They train teachers to recognize and manage the signs of overload or trauma. These and other practices set the foundation for teachers to weave social and emotional literacy into the curriculum.

They also teach young students about their brains, how to recognize and regulate breathing, the body, feelings, and impulse control. Students also learn emotional maturity, gratitude, optimism, grit, and resilience. These habits and skills allow the development of empathy for, and understanding toward, others. In the same developmental stage, students develop listening skills. They also learn to accept diverse or new perspectives and how to share personal views in constructive dialogue. Students build the capacity for kindness, compassion, and hope.

The Momentous Staircase of Growth

- *Safe relationships*
- *Self-regulation*
- *Awareness of self*
- *Understanding others*
- *Change-maker*

Momentous uses the same social-emotional practice with their teachers they use with students. Tina explained, "We do that because the students will know if it's not authentic. If you are pretending to have a conversation with a child that is on your last nerve, that child can read every bit of that. It doesn't matter what you're saying, because that little boy or little girl looks at you and knows that you have fire in your eyes. So, we have to do exactly what we're teaching kids to do. We're known for teaching kids to 'settle your glitter.' Well, we have to settle our own glitter too."

Wrapping Up

- Invest in kids as early as possible.
- Real value comes from the organic solutions more than the organizational.
- Maintain a local and human touch.
- Reduce social isolation.
- Build participation bridges with your community.
- Grow support for coalitions and local partnerships.
- Most of the lessons through early social and emotional learning will last through life.
- Take a close look at early learning through an economic development lens.
- Provide the same social and emotional health for teachers that is provided to students.
- Create relational connection and reduce anxiety.
- Build the capacity for kindness, compassion, and hope.

Practical Reflections

1. Consider a field trip to see Joan and her team at the Childhood Development Institute or similar organization.
2. Consider attending the next Momentous Institute *Changing the Odds* conference. Perhaps you could bring others.
3. Read Heckman's book, *Giving Kids a Fair Chance: A Strategy that Works.*[11]
4. Read Robert Putnam's book, *Our Kids: The American Dream in Crisis.*[12] It will amplify Chetty's concern that current and future generations are losing the ability for upward mobility.

Notes

1. James J. Heckman, "Invest in Early Childhood Development: Reduce Deficits, Strengthen the Economy." The Heckman Equation, Feb. 15, 2017. www.heckmanequation.org/resource/invest-in-early-childhood-development-reduce-deficits-strengthen-the-economy/

2. Child Development Institute. website: https://cdikids.org/about-us/whats-at-stake-what-do-we-risk/

3. James J. Heckman, "Four Big Benefits of Investing in Early Childhood Development." The Heckman Equation. www.heckmanequation.org

4. James J. Heckman, "Make Greater Investments in Young Children to See Greater Returns in Education, Health, and Productivity." The Heckman Equation. www.heckmanequation.org

5. Melissa Horton, "What Rate of Return Should I Expect on My 401(k)?" Investopedia, July 6, 2019. www.investopedia.com/ask/answers/041015/what-rate-return-should-i-expect-my-401k.asp

6. The Heckman Equation, "13% ROI Research Toolkit." The Heckman Equation, May 10, 2019. www.heckmanequation.org/resource/13-roi-toolbox/

7. Heckman, "Four Big Benefits."

8. Centers for Disease Control and Prevention, "Health Impact in 5 Years. Health System Transformation. AD for Policy. CDC." Early Childhood Education, Aug. 5, 2016. www.cdc.gov/policy/hst/hi5/earlychildhood-education/index.html.

9. Tyler Cowen, "Raj Chetty on Teachers, Taxes, Mobility, and How to Answer Big Questions (Ep. 23)." *Medium*, conversations with Tyler, Nov. 21, 2018. medium.com/conversations-with-tyler/raj-chetty-tyler-cowen-inequality-mobility-american-dream-d5ea7f4742b1

10. Ibid.

11. James J. Heckman, *Giving Kids a Fair Chance: A Strategy that Works* (Cambridge, MA: MIT Press, 2013).

12. Robert Putnam, *Our Kids: The American Dream in Crisis* (New York: Simon & Schuster, 2015).

CHAPTER 8

The Teacher Athlete

After 17 years of teaching, I was diagnosed with "burnout" and needed to take some time off. I fought it, but when the lab results showed body systems shutting down, I complied . . . for a while. Part-time only made it worse. I couldn't believe this was happening to me. I LOVED my job, my students, my teaching.

—Joel Wagner[1]

Athletes don't run, leap, swing, or soar for exercise. They compete for a prize.

So do teachers. They fiercely compete for the hearts and minds of their kids. They strive to see that light come on in a student. We've all seen that movie; teachers live for the moment when a disconnected, angry, or fearful student walks out of the shadows and into the full joy of learning. The teacher's prize is feeling that sense of accomplishment for building a fire of curiosity in another human, equipping kids for success, and coaching young minds to excel.

Teachers compete as caregivers of the next generation, even those who don't want to learn. That worthy purpose drives many teachers to push themselves beyond their limits. And, that's why too many drop out of the race. Pushing beyond limits takes a toll. However, new breakthroughs in the field of resilience bring great help. Professional sports technologies and insights lead the way. They help to ensure our *teacher athletes* can stay in the race and finish well.

Our educational system and practices set up too many teachers to fail. They were probably not adequately prepared to teach kids who are not ready to learn. And, they may have little or no support, coaching, or means of recovery. Many live with acute and chronic stress. Their bodies try to tell them they are pushing beyond natural capacities; their stress creates mental and physical pain. Without healthy ways to release our stress, our bodies will look for unhealthy ways to do that.

What if the teachers I've described here had been star athletes? They would have been trained for the demands of the position. A coach and trainer would monitor each teacher's ability to handle the stresses. Each would be given rest as needed. On extreme days, a trainer would help the teacher work out the stress and bruises. If teachers were athletes, they would also have a tailored regimen of exercises, meals, and rest overseen by strength and fitness trainers. Why do athletes receive such care? Because losing one to burnout or injury can be very costly.

The sheer economics of sports has forced teams to take care of the players. Within the last few years, we have seen dramatic shifts in the protocol for football players who get knocked out. Not very long ago, a coaching assistant waved smelling salts under the player's nose and sent him back on the field. The recent and damning evidence of long-term neurological effects from concussion radically changed that.

So, why do we not extend the same quality of care toward teachers? When will we stop waving smelling salts to push teachers back into the game? How much more evidence of teacher trauma do we need before we take their health and care seriously? We can and must do better!

In pure economic terms, each teacher will steward a treasure of close to $4 million in every class of twenty-five they teach.[2] So, assuming graduation and full employment, each of those classes will collectively earn more than $61 million over their careers.

— Lam Thuy Vo[2] and Anne Sraders[3]

At some point, that view should motivate schools and all of society to take better care of those stewards.

Because of recent sports technology breakthroughs, players can now monitor their level of readiness to work out or compete. It guides an athlete in how much recovery time they need, how much strain they can take, and even how much sleep they need.

At MindShift, we have also been using that technology in the workplace. The parallels between the strain of athletes and that of office workers surprised us. And, we know teaching takes an even greater toll as the fourth most stressful occupation. These new insights have dramatically shifted the old traditional attitude of "no pain, no gain" to a new perspective that prioritizes recovery.

Houston Astros All Star pitcher Justin Verlander is considered the Tom Brady of baseball; he just gets better with age. At 36, he is having one of his best years and still pitching 90-mile-an-hour fastballs. Why? His insistence on recovery time. He gets 50% more sleep than most Americans.

In 2018, Verlander intervened to help third baseman Alex Bregman, who was struggling with only one home run midway through the season. Verlander asked how many hours of sleep Bregman was getting. He admitted six or less. Verlander said, "I get ten." When Bregman tried it, he went on to hit 30 home runs that year.[4]

MindShift has been using technology (see below) to provide new health patterns for our "corporate athletes" who work under high stress. At 64, I am experiencing that Verlander boost of youth; so are our clients. Understanding and developing good recovery habits may be the single biggest improvement you can make for your health, effectiveness, and satisfaction.

Addicted

Do you know why athletes push themselves to the breaking point? It's called "over-training syndrome," and it exists because physical exercise, intense work (including the demands of teaching) can become addictive. The natural endorphins and dopamine from sports or intense work can create a psychological reinforcement that characterizes addiction.

Dr. Amit Sood, Chair of the Mayo Clinic's Mind-Body Initiative, explained to our MindShift group that our brains do not have nerve endings; they don't register pain. But, when we go beyond 45–90 minutes of intense mental focus, we damage our brain nerves. We must find ways to manage brain fatigue.

Our brains require more energy than any other organ or muscle. On average, they consume 25% of our calories. The first sign of mental fatigue is a signal from your brain to STOP before you do damage.

Stress propels you to act. That's normal. But, when it builds up in your body and finds no release through physical activity, you feel the pain in the form of exhaustion, a headache, or mental fatigue. That too often leads to unhealthy patterns of pain relief: smoking, drugs, alcohol, sitting too long, or eating too much starchy, fatty food. That's why it's called "comfort food."

Heart Rate Variability (HRV)

Since receiving my professional tennis certification thirty-five years ago, I have followed the health and technology side of sports. About a decade ago, I began noticing a new trend. Many top athletes exceed eight hours of sleep each night; many hit ten or more.

That trend results from discovering a *resiliency sign*, like a vital sign, called heart rate variability (HRV). That resiliency factor forms the secret behind the longevity of athletes like Lebron James, Tom Brady, Justin Verlander, and Roger Federer. That's why it is becoming a standard protocol in sports. Today's extreme level of performance requires a comparable offset of recovery.

If heart rate measures the number of heart beats per minute, HRV measures the variation between beats. If your heart rate is 60 bpms, that does not mean your heart is beating one time per second. The time of each beat actually varies, and more variation means more resiliency.

That brings us back to the central role of our autonomic nervous systems. The sympathetic side tells your heart to speed up, and the parasympathetic side calls for a slowdown. That creates a constant and necessary up-down, up-down dynamic between the two sides. When the sympathetic side overrides our parasympathetic impulses for recovery, it builds an acute or chronic stress condition. Extending that condition places your body in distress. If not treated properly, you cannot recover.

When HRV is low, recovery is low. Your body is asking for more downtime to catch up. When HRV is high, recovery is high. Your body can quickly respond to strain and quickly bounce back into recovery.

HRV is like the idle of a car. Low HRV runs like an 82 Plymouth. Stepping on the gas pedal actually decelerates because of the demand suddenly placed on it. But, just tapping a Porsche's accelerator creates high RPMs. And, just as quickly, it settles back to a low purr when you take your foot off the accelerator. High HRV is the balance and sensitivity to speed up or decelerate.

The heart rate of the teachers who took part in the Next Jump Academy (the story told in Chapter 1) decelerated at the slightest demand (like just sitting up from a prone position). That's what caused Charlie Kim's alarm. They didn't know that was subnormal; they had adjusted to their depleted state.

WHOOP and HRV Technology

WHOOP, a sports technology firm in Boston, developed a breakthrough sensor capable of measuring HRV. In 2016, when I discovered them, the WHOOP wrist strap was used almost exclusively by professional and collegiate athletes and teams. WHOOP designed it to help athletes know when they cross the threshold into overtraining. It also provides data that allows them to optimize their training.

Based on my research, I thought the WHOOP device might open a similar window and warning for stressed or overworked employees. I bought my band in December 2016; I used it primarily as a warning device for myself and clients. Then, I started experiencing what reaching full recovery over time felt like.

HRV levels are relative to each individual. What is high for me may be low for someone else. Users first establish a baseline for sleep needs, sleep efficiency, resting heart rate, HRV, and maximum strain levels. Then they work to improve the numbers.

Restoring Vitality

You and I can also experience the Tom Brady effect. I began using the WHOOP system in December 2016. In the beginning, I registered a low resting heart rate (RHR), probably because of my days in tennis. A lower RHR usually means a stronger heart that can pump slower with less wear and tear. That was the good news.

My sleep numbers told another story. They said I needed eight hours and twenty minutes of sleep a night for a full recovery. I was seldom in bed more than seven and a half hours. I learned I'm also awake up to an hour and a half during the night. So, to get enough sleep, I needed to be in bed ten hours. That seemed impossible. The second piece of bad news was my resiliency number, my "HRV." It was 44; some athletes I researched were above 120.

My sleep habits were actually shortening my life, robbing my brain of its needed recovery and setting me up for early dementia. That jolted me into radical change.

My road back began by improving my sleep; I describe what I learned in Chapter 14. After thirty months, my sleep need dropped by an hour. My ratio of bed-to-sleep time improved. My heart got stronger and my resiliency (HRV) jumped up 250%.

At 64, I am statistically younger than I was three years ago. And I certainly feel younger. We also set up a colleague, an educator and assistant middle-school superintendent, for a very challenging school district, with the WHOOP.

In the beginning, her baseline numbers showed a resting heart rate in the high normal range at 71 beats per minute. She needed eight hours of sleep, but rarely achieved that. Her resiliency was similar to the teachers in Chapter 1. Her HRV was 28.

After eight months, she saw significant improvement. Her resting heart rate fell, her sleep improved by an hour, and her consistency increased by 15%. But, her resiliency shot up to 116!

Is the Strain of Teaching on the Level of Professional Sports?

WHOOP's dashboard lists specific athletic activities, like running, tennis, or weightlifting. It contains no categories for meetings, presentations, workshops, or classroom sessions. What if we could use an HRV monitor to gain insight into both the stress load of work and teaching? Could such a device help us coach others?

Bill Latham—CEO of MeTEOR Education, co-author of this book, and a champion martial artist—saw the benefit of such feedback immediately. After a few months of using it, we designed an experiment to outfit his leadership team with straps. We worked with WHOOP to create a "team dashboard" so I could monitor everyone's activities.

Bill is competitive. He frequently sends me screenshots of his strain level for the day after a workout, levels reflecting the insane output of a world-level athlete, ranges I will never reach. But his weekly results prompted an experiment.

I looked for a way to track an upcoming all-day workshop. I finally discovered the "Other" activity option; I could use it to measure that workshop. When Bill texted one of his screenshots of another day of "Extreme Strain," I noticed that my strain level was in that same level as Bill's.

That did not seem possible. So, I called Kristin Holmes-Winn, the Vice President of Performance Optimization at WHOOP. When I explained the issue, her reply rocked me: "Rex, cognitive load and emotional load operate the same as physical load on your autonomic nervous system. Your SNS activates by releasing cortisol, elevating your heart rate, and making your breath shallower. Your pupils dilate and your blood pressure increases."

She also explained the difference between work strain and athletic strain. Physical exertion flushes cortisol and restores the balance to your ANS. Work strain does not; it stays in your system.

I started measuring my presentations and workshops, and even a stressful commute through Los Angeles. My strain levels were comparable to my workouts. During an average 30-minute workout, I will burn between 400–450 calories and reach a maximum heart rate in the mid-150 range. When I gave a keynote to a technology firm in San Francisco, I saw it as a big opportunity, and that added pressure and stress. When I tracked my one-hour rehearsal and the actual presentation (90 minutes with questions), I saw I had burned 1818 calories! I thought that was crazy, but that is what running on adrenaline does to the body.

I attended a reception that evening. Exhausted. My WHOOP calculated the strain from the day and told me I had to get an extra hour of sleep for recovery. If I wanted to get up at 6 a.m, fully recovered, I needed to be in bed by 8:30 p.m. So, at 7:45, I excused myself from the reception, showing my host my bedtime on the WHOOP, like a note from the doctor.

We have also tested the Biostrap and Oura rings and other HRV sensors. The best ones are designed for active athletes. At MindShift and MeTEOR Education, we have expanded the research and now provide coaching to individuals and teams who would like to become part of our Corporate and Teacher Athlete training.

Overtraining syndrome, just like teacher overwork or burnout, looks like disengagement, but it's not. Teacher strain is similar to high-performance athletes. Athletes require recovery time, activity rotation, and rest. Recognition of the physical strains of teaching, and leading like a coach, can increase the effectiveness of these Academic Athletes.

Finally, I am somewhat startled to realize that my grandparents, if they were still alive, would not understand what this chapter says. Teacher athlete? HRV? Resiliency factors? WHOOP? We all live in continuous change. The ideas, technologies, strategies, and languages of any age twist us into new shapes and possibilities. Most people eventually adapt to the future.

But, sometimes those new lines and structures camouflage what is truly important. And, *this* is truly important: extending care, respect, and service to those who shape our children as students. We *must* take care of them. And, we must give a damn about the students they teach. The legal and logical nuances of a culture cannot distract us from doing the right thing for both teachers and students.

My grandparents may not have understood what I write, but they certainly understood serving others. They probably gave chickens, fruits, and vegetables to the new schoolmarm. They did what they could; they gave what they had. So did my parents. Lisa and I have done the same for our various communities.

We cannot allow the dazzling sounds and lights or provocations of a new era to obscure what it has always meant to be human.

Wrapping Up

- Teachers compete for the hearts and minds of their kids.
- Pushing ourselves beyond our limits takes a toll.
- Too many teachers are not adequately trained or emotionally prepared to teach kids who are not ready to learn.
- The collective life-time earning power of each class a teacher will teach is estimated at $61 million or more.
- We can handle between 45–90 minutes of intense cognitive work before we damage our brain nerves.
- Stress that leads to unhealthy coping habits also leads to fatigue and poor health.
- HRV is the measure of how well your heart can modulate between demand and rest.
- Low HRV is a serious warning sign of pushing yourself beyond your limits.

Practical Reflections

1. What does it mean to be a teacher athlete? What do you strive to excel at as a teacher?
2. If you feel continuously tired, what are the key contributors? If you had a trainer, what would they say you need to recover and be better prepared to handle the strain?

3. How strong and balanced is your heart? Do you know your Resting Heart Rate or your Heart Rate Variability?
4. What might your school offer to provide opportunities to restore and recover during the school day?

Notes

1. Joel Wagner, "Teacher Burnout: A Sad Story." So You Want to Teach?, June 30, 2010. www.soyouwanttoteach.com/teacher-burnout-a-sad-story/
2. Lam Thuy Vo, "How Much Does the Government Spend to Send a Kid to Public School?" NPR, June 21, 2012. www.npr.org/sections/money/2012/06/21/155515613/how-much-does-the-government-spend-to-send-a-kid-to-school
3. Anne Sraders, "What Is Middle Class, Really? Income and Range in 2019." TheStreet, Jan. 21, 2019. www.thestreet.com/personal-finance/what-is-middle-class-14833259
4. James Wagner, "Justin Verlander: The Astros' Ace and Sleep Guru." *New York Times,* July 9, 2019. www-nytimes.com.cdn.ampproject.org/c/s/www.nytimes.com/2019/07/09/sports/baseball/justin-verlander-all-star-sleep.amp.html

CHAPTER 9

Are Schools the New Field Hospitals?

The answers you get depend on the questions you ask.
—Thomas S. Kuhn

One of the big questions in America, or any civilized society, is, "How do we improve schools?"

But, what if that's the wrong question?

Forget bureaucracy, politics, low pay, tests, and all the other peripheral issues. Let's focus on one thing: the child who enters the school. How are school-age children doing?

I presented that question to Laura Lockhart, Area Director of Student Services for Keller (Texas) ISD. Laura has worked in that stable, upper-middle-class community for more than twenty years.

"We have five core values," she told me. "The number one is, Care for our teachers because the impact of their work prepares students for their future. We start with the teacher because we can't teach what we don't know and experience."

Because of her twenty-year vantage point, I asked what—considering safety concerns, school shootings, trauma, politics, racial tension, drugs—had changed for teachers, kids, parents, and the community. Her tone shifted as she described the alarming rise in stress, anxiety, and depression among students. She continued, "We have suicide outcries almost daily. The level of self-medication we see in our kids—vaping, online, phones, etcetera—is simply a symptom of their massive self-pressure and fear of failure. We are seeing a rapid rise of students coming who are not ready to learn."

A System at the End of an Era

Knowing that the external and unexpected demands on any system divert resources from mission, I always examine the other stuff that gets loaded onto hard-working people in any organization. That is especially true in K-12 education. And, sure enough, I discovered some of what has been added on to the Keller ISD's work:

- Social Emotional Literacy (SEL)
- Evening classes on health
- Mindfulness training
- Beginning of class and ending rituals
- Restorative practices
- Culture circles
- Climate and culture surveys
- Teacher round tables
- A new Career and Technology Center (CTE)
- A facility refreshing program
- Updated discipline protocols so recess is not removed
- The Collaborative Social Emotional Learning (CASEL) model and its 5 Essentials
- Positive Behavioral Interventions and Support
- The Leader in Me
- Character Strong
- Threat assessment protocols
- Trauma Informed Care
- Addressing privilege and inclusiveness

I asked Laura how teachers on the front lines keep up with the add-ons. Her answer was correct, but frustrating, "We have grown so fast in the last ten years that demand has outstripped our capacity." That's the same summary I hear in every school or district, anywhere in America. Our obsolete educational system and mindset force everyone to run in the Red Queen's Race. Remember how she explained it in *Alice's Adventures in Wonderland*?

"The Red Queen told Alice, 'Now, here, you see, it takes all the running you can do, to keep in the same place. If you want to get somewhere else, you must run at least twice as fast as that!'"[1]

That is where we are. K–12 education takes all the running anyone can do just to stay in the same place. What if that unsustainable level of pressure just confirms that the current system is simply incapable of closing the gap? What if it means our paradigm of a teacher is obsolete?

Here is a clue we have reached the beginning of the end: Stakeholders start grabbing specialty roles and interventions just to plug the leaks in the dam. In education, those band-aids and bolt-on solutions just add counselors, school resource officers, nurses, SEL coaches, teachers' aides, and campus police, just to keep the levees from blowing.

Each of the add-on pieces address what Thomas Kuhn calls an anomaly to the system. Problems the organization was not designed to handle will always confront any system; an effective system can absorb exceptions up to a point. When exceptions become the norm, what was once considered absurd becomes commonplace. That's when the prophets, the coal mine canaries, and those who feel a "splinter in the brain" begin scanning the horizon because they sense the end of an era and the hope for a new birth.

I keep going back to Laura Lockhart's statement, "We are seeing a rapid rise of students coming who are not ready to learn." If I was a dog, I think I would hear that as a tsunami warning.

How will we accommodate the new norm of students whose emotional, social, and psychological needs keep them from learning? Who can help integrate healing and learning? What kind of institutions can respond first to that wave crashing on our beach?

First, let's start with an accurate picture of the social landscape and needs.

Kintsugi: Golden Joinery

In Kintsugi, an ancient Japanese art form, the artist fits broken pottery pieces back together with liquid gold. Because the gold highlights the pattern of brokenness, the art presents the beauty that comes when broken humans are restored. The art displays the human reach for wholeness. That metaphor spoke to our team in our final summit for the WHOLE Project. It perfectly and vividly captured the highest yearning of every person.

That probably connected because so many on our team and in our MindShift network function as "healing" practitioners in education. They face a constant uphill battle to get buy-in, to find and then allocate resources, to do more than desperate interventions. They all lean into artistic expressions that lift the learning-healing dynamic and imperative.

That allegorical image found practical application through Dr. John Gasko, former Dean of the University of North Texas at Dallas (UNTD) School of Education. When he joined our final summit in Dallas, he introduced us to a new vision for schools as field hospitals.

He first helped us to understand that schools have been serving as field hospitals for a long time. That has come about because of the collision between accountability systems and the great demands for services wrapped up in the needs that students bring to school. That collision takes everyone beyond the traditional purpose of schools.

The normal and proper domains of accountability make it difficult to attend to those needs because schools remain focused on specific

blunt indicators, like standardized test scores. Accountability dictates the training and professional development that can be extended to administrators, teachers, and other adults in the system.

Dr. Gasko believes the reasons the field hospital metaphor is accurate and needed is because of the new level of needs showing up in public schools across America. Those needs arrive mostly through students in low-income and non-English-speaking families, and from vulnerable neighborhoods. About 45% of all Dallas ISD students speak languages other than English.

*M*A*S*H* and Pope Francis

In fact, Gasko found a working model of the idea while watching reruns of *M*A*S*H*. For those too young to remember the hit movie and TV show, *M*A*S*H*—Mobile Army Surgical Hospital—was a comedy about a field hospital (housed in a compound of tents) during the Korean War. Situated near the battlefield, the M*A*S*H unit formed a real, somewhat insane, community of healing as they coped with the acute cases of battlefield casualties brought to the tents.

Dr. Gasko told our summit, "*M*A*S*H* reminded me of the life of a public-school teacher. Today, we have students coming to public schools that have resettled from different parts of the world, and many have suffered acute trauma. Our schools expect students from poor neighborhoods, stressed families, chaotic schedules, and those exposed to violence to perform like kids who come out of affluent, stable, and managed environments.

"Wounded students arrive with a lot of need and trauma; that puts great strain on the system. The good people in the tent hospital are scrambling like they did in *M*A*S*H* to triage and do their best to keep up. Trying to serve the 'patients,' stop the pain, and bring hope takes a significant toll on those providers. Teachers not only teach, but provide care that goes beyond the definitions of teaching."

Pope Francis used the same metaphor to describe the new mission for parishes who are caring for the dislocated and the global social disruption. In a 2013 homily, the Pope said, "I see the church as a field hospital after battle. It is useless to ask a seriously injured person if he has high cholesterol and about the level of his blood sugars! You have to heal his wounds. Then we can talk about everything else."[2]

Just as Pope Francis sees a transformation of the role and application of the priestly vocation, education must quickly adapt to the same kind of practical human response to the surrounding crises. Just as medical personnel in a M★A★S★H unit could not afford the time to treat high cholesterol or high sugar, schools may have to eliminate some programmatic add-ons in order to become more relevant to the needs that arrive in the classroom every day.

Teachers at Risk

A recent NPR poll lists teaching as the fourth most stressful profession in America, behind active duty military, first line responders, and working parents. When we relate to people according to their roles or titles—teacher, police officer, judge, truck driver, soldier—it becomes easy to forget they are real human beings. Guess what? Teachers are humans. They have an autonomic nervous system, a central nervous system (CNS), and all the aches, pains, weaknesses, and emotions that you possess.

We can't pile on the pressure and programs to teach kids to reach grade level and ignore the central nervous systems of the adults. If we expect the adults to grit through it, we set them up for failure and burnout. And illness and death.

If we don't rethink the competencies, attitudes, behaviors, skills, and resources needed to help teachers, we will continue watching waves of teachers and administrators leaving the profession. And we also will see fewer and fewer students graduating and going on to college.

If we reimagine schools as field hospitals, both pre-K–12 and universities, we will have to determine and then deliver the services, training, and support necessary. Operating a field hospital while keeping focused on learning means we will need to do things radically different. We must start by having real conversations at every level of our educational mandates.

Perhaps the first step is to make sure that the adults in the building are being genuinely cared for. We must prioritize the collective well-being of those charged with teaching children. They cannot do that if they are stressed, sick, broke, or hopeless.

Start with the Basics

Schools are in the care business. So, what if they start by extending care for one another? Could they begin providing basic health fundamentals that have been neglected? What if every school worked to develop a well-being plan for adults and then did that for kids? Start with basics. First question: "When was last time you had an annual physical?" Yes, that is a very simple step. But it can be a starting point. Schools should promote the importance of getting a checkup every couple of years.

Second, many do not even know what is available or how to access their benefits. Yes, again, very simple. But, if we don't start with basic health regimens, we can't even begin to handle the bigger challenges.

Third, educate the adults about health and money. Many people don't seek medical attention because they think they can't afford it. Because insurance premiums are high, many people will only use their insurance for emergencies. They don't see a way to take care of the basics. Educating them on how to find sufficient care—regardless of financial strength—would be profoundly helpful to many people.

Fourth, work to mitigate stress from the workplace. We cannot pretend it doesn't affect a teacher's performance or health. *If stress is a killer and educators are at high risk, we set up teachers for disasters that could lead to disease and death. That makes us complicit, and that is morally unacceptable.*

We must pay attention to symptoms of stress in the collective nervous system. Every school (and every workplace) should monitor stress levels. Various tools can help. For example, the *Perceived Stress Scale*[3] is a classic stress assessment instrument that gives an excellent starting point. The *Ardell Wellness Stress Test* provides a more holistic assessment.[4]

Fifth, educate the adults about the positive approach to mental health. Kick the stigma out of the building. Dr. Martin Seligman, known as the "father of positive psychology" and the Director of Cornell's Positive Psychology Center, has worked long and hard to create an environment of positive attitudes and approaches to mental health. His latest book, *The Hope Circuit,*[5] examines the neurological process of how people move from helplessness to optimism and resilience. I recommend the tab, "Questionnaires," on Dr. Seligman's website, Authentic Happiness.[6] It includes, at current count, twenty-six free assessments. We work with several of them.

The "contagion" effect is also relevant to this issue. When the needs of students outstrip the capacity of teachers to absorb and recover, that negative energy bouncing around in the classroom can spark conflict. But a happy and healthy person boosts the well-being of everyone nearby. By bringing more positive energy to staff and students, we can release a positive contagion within our learning spaces.

I agree with Dr. Gasko: "We have to change our mental health framework from a 'disease' mentality to one of building wholeness, strength, optimism, and resilience. If the teacher isn't healthy and happy, her compromised presence and state will transmit to every student. And, if the system within the school and with the community isn't healthy and supportive, it is an uphill battle for everyone. Only the resilient and the heroic will survive."

What Does a Field Hospital Need?

When administrators and teachers really think about the implications of a school as a field hospital, it will force them to identify skills, standards of care, metrics, and new training and resources. And that will include educating and supporting parents. *Better parents mean better students.* Schools like the Childhood Development Institute, the Momentous Institute, Canyon View High, and the Purpose Built Schools Atlanta, reach out to parents with training and support. The field hospital image allows schools to see themselves as part of an interdependent ecosystem. Schools cannot begin healing without that health and care spreading to the surrounding community.

In our site visits across the country, we saw examples of schools doing exactly that. In some cases, teachers visit students' homes to gain a better understanding of the home conditions, but also to build a bridge of trust and support with the parents. We have also seen schools providing on-campus classes in life skills for parents and others in the community. Many schools help parents discover how to support their children with homework. Including health and well-being in our conversations may be a natural extension of a school's roles and relationships.

Dr. Gasko reminded our summit participants, "The most vulnerable neighborhoods in America hold many different levels and types of hospitals. If we provide differentiated support for classrooms, I think we need to also think about different levels of support for communities through different kinds of schools or field hospitals.

"When I was at the University of Chicago, we developed a powerful forensic tool to help schools build a foundation around five essentials.[7] In addition to tip-of-the-iceberg stuff, it also looked into deeper symptoms within a school. As we began to pay more attention to what was beneath the surface with the same level of urgency as test scores, schools in Chicago started to change dramatically."

The Five Essentials

1. *School Leadership*
2. *Parent–Community Ties*
3. *Professional Capacity*
4. *Student-Centered Learning Climate*
5. *Instructional Guidance*
   —*UChicago Consortium on School Research*[8]

When Dr. Gasko visited schools in Singapore, he saw why that country remains one of two best countries in the world in terms of academic achievement. Every school focused on achievement, but also addressed the human side of the equation. Every school had a collaboration space for teachers called a PULSE, representing the heartbeat of the school. Every school provided a room designed for the social and recovery needs of the adults. It was called the Living Room and served as a teacher stress decompression chamber. The comfortable and peaceful room offered healthy food choices, water, and periodicals that focused on well-being. In some cases, the room contained a massage station.

He and other educators know these kinds of human renewal spaces fall within the responsibility and ability of every school. Developing a healthy central nervous system (CNS) should be one driver for how we design and build healthy schools. Teachers and administrators must find the time and space in which to talk about health and care.

And, on that subject, Dr. Gasko sees that we must "reimagine what teacher lounges look like. They are typically a disaster. They are little more than stark break rooms. They provide sugary snacks and drinks.

Bathrooms are unpleasant. Most teachers avoid them like the plague; the setting is a perfect stimulus for negativity and complaining. One break room we viewed posted teacher test scores, by name! It would not take much to make some simple shifts in how we think about spaces throughout the school. Most times, space can be easily redesigned to accommodate how humans learn, how they connect, and how they recover.

"The Singapore schools bring in well-being experts monthly to address teachers on different topics. As teachers have their planning periods and spare time, they helicopter in and out of the living room on campus and learn from an expert about how they can take better care of themselves.

"One of the most stressful times of the year for parents and teachers is just before the start of school. Imagine if parents knew how stressed out the teachers were for that open house before school starts. I think parents would jump at the opportunity to help support ways to nourish teachers so they can take better care of their kids."

The challenge we face is that the whole district would have to approach well-being as the district's ecosystem priority. That includes reimagining what some functions of central office support staff will look like. When we don't approach this as an ecosystem, we create fixes that will fail.

Teacher Physicians

We are asking teachers to perform roles similar to those of physicians. They have to make high-stakes decisions throughout the day with different "patient" needs. As the cognitive load to learn new skills, apply new protocols, and manage complex student needs increases, we must also consider the increased demand on the teachers' sympathetic nervous system.

If an athlete does not fully recover from workouts or competition, they strip their body's natural capacity to perform. We train athletes to push beyond the pain or fatigue, but have to draw upon their adrenal systems to do that. We can do that over short periods of time, but the body will eventually shut down emotionally and physically. That's why many teachers are running on fumes.

Or, as Dr. Gasko summed it up, "If we make instruction more sophisticated and increase cognitive load, we must simultaneously attend to the human vehicle that needs to carry the load. That's why the school of the future will look and function more like a field hospital."

What Is a School?

We thought that we had the answers; it was the questions we had wrong.
—Bono

After Dr. Gasko introduced the concept to our group, we saw that we were being pushed back to rethink definitions, frames, and assumptions: "What is a school?" Instead of taking the linear leap into a discussion we imagined the future by playing with a set of blocks from the Froebel Gifts.[9] The blocks are instructional tools using simple geometric shapes. They allowed us to deconstruct our thoughts and build our ideas into shapes and patterns. Each participant shared the story behind their display. This freed us from the usual limitations and opened a broader and richer set of questions:

- Where is the teacher in this setting?
- What is a teacher's role?
- What do we call that role?
- Where is the student?
- What is the student's role?
- What do we call that role?
- What skills and training do we need?
- What are new standards for care?
- What does an institution look like that is a blend of social, psychological, medical, and educational disciplines?
- Might this look like models the Cleveland or Mayo Clinic have developed around integrative and team-based medicine?
- What is the relationship between field hospitals and families or the community?

These and other questions led us and will lead you down very different lines of inquiry. The answers ultimately depend on the questions we ask.

Wrapping Up

- What if caring better for teachers was the most effective strategy for improving schools?
- Self-pressure and fear of failure are causing an unprecedented rise in suicides and self-medication. An obsolete system forces everyone to run twice as hard just to keep up.
- Schools as field hospitals reflect an accountability culture colliding with the new level of needs entering school.
- The mission of a M★A★S★H unit to triage, serve patients, stop the pain, and bring hope takes a significant toll on providers.
- Teaching is the fourth most stressful profession in America.
- Schools can begin with basic health fundamentals for teachers and staff.
- In addition to restoration, we should also provide positive approaches to mental health.
- If teachers carry more complex loads, they need a different level of human care and support to carry that load.

Practical Reflections

1. How do we accommodate the new norm and demand for emotional, social, and psychological support?
2. What are the new services, training, and support necessary in a learning field hospital?
3. How would you assess the different kinds of field hospitals needed and the different levels of care for different communities?
4. If stress kills, and teaching is among the most stressful professions, what is the moral obligation of leaders and communities to address the risk?

Notes

1. Lewis Carroll, *Alice's Adventures in Wonderland* (New York: Macmillan, 1865).
2. Dennis Coday, "Pope's Quotes: The Field Hospital Church." *National Catholic Reporter*, Oct. 26, 2013.
3. https://www.mindgarden.com/132-perceived-stress-scale
4. Donald B. Ardell, *High Level Wellness: An Alternative to Doctors, Drugs, and Disease* (Berkeley, CA: Ten Speed Press, 1986).
5. Martin Seligman, *The Hope Circuit* (London: Nicholas Brearley, 2018).
6. https://www.authentichappiness.sas.upenn.edu/
7. UChicago Consortium on School Research, "The Essential Supports for School Improvement." www.consortium.uchicago.edu/publications/essential-supports-school-improvement
8. UChicago Consortium on School Research, "Organizing Schools for Improvement." www.consortium.uchicago.edu/publications/organizing-schools-improvement-lessons-chicago
9. http://www.froebelgifts.com/gifts.htm

CHAPTER 10

"Shots Fired"

In August 2012, Chris Erwin, Superintendent for Banks County School System in Commerce, Georgia, received the call, "Shots fired, a student is down." Between twelve and eighteen superintendents will receive that call this year.[1] About sixty students die each year from what most classify as an "active shooter incident." The episode described by Superintendent Erwin was a student suicide.

Security and safety are tough problems for schools, but most are not openly talking about them. Officials are afraid, and understandably so. The issues around guns invite criticism, second-guessing, and liability. That's why it is increasingly difficult for school officials and experts to address hard topics like school threats, violence, student depression, bullying, stress, and why so many kids are not ready to learn. But, we believe those conversations are the only path to sanity. The simple fact is that expert-driven solutions have failed.

Welcome to the Era of Wicked Problems

These school safety problems cannot be understood or confronted in a classic sense. We cannot solve any of them and they will not go away. They are "wicked problems"—social or cultural issues that are difficult or impossible to resolve because of incomplete, contradictory, or changing requirements. But beyond that definition, it seems that many problems today have no known frameworks or formulations. They are complex, vague, vexing, and shifting; we are never sure when, how, or if we have solved them. Many of the problems we deal with today are, in that sense, wicked.

"Many business leaders understand that we have left the age of 'solving problems.' Today, problems must be navigated. To 'solve' a problem means that you can walk away from it. To navigate a problem or dilemma means that we must find a path between competing pressures."[2]

Wicked problems are deceptively enticing to expert and blue-ribbon commission rescue objectives. They jump in with both feet and open wallets, only to learn the hard way that the problems cannot be solved. The best efforts resist change and any kind of intervention creates a ripple effect of new unintended consequences. MindShift has learned to develop the same mindset and skills found in sailing. You must sail in a zig-zag pattern if you want to make progress against the current and the wind.

Myths about School Shootings

I have been researching deadly force incidents in schools for five years. But every time I think I understand, a new incident destroys my certainty. To dig deeper into the wicked problem of school shootings, I interviewed Carl Chinn, President of the Faith-Based Security Network, and Vaughn Baker, President of Strategos International. Both serve as security consultants to schools, businesses, and churches. They walked me through several areas that many schools underestimate or overlook.

Myth 1: Our primary threat is an active shooter.

Vaughn: "We are losing three times as many students to suicide than to active shooters. Suicides are kept quieter; they just don't command the attention a dramatic shooting does."

Myth 2: We must focus our preparation on an outside threat.

Vaughn: "If you look at the Massachusetts Fusion Study that analyzed sixty-seven school shootings between 1992 and 2012, 82% of those school shootings were committed from an insider threat."[3]

Myth 3: School shooting is an epidemic and rising.

Vaughn: "The U.S. averages between twelve and eighteen active shooter events a year. That has remained constant since the 1980s. We're losing an average of about sixty lives a year in school. Fifty-plus million students are enrolled in 100,000 public schools. With sixty student deaths per year, the odds of any student losing his or her life in school is almost a million to one. However, it is not the likelihood that makes security a priority; it is the impact on the families and communities. Schools are a sanctuary for learning. When that is violated, it threatens our security and sense of well-being."

Chris Erwin told me his number one priority as a superintendent was to ensure the security and safety of the children. Educating them was second.

Myth 4: We need to arm every teacher and staff member.

Both Carl and Vaughn see this as an impossible mission and one that can lead to greater vulnerability.

Carl: "Some folks have it in their DNA to fill such a role. It might be a math teacher like Dr. David Benke at Deer Creek Middle School in Littleton, Colorado. Dr. Benke tackled a gunman who had shot and wounded two students. Then, with the help of other teachers, administrators, and an on-site contractor, held the shooter until police arrived. He took his role as a protector very seriously. But, that is simply not a viable role for many people."

Myth 5: We need to get the police here, now!

Carl: "After every incident, we hear statistics about officers arriving within two, three, five minutes. But that measurement is from the time they were dispatched from the 911 center, not from the time the first shots were fired.

"Initial responders are those who work at the school (or other site), but have signed up to be on the response team. They are typically the only responders on-site when the attack starts.

"Most (or all) of the threat stops by the time police arrive. While every community should improve response times, it is not possible for police to arrive as soon as the victims needed them. But, Dr. Benke was there."

Three Schools, Three Strategies

High Tech High in San Diego, Gainesville, Georgia's Riverside Military Academy, and Canyon View High School in Waddell, Arizona, offer three very different but effective strategies for responding to deadly threats on campus.

High Tech High: Building a Safe Culture

I asked Larry Rosenstock, CEO for High Tech High, how security in a tough neighborhood challenges their open school environment. He said, "We don't do rigorous checks. We know our kids and we know our families." When I asked Vaughn and Carl about that, they looked at me like a West Texas rancher looks at a California surfer dude.

Carl: "I've heard too many schools try to explain why it won't happen in their school. But, ask the administrators of schools that have had a shooting. Many had done some level of precautions, but still assumed *'that would never happen here.'* Unless you assume it *will* happen here, you won't be prepared. If you think it *might* happen here, you are starting one step behind the attack."

Canyon View High School: A Velvet-Covered Brick

David Schmidt, the lead architect, explained the security strategy for the design of Canyon View. They wanted to create high security without compromising an open campus. That security starts with a high perimeter fence that disappears into the background. The lobby and an advanced guest check-in system appear friendly because of natural lighting and interior glazing. But the school uses 100 cameras to monitor the interior and exterior spaces.

Beyond the physical security measures, Principal Nowlin has created a culture and a system of responsibility and team collaboration. There are no bells. Teachers office together. They also work by a philosophy of helping each other succeed. Canyon View also features a time four days a week that allows students needing help to meet together, help each other, and get coaching from teachers.

They designed most classrooms as open learning labs with movable perimeter walls. Teachers and students in most classrooms are visible to everyone. "See and be seen" fulfills a safety strategy.

When I met some students, I saw their collaborative learning model also plays a safety role; it creates more and deeper relational connections. Every student is also required to take part in some on-campus extra-curricular activity. An administrator told me, "We believe in the value of our extra-curricular opportunities but we also want to ensure no student feels or gets isolated."

Riverside Military Academy: Hardening and Rigor

Riverside assumes a tragic event will happen. Their strategy hardens the facility and creates rigorous preparation, on-site response capabilities, and reduces access to the facility.

Riverside's president, Stas Preczewski, and the school's counsel, Britt Daniel, outlined surprising levels of issue complexity. When Stas was president of Georgia Gwinnett College, four campus incidents exposed him to the challenge leaders face when making decisions in real-time, but under ambiguous and fluid circumstances. He learned those lessons well.

For example, do you lock down or escape, withhold information or share it, conclude the shooting is an attack or suicide, hold back or send in the police, create a diversion or apprehend?

Even if an administrator makes all the right calls and contains the damage, parents, media, and social media may still second-guess and create doubt about the actions.

Schools also face liability. That's because schools act in place of parents; that is the meaning of the legal designation, "loco parentis." When parents entrust their children to the school, the school accepts responsibility and liability. In today's environment, that can easily and quickly lead to litigation. And that creates numerous other issues for schools.

For example, Vaughn Baker explained that his company does not give schools threat assessment scores. They give it to the school's attorney so that the report will be protected by attorney-client privilege.

Britt Daniel gave another example. "Assume that we decide to upgrade the security system. Should we upgrade the entire campus at one time, which could be financially unfeasible? Or, do we phase the installation over two or three years? One decision creates a financial risk; the other opens the door to litigation if a shooting were to take place in an area not yet covered by the new surveillance system."

Britt also said the one big event doesn't keep him up at night, but the potential small violence issues do. Studies show that 82% of in-school violence will be from inside the school, someone known within the school. And of those, it is three times more likely to be a suicide. Britt and Chris both talked about the difficulty of getting funding for preventative measures like training and mental health support. It is much easier to raise money for hardening a point of entry. Making the prevention side more difficult is that it is impossible to prove a negative. In other words, schools cannot prove that increased surveillance prevented a shooting.

Riverside and North Park Elementary in San Bernardino faced the same funding challenge. Without an imminent threat or a recent tragic event, communities and legislatures find it difficult to embrace an expensive, uncertain, and complex issue. How much is enough? What guarantees will it buy?

During our visit to San Bernardino, California, we found the post-shooting security improvements for North Park Elementary were very expensive. The funds had to come out of other budgets. The superintendent made his challenge clear; unless the state legislature provided more funding, the district could not provide the same level of security over seventy-one other schools.

At the other end of the spectrum, Gainesville, Georgia, exhibits a community ethos of pulling together and supporting the public good. Carroll Daniel Construction, a third-generation firm that just moved its headquarters from an industrial part of town to the town square, is what James Fallows describes as a "business patriot." They donated their services to develop the plan and the funding to upgrade the security.

Common Traps

Stas Preczewski at Riverside explained that the most common trap in developing a sensible security plan is setting unrealistic expectations with parents and staff. He explained the importance of detailing the extent of measures the school is taking to ensure the safety and security of their children, while also explaining the unforeseeable. According to Vaughn, schools tend to underestimate their risk and overestimate their readiness.

That leads into the second trap of deciding that "We can do this ourselves." Because of the complexity of considerations and the tendency to validate one's assumptions, every organization needs outside eyes and guides. Vaughn says confirmation bias is common; he helps schools see what they overlooked, often hiding in plain sight.

The third trap springs shut when the outside experts (perhaps even an official agency) end up running the security process, allowing school leaders to relinquish their role. Chris recalled a situation when a bomb squad entered and removed a student backpack by robot and prepared to drop it into a detonation container and blow it up.

Facing the prospect of 1,000 parents watching and students hearing the detonation, Chris challenged the law enforcement decision because of the emotional impact of blowing up a backpack. When he expressed his strong concern, the law enforcement leader agreed to take the backpack off the premises before detonating it. Although the legal authority resides with law enforcement, the moral authority rests on the school administration as it considers the welfare of their students and families.

The fourth trap is channeling most school energy into the response. All those we interviewed agreed that the better path reinforces readiness. By assuming a shooting will happen, that mind shift makes the critical difference when implementing proactive efforts. They also see the need to prepare for the aftermath of trauma on staff, students, themselves, and the public.

Hard Conversations

I think it reminds us not to be so disconnected. Sandy Hook happened when we were all young, middle school ... I think we've always grown up surrounded by guns and by mass shootings ... and Sandy Hook made it a national topic.

—Student from Cry Havoc

Under Mara Richards Bim's direction, the Cry Havoc Theater Company in Dallas digs deep into current events and contemporary issues, releasing student artistry to research and recreate traumatic experiences. Through the magic of theater, they help individuals and whole communities and cities to step into the hard conversations that often remain in the shadows.[4]

Cry Havoc joined our last summit to help us see how to bring those conversations to all stakeholders. When they considered the wide topic of guns and schools, Mara's students traveled to Sandy Hook, attended the national NRA Convention, spent time in Washington with their state representatives, and shot guns on a firing range. They also conducted first-person interviews and reformulated those interviews into the script for *Babel*, an exercise in "verbatim" or "documentary" theater. So, the students who conducted the interviews played their interviewees.

The students told us about that experience:

"I think it reminds us not to be so disconnected. Sandy Hook happened when we were all young, middle school ... I think we've always grown up surrounded by guns and by mass shootings ... and Sandy Hook made it a national topic."

Another said: "At one point we were pulled back into the experience. We were reading the lines, but it felt distant. One of the theater coaches responded, 'You guys can't protect your heart from this. You can't sit there and protect yourself because you don't want to feel the emotion, feel it now and then deal with it. But you can't just keep protecting yourself and avoiding it entirely.'"

I asked Mara what it was like to walk so deeply and personally into the trauma of Sandy Hook. "How did you and your students process and deal with it?"

Mara answered, "While they expected to be affected by the interviews and talked a lot about self-care, they had not developed the protocols to deal with the emotions the interviews brought up. Conducting the interviews and taking on the roles took a deeper toll than anticipated. For the most recent show on immigration, they brought in a therapist to work with the cast before and after conducting interviews. They also set up clear protocols to deal with the emotions that came up."

With Mara's permission, we asked the students to present an extract from the play. They selected an interview with a family whose teenage daughter had committed suicide. Most of our participants were parents of teenagers. The scene transported all of us into the scene.

Student Cara Lawson read the part of Sue Loncar:

It's just really still hard to believe that somebody that was so full of life … I can still picture. When we found her feet. Something about feet, babies' feet when they're little and … when she was laying on the floor I looked at her feet. I tried to pick her up. It was, like, if I could just pick her up, and it was just, like, if I could just will her back to life. Even though it was obvious she was gone, I tried to sit her up. It was ... I mean, the image is looking at her feet. It was just the most shocking sight ever, just seeing her laying there on the floor. Your mind can't even take it in.

The day that she died she had been to the mall. She had bought face masks. She'd always took really good care of her skin and she was real proud of her skin. Because she had porcelain skin and it was just flawless.

And you know to me that's not the sign of someone who's getting ready to take her life. So, I don't think she was planning on taking her life. She had a party she was looking forward to going to that Saturday night. But she got in trouble that night. And a lot of research shows that that's what happens sometimes with kids, that a family altercation or arguments, kids will in a fit of rage or anger just react. And that's why I think it's so important not to have guns in the house. I think she didn't think it through. I think she was just really angry.

She got in a big argument with her dad that night, and I think she just thought, "I'll show them." And because her dad had said, "You can't threaten suicide to get out of trouble." And she thought, "Oh?" Because she was very strong-willed, I think she thought, "Well, I won't just threaten it; I'll do it." And I think it was very much just an impetuous spur of the moment decision. Because teenage brains are not completely developed.

The next morning, we went into her room and her bed had not been touched. We'd stayed up talking to her until about 3:00 a.m. and then we went to bed. And then I just think she just Googled. And my son looked on the computer. She Googled how to load. She didn't know how to load the gun and she Googled how to load the gun.

Cara's reading was emotionally difficult for many of us. Some cried, some stood and paced, others practiced deep and slow breathing and exhaling. After Dr. Gasko took us through exercises to address trauma and stress, Will Richey spoke, "Part of what we just experienced is a process for stepping into emotional spaces. We need a process when walking into potentially traumatic zones. Process and dialogue, process and listening. We just went through Dr. Gasko's process of re-centering and getting the parasympathetic nervous system reactivated. I mean, we were pretty agitated, right? And so it's hard to do good work or even think clearly in that frame of mind. When we are agitated, our narratives go down roads where they loop back and don't move forward."

Throughout our journey in the development of this book, various guides—Hamilton High, Karen Blessen, UNTD's Jovi the Superhero, and Cry Havoc—built bridges to bring stakeholders into productive conversations around complex and hard topics. They helped plant the material in emotional maturity by providing symbols based on real life. So, instead of fifteen opinions of what is most important, they gave us a common reference point as an anchor for the hard conversations.

If schools continue to avoid that dialogue, they will continue to incite the opposite result. People won't feel safe or included, and that will permit their fear instincts to kick in. If you don't create a framework for extending trust, then you lose the very thing you are trying to create.

Whatever you do for me but without me, you do against me.
—Mahatma Gandhi

What Can We Do?

Commercial construction may hold wise and practical help for schools. Twenty percent of all occupational deaths occur on construction sites. That translates to about eighty lives a month. So, more die in one month at construction sites than die in a year of school suicides and attacks. Construction tackles this on two fronts. The first is the data; that identifies the most common risks. Since 40% of construction deaths are due to falls, the industry focuses on eliminating or reducing those accidents. Second, the construction industry addresses the problem through a process called, "Safety Culture," a specific effort to embed a safety mindset throughout a project, organization, or system. That approach has also become common to heavy industry, manufacturing, airlines, and nuclear power plants.

So, how does that help schools?

The data tells us 80% of a school's risk comes from people present or known within the school, and, therefore, not considered as suspects. And, data also confirms that 66% of school shootings will be suicides. Creating a "safety culture" is the most effective means of protection. The best on-ramp to creating a safety culture would be through investing in the following:

1. *Clarify values:* This includes explaining why safety is important to the school, the students, the families, and the community.
2. *Define safe behaviors:* Schools should study and clearly communicate behaviors that are safe and those that are not.
3. *Leaders must embody the values and behaviors:* If leaders do not walk the talk, no amount of training will make a difference. I worked with the senior leadership team in a global construction firm, as they tried to examine why injuries (and deaths) had increased over the last quarter. We discovered the CEO violated safety by taking a shortcut out of the parking lot and going the wrong way; employees saw him do it. I also learned that no member of the leadership team had visited the sites where the accidents occurred.
4. *Design the environment to support a culture of safety:* The campus and buildings are one of the greatest tools for influencing behavior. An environment that is open and provides easy visibility creates a sense of protection and accountability.
5. *Invest resources, both time and dollars:* A plan without sufficient resources will shrink and die.
6. *Incentivize positive behaviors:* Humans naturally take the path of least resistance. To do the right thing requires clarity and alignment. That also calls for external reinforcement to support the clarity and alignment.

If you visit a construction site, you will hear two things. First, they will show and tell you the best way to exit the building in case of an emergency, and where to gather after exiting the building.

Second, you will hear a recent story illustrating someone taking positive steps to prevent a potential accident, or one describing the outcome of someone *not* taking steps.

Chris Erwin said that after the suicide at one of his schools, every staff meeting began with a reminder—including vivid stories and solid tips—to pay attention to how their students are doing.

The Real Villain

No other subject in this book provokes more controversy and anger than firearm assaults. Because the issue generates such intense anxiety, frustration, and anger, all sides claim the high ground, but use it to attack every other side and idea.

But, it all comes down to fear. That is the real villain. And fear makes us all do and say things that are too visceral, volatile, superficial, and distracting. Fear usually invites the wrong people to the table and keeps the right people away.

Moral and integral responsibility cannot be delegated or contracted out to others. Schools and other organizations will bring better and more enduring change by inviting all the true stakeholders into a process that remains locally led, resourced, and focused. Everyone who belongs in the room must leave their Superman capes at the door and pay the personal price to work together. That requires humility, integrity, honesty, and collaboration. It may also require admonitions to "settle your glitter."

As long as fear drives thoughts and responses, school safety will remain a difficult discussion for schools and communities. It will also drive decisions to treat the symptoms because they are tangible and technical in nature and end up leaving the school more vulnerable because of a false sense of having "solved" something. But, if schools develop the long view, ignore the distracting voices, work toward a Safety Culture, follow the six principles, and focus limited resources on the few areas that are the highest risk, they will be among the best prepared. They can help defeat fear by creating a safe bridge for teachers, students, their families, and the community to meet, engage, and maintain an ongoing and deepening conversation about what kind of community they want to be.

Together.

WHOLE

Wrapping Up

- We live in an era of "wicked problems," problems that cannot be solved because of incomplete, contradictory, or changing requirements. They are also complex, vague, vexing, and shifting.
- Rather than solving wicked problems, we must navigate them.
- Public hysteria tends to create myths about the nature, intensity, and scale of problems. That is certainly true of violent invasions of schools (and other institutions).
- The most effective responses to incidents of school violence may be to let data reveal the best investments of resources, and build a safety culture by specific and solid measures.
- Those schools (or other organizations) who do that best will be among the most prepared.

Practical Reflections

1. Think through how problems in government, culture, politics, or your own school or company seem to defy solutions. How do (and how should) you approach them?
2. You read about the three schools that developed three different strategies for combatting school violence. Can you think of other viable approaches?
3. How does fear impact your world of work or education? What does it do to you as you face crises? Does this chapter help you to defeat or avoid fear? How?

Notes

1. https://everytownresearch.org/gunfire-in-school/#13201 and https://www.cnn.com/interactive/2019/07/us/ten-years-of-school-shootings-trnd/
2. Rex Miller, Mabel Casey, and Mark Konchar, *Change Your Space, Change Your Culture: How Engaging Workplaces Lead to Transformation and Growth* (Hoboken, NJ: John Wiley & Sons, Inc., 2014).
3. Public Intelligence, "(U//FOUO) Massachusetts Fusion Center School Shootings Analysis 1992–2012," Sept. 27, 2013. www.publicintelligence.net/ma-school-shootings/
4. Available at: youtu.be/s3uehDK51C8

CHAPTER 11

Do Healthy Buildings Improve Learning?

I don't think that architecture is only about shelter, is only about a very simple enclosure. It should be able to excite you, to calm you, to make you think.

—Zaha Hadid

1925 marks the first time more than 50% of American homes had electric lights. Since then, with increased climate control and convenience, much of life has moved indoors. In fact, if you multiply your age by 90%, you will see the number of accumulated years you have spent indoors.[1] Think about it; if you're 42 years old, you have spent almost 38 years inside your home, office, factory, school, grocery store, place of worship, or other built environments. And, according to health experts, that percentage has increased with those born after 1984.

That creates a whole new milieu of illness. Sick buildings. When buildings get sick, they can infect the people who pass through them. The most famous building-borne illness, Legionnaire's disease, can be fatal. Beyond that, buildings spread colds, flu, allergies, edema, occupational asthma, pregnancy complications, and many other ailments. Sick buildings increase expenses through reduced efficiency, lost time at work, and increased medical expenses.

Keeping buildings healthy should be a high priority, but often it is not. Budget squeezes tend to constrain the policies and expenditures that make buildings well.

Building sources that make people sick

1. *Inadequate ventilation*
2. *Chemical contaminants*
3. *Biological contaminants*
4. *Electromagnetic radiation*
5. *Psychological factors (i.e. stress and toxic culture)*

That is certainly true of schools. The Center for Green Schools estimates schools spend less than half of the $482 billion needed for proper upkeep.[2] That comes to about $2.5 million of neglected maintenance and repair for each of the 100,000 schools in America.

From Green to WELL

In 2013, medical science and building science finally collaborated to create a standard and a process to help build measurably healthy facilities. Even though research confirmed the positive effects of natural light, proper CO_2 levels, the use of color, and properly managed temperature and sound on learning, the K–12 world did not quickly or fully embrace that new science. But the inevitable progression from environmental sustainability to human sustainability could not be more relevant and timely for educators. Thankfully, because of progressive educational architects and increasing scientific evidence, schools are starting to catch up.

The idea of healthy buildings grew out of the Green movement. But, it took thirty years for that movement to go from a fringe idea to a high-end solution for premium buildings, to a smart business choice, and finally today when some form of LEED® Certification has become expected for new commercial construction. Although education fell behind the curve on healthy environments, schools can learn from the business world's knowledge that healthy and happy employees produce a high return on investment. Healthy and happy teachers and students likewise produce high returns on learning (ROL).

The time for healthy buildings has fully arrived. Today, the financial logic completes the case. Business ventures will spend an average of 5% of their budgets for design, construction, and interior finish out. Another

15% will cover technology and operations. And, about 80% of a company's budget goes to employee salary and benefits.

We know green buildings improve health and human performance. And, they only cost *up to* 1% more to build. So, what if, instead of spending 5% for design, construction, and finishing on the building, a building owner spends an additional 1% (or less) to achieve WELL Building certification, which will improve human sustainability? Could an owner attract and retain people better with a healthy building? Might that give people more incentive to come to the office? Would they take fewer sick days, feel better, think better, and work better? What if that single penny out of each dollar spent in construction makes a 1% or more improvement in the lives of the employees?

That 1% improvement is an 8 cent return on the single penny. Real estate investment experts estimate actual returns in productivity are many times higher.[3] Who would not make that investment?

That is how the heavy lifting of the Green movement and consistent cost improvements finally connected healthy buildings to human sustainability. And, in a school, that means healthy buildings improve learning.

How to Live and Work Healthier

The International WELL Building Institute (IWBI) is a public benefit corporation that serves to improve human health and well-being in buildings and communities around the world through its WELL Building Standard.

Ergonomics specialist Angela Spangler, who leads IWBI's Education and Healthcare sector, knows how space impacts people. In her role at IWBI, every day she observes the ways a healthy environment improves the health and performance of every employee, every hour of the working day. Space forms a passive delivery system of positive health benefits by improving air quality, matching lighting with human circadian rhythms, reducing stress, decreasing noise pollution from poor acoustics, and displaying the design nudges that shift behavior.

In my recent interview with Angela, she captured the opportunity of this historic moment for education. "The education sector really popped up as a prime opportunity to practice preventative care. Schools can instill these principles at such an early age, giving them a great educational advantage. And, students in healthy schools also have the opportunity to take that home and impact their family, make bigger ripple effects into the communities where they live.

"Attracting and retaining students and faculty are a primary driver for higher education. Wellness and facilities reflect the brand. They tangibly express if school leadership has a strong commitment to health and well-being, or not."

I pressed her for clarity in the K-12 market, "Angela, all of that sounds good, but what about a K-12 principal or ISD superintendent who wants to begin creating healthy space, but has no budget?"

Angela explained that she has those conversations often. She told me when a principal recently told her they have to choose between WELL certification or a new roof, she told him, "Roofs are important. You probably ought to do that." But, she also knows starting points can be simple and inexpensive, things as simple as updating the cleaning protocol. A healthy cleaning process immediately impacts everyone; get the chemicals out of the system. That will not cost a lot of money and it achieves a quick, fast, low-hanging impact that touches every single person.

"Or, a school can look at policies that promote health and reduce stress. A next step might be to layer on some environmental fixes. Add circadian appropriate lighting; that will improve students' attention, mood, and ability to learn. Schedule a recess period at noon; allow students and teachers to gain the benefits of peak sun exposure. Better regulated hormones carry over to home. It also improves sleep. It's hard to quantify the value of a well-rested educator or student [see Chapter 14, in this volume]. These are some of the easy and low-cost opportunities that add high impact. There's no one size fits all, so the IWBI provides coaching to help people develop a strategy that works for them.

"For example, solid research verifies the impact of noise on growth and development. Particularly if you are from a low-income environment. If a student lives next to an airport or a freeway, he or she lives in a continuous barrel of loud noise. That is also true inside a school! Draining and debilitating noise can come from a lot of kids jostling in the hallways, bells ringing, and loud talking inside the hard surfaces that act as echo chambers. Of course, teachers also suffer the impact of the bombardment of their surroundings.

"The WELL Building provides strategies for the behavior in the building. We often start there by identifying the major goals and principles. Is the school promoting healthy food or physical activity? Can we easily and efficiently shift the schedule? Maybe they don't need 50 minutes of teaching time; maybe they could get by with 45 minutes. Then all of those little chunks of saved time can shift to physical activity breaks or recess. And those little changes cost nothing.

"The same thinking applies to food and hydration. And, that can start with the simple design of a cafeteria and food presentation. First, make healthy options the easiest and most appealing choice. Label food with nutritional information. Group healthy foods in one area and less healthy foods in another. And what about plate size? What does that do to your perception of satisfaction, of being full?"

When you listen to Angela, you realize that a positive attitude and energetic posture may be the most important resources to making life in buildings healthier. After all, dollars tend to follow vision. When that all comes together, the building becomes a fully functioning part of the learning process. Let's now look at what that looks like in the real world.

The Building Is a Teacher

When Dr. Marilyn Denison was the Assistant Superintendent for the Coppell, Texas, ISD, she led the design team for the new Richard J. Lee Elementary PK-5 school. Lee became the first school with net-zero energy consumption in Texas. Dr. Denison also partnered with architect Taryn Kinney (who worked at Stantec at the time) to help rethink the learning environment. The two have since reconnected after both individuals joined DLR Group.

It worked. Marilyn told me of her conversation with a fifth grade student who had transferred to Lee in third grade. When she asked the student to compare her old school with Lee, "This girl just lit up and said, 'I feel happy when I walk inside the school.'

"So, I asked why.

"And she gave her reasons: 'The color, the light, I can choose where I do my work. And, the teachers respect me to get my work done.'

"This young girl was so articulate I wanted to bring her on the road to help others understand how powerful a school building can be on engagement and learning." This young student was just one intonation of Lee Elementary's compelling voice. The school's exemplary results speak even louder.

Lee Elementary: The Bridge between Green and WELL Buildings

Richard J. Lee Elementary was not only the first net-zero energy school in Texas; it is LEED® Gold certified by the U.S. Green Building Council. LEED®, which stands for Leadership in Energy and Environmental Design, recognizes best-in-class building strategies and practices. Through the certification, Lee has created a circle of influence far beyond the Coppell community. They have paved the way for others.

The building is an additional teacher. The unique architecture, grounds, energy management, and the structure are all built into the curriculum. Marilyn and Taryn dropped the traditional approach of relying on experts to determine how learning would take place. The design instead expressed how teachers and students would learn by bringing other stakeholders into the process. According to Principal Chantel Renea Kastrounis, Lee designed a unique culture around "five K-5 vertical houses throughout the building where there are flexible uses of space and furnishings. Five collabs are in each house where learners can work together to learn from one another in small groups."[4] The school is also designed to engage the community.

Students are not the only ones rejoicing about Lee. Teachers also describe the joy of teaching there. Students are also teachers. The House structure brings the same kids and teachers together over several years and builds a safe, tight-knit supportive community. The building motivates students, teachers, parents, and the whole community.

The Score Sheet on Lee Elementary

Lee Elementary's 99,000 square feet for about 900 students equals about 110 square feet per student. Taryn says that they frequently see 150–160 square feet per student in school designs. So, even with about 25% less space, Lee Elementary provides 39% more instructional space than a traditional school by leveraging circulation space for learning.

The National Renewable Energy Laboratory in Golden, Colorado, published a document outlining why conserving energy should be a priority for schools:

> *In many school districts, energy costs are second only to salaries, exceeding the cost of supplies and books. Nationally, K-12 schools spend more than $6 billion a year on energy and, according to the U.S. Department of Energy, at least a quarter of that could be saved through smarter energy management. Energy improvements could cut the nation's school bill by $1.5 billion each year.[5]*

Solar panels, building automation, recycled materials, a wind turbine, geothermal HVAC system, rainwater collection, LED fixtures, and other energy-saving measures allow Lee to function as a net-zero energy user. The average school in 2008 paid $1.25 per square foot for electricity.[6] The energy inflation rate since 2008 would increase that to $1.38 per square foot.[7] Their net-zero school saves approximately $136,000 annually, savings that go back into the classroom.

It's Time to Play Catch Up. Fast

Sustainability is not a new topic for schools. But, it's also not a high priority. Fewer than 2% of K-12 schools hold any form of LEED® Certification; that's 2,000 schools out of 100,000!

Angela explained that her primary hurdles with public schools revolve around their budget and procurement process. But, in reality, that is an old and increasingly baseless constraint. It costs no (or very little) more to build a healthy and sustainable building if you use a cross-disciplined collaborative or integrated delivery. But most of the commercial construction world still operates under a 1950s' structure and mindset.

Most construction projects, including schools, still follow a now-ancient process called Design-Bid-Build (DBB). That means an architect develops the design, procurement bids the design to contractors, and then the contractors build it. Seventy percent of projects that follow the DBB model come in late and over budget. Complexity is the culprit. At one time the architect's general knowledge was sufficient to produce workable drawings. Today 80% of the knowledge and cost resides in specialty trades and consultants that never have input until someone hands them a drawing and says, "Go to work."[8]

Twenty-first-century projects flip that sequence. Because new buildings are so much more complex, the process requires deep and early coordination to manage the interdependent systems, interior flexibility, advanced technology, security, safety, culture support, adaptability to change, energy conservation, and occupant health and well-being. All the specialty trades need to enter at the earliest possible time frame, preferably prior to design.

Projects that follow that pattern will cost less, create more efficient and better use of space, and improve the business or learning outcomes. The power of design will also transform the experience and even the lives of those who enter those spaces each day.

Things You Can Begin to Do Now

Completely shifting from traditional building construction to WELL building standards can be a long and expensive process. But, there are many effective steps that can be taken quickly and at low cost now.

The first step is education; learn all you can about the science behind WELL. You can begin by downloading a free copy of the WELL Building Standard,[9] a comprehensive instructional manual on all the elements within a building that contribute to health and well-being. Each element links to medical research. The manual can be a valuable guide to facilities and capital projects departments.

Beyond that, let me recap steps presented earlier in this chapter; all those can be implemented rapidly, easily, and economically.

- Update the cleaning protocols.
- Adapt policies that promote health and reduce stress.
- Add some of the environmental upgrades and policy revisions described earlier. These are some of the easy and inexpensive opportunities that add high impact.
- Lower noise within all learning areas.
- Promote healthy food choices and increased physical activity.
- Consider ways to shift the schedule which can increase time for physical exercise and outdoor activities.

These are some of the low-hanging opportunities that add high impact—quickly and reasonably. Because every school has different needs and a different starting point, we provide coaching to help develop a strategy that works for them.

Wrapping Up

- In 2013, medical science and building science converged to provide a framework for creating a healthier environment.
- Improving lighting, CO_2 levels, and temperature improve mood, cognition, comfort, and learning.
- Schools can instill healthy habits at an earlier age by providing healthier environments.
- Schools should bring the right expertise in earlier than is typical in traditional capital project acquisitions. Review the WELL Building Standard to understand how to start.
- Start with the low-hanging fruit listed in the chapter.
- District energy costs are second to salaries.
- Sustainability and WELL buildings should be part of every district's agenda.

Practical Reflections

1. What is the Return on Learning from a healthier building?
2. How can you use your building as a teacher?
3. What could your school do with savings if it cut its energy costs in half?
4. How can your school start its Green to WELL journey?

Notes

1. Roberts, "We Spend 90% of Our Time Indoors. Says Who?" Building Green blog, Dec. 15, 2016. www.buildinggreen.com/blog/we-spend-90-our-time-indoors-says-who

2. Rex M. Miller, et al., *Humanizing the Education Machine: How to Create Schools That Turn Disengaged Kids into Inspired Learners* (Hoboken, NJ: John Wiley & Sons, Inc., 2017).

3. Scott R. Muldavin, "Value Beyond Cost Savings: How to Underwrite Sustainable Properties." Muldavin Company, San Rafael, CA, 2010.

4. Stantec, "Richard J. Lee Elementary School Is Texas' First Net-Zero School." Oct. 20, 2014. https://www.stantec.com/en/news/2014/richard-lee-elementary-school-is-texas-first-new-zero#.VQXNW1qJmJX

5. National Renewable Energy Lab (NREL), "Myths About Energy in Schools." Feb. 2002. www.nrel.gov/docs/fy02osti/31607.pdf

6. Electric Choice, "Schools and School Districts." www.electricchoice.com/business-electricity/schools-and-school-districts/

7. Electricity price history from 2008 through 2019, "Inflation Rate For Electricity Between 2008–2019." www.in2013dollars.com/Electricity/price-inflation/2008-to-2019?amount=100

8. Rex M. Miller, *The Commercial Real Estate Revolution: Nine Transforming Keys to Lowering Costs, Cutting Waste, and Driving Change in a Broken Industry* (Hoboken, NJ: John Wiley & Sons, Inc., 2009).

9. Available at: https://resources.wellcertified.com/tools/well-building-standard-v1/

CHAPTER 12

The Heart-to-Head Connection: Managing Emotions to Support the Brain

The human heart has hidden treasures, in secret kept, in silence sealed.
—Charlotte Brontë

Lisa and I recently went to brunch with Jan and Mike. Jan teaches first-grade at an elementary school on the northeast edge of Fort Worth. Mike, her husband, helps as a volunteer. The school serves a mostly blue-collar community. Several of her students are "Simply not ready to learn." Mike's main role is working with two young boys from backgrounds of heartbreaking abuse, Jamal and Jaime (not their real names).

Jamal is about a foot taller and 50 pounds heavier than his classmates. In his frequent outbursts, he sometimes flips desks. He once threw a student over a desk and into the wall.

And Jaime just curls up in a ball under his desk.

Recently, Jamal picked up scissors and threatened to poke out the eye of another student. Mike ran over, grabbed the hand with the scissors, and wrapped his 6-ft body around the boy in a big bear hug of compassion.

Over brunch he said, "I know you're not supposed to touch these kids. I was reacting to the situation." Jamal and Jaime compete for Mike's attention. One tips over desks and the other cocoons beneath them. The drama often spills into the class. While Mike smothers one fire, Jan deals with the sparks that land on other students.

Experts say Jamie's and Jamal's emotions are "dysregulated." That means their early life experiences have conditioned their brain so that they can't self-regulate. At least not yet.

Emotional dysregulation often results from early psychological trauma, abuse, or neglect. It affects the frontal cortices of the brain, the logical portion.[1] SPECT brain scans show exactly what chronic stress, trauma, and abuse look like. Regions of their brains are dark; that means the neurons have stopped firing and blood no longer flows to those areas. The surface of their brains is bumpy, like broccoli.

Dr. Jay Faber of the Amen Clinics walked me through a trauma scan. When looking down at the top of the brain, you see an inflamed triangle pattern called the "ring of fire." According to Dr. Gasko, that pattern creates a default mode network.

Emotional dysregulation: impairment of a physiological regulatory mechanism (as that governing metabolism, immune response, or organ function).
— Ryan W. Carpenter, and Timothy J. Trull[2]

Triggers go directly to that part of the brain and are trapped in a Bermuda triangle of thought and behavior response.

I wish the professionals in the various fields would use a better term than "dysregulation." That description is far too antiseptic for the tragic reality of what happens in a child's brain. Perhaps school protocols and policies (as required by lawyers and insurance companies) keep us too detached from these kids' realities. Mike's instincts are probably accurate; what they need most is that bear hug of protective compassion.

The classroom challenges cannot be solved through cognitive means of persuasion or discipline. These boys have more primal issues. Their central nervous systems (CNS) are in chaos and need restoration and retraining.

But, their chaos becomes our chaos.

That sentence may be the most important observation in this book. When you follow the trail of teacher burnout, stressed-out students, disrupted families, and chaotic communities, it leads back to this posted warning: *Our students come to school not ready to learn.* Translation: children come to school with unregulated central nervous systems. The real issue goes deeper than clinical pronouncements. It's a matter of the heart.

Chaos in the brain builds chaos throughout the whole community. Education and society depend on self-regulated individuals who engage their frontal cortices. Perhaps we are entering a limbic era, where the emotions of survival dominate. If that is true, then re-educating the heart must start earlier. Dr. Gasko says education's focus on cognitive learning neglects the iceberg that controls our readiness to learn: our central nervous systems.

In the past, life was stable enough for society and schools to function on top of the iceberg. Then, almost a half-century ago, Alvin Toffler warned, "Unless man quickly learns to control the rate of change in his personal affairs as well as society, we are doomed to massive adaptational failure."[3] *That is the iceberg lying dead ahead.*

The Contagion Effect

How does a teacher like Jan cope with today's classroom conditions? At 6, Jamal is already as tall as Jan. Without Mike's service as a volunteer, the two boys would consume all her attention and energy.

Without skilled intervention, a classroom can mirror the behavior of the least regulated students. Dr. Gasko explains that groups learn to synchronize into a collective central nervous system. Jazz ensembles, for example, develop an ability to anticipate where the music is headed and perform as a fluid collective creative expression. Their central nervous systems, the mirror neurons, allow them to regulate and develop deep social synchronicity.[4]

Protesting mobs can likewise detonate spontaneous violence. Here the agitations jump out of dysregulated CNS. Both phenomena, jazz ensembles and mobs, create network effects. They override conscious control. One achieves creative flow; the other sparks a flame. According to Dr. Nicholas Christakis, group structures create different network effects. He uses the example of carbon atoms. Combining them one way produces graphite. Arranging them in another structure forms diamonds. The property (or behavior) does not reside in the makeup of the atoms, but in their configuration.[5]

Imagine Augmented Reality and Classroom Management

Class management strategies are designed to help teachers handle students who get distracted, act impulsively, or fall behind. A slight redirection of that student's attention or energy may be all that is needed to restore harmony in the classroom. But, most teachers are not trained to see their students through the lens of the central nervous system. They are not taught the role of body, mind, and heart connections and how to dissipate or channel energy into positive behavior.

Imagine tomorrow a teacher walks into her classroom with a special set of CNS-augmented reality glasses. She can magically see the energy levels of each child's central nervous system. Her glasses provide a color meter for seeing red SNS (stress) levels and blue PNS (calm) levels. As she scans the classroom she notices energy from one student shifting the color tones of another. A word or a phrase from one student shifts the colors among the students next to him.

When the class sits, she sees a jagged variegation of color patterns filling the room. The atmosphere feels electrically charged. She takes a few steps forward; immediately some zones turn crimson, apprehensive of what's next.

When the teacher places her chair in the middle of the students, they shift their desks to face the center. The students can now see her and one another. She welcomes them with a smile; the red meters morph into a slight blue tint. Then, she notices red hues toward the back corner surrounding two students. Their red begins to expand; now another student displays red. Before it expands further, she asks the class to stand up, close their eyes, and enter a breathing exercise. Soon, the color throughout most of the room slides into a soft canopy of blue. "Okay," she whispers, "Let's take a seat and go back in time to visit the Constitutional Convention in 1787."

Response-to-Intervention: The Conventional Approach

The Response-to-Intervention (RTI) divides students into three tiers.

Tier 1 students function emotionally and academically at benchmark levels (about 75–80% of students). Tier 2 students fall short in some areas, but with "strategic" intervention can remain in class and get back on track. For example, if Jimmy is a grade behind in reading, he may be paired with Sally to help him. Tier 3 students require intensive (sometimes professional) help.[6]

Tier 3 students are the Jamals and the Jaimes. Those students require a special kind of teacher, one who can stay calm and not get triggered. If Jamal's outburst elevates a teacher's stress, she can inflame the atmosphere by simply raising her voice. As Michelle Kinder says, "You can't logic a student out of an amygdala hijack."

Mike's bear hug, although unauthorized, produced the magic, calming Jamal's agitated body and releasing the affection hormone, oxytocin. Jamal's limbic brain anticipated a fight, but Mike's hug and soothing words shifted the body chemistry. After that dramatic encounter, Jamal came to class each day and gave Mike a fist pump. During class, he often sought eye contact with Mike; he needed a reassuring signal, a thumbs up, a smile, a wink, something.

If schools are facing the growing problem of *students not ready to learn*, perhaps schools should begin by retraining the heart-brain connection. Schools adopting Social Emotional Literacy as their platform are doing exactly that. However, those programs seem to be used primarily in schools serving high-risk children. But, what if schools could educate all students in how to manage their heart-brain reactions? If teachers need the same SEL care as students who struggle with self-regulation, perhaps everyone needs it.

Educating the Heart–Brain Connection

"The heart" can mean several things. It's a pumping organ, the seat of love and affection, the visceral human core, etc. For my purpose here, it means the seat of control of the emotions. *That* heart continuously responds to the demands of its environment, adjusting heart rate up or down. We know the heart rate is controlled by the autonomic nervous system (ANS), that the sympathetic side accelerates the heart rate, and the parasympathetic side decelerates. The rapid dialogue between the heart and the ANS gets measured as heart rate variability (HRV). High variability confirms the heart's ability to regulate the demand. Low variability means the heart has a hard time regulating.

Doc Childre, Founder of the HeartMath Institute says it well, "Since emotional processes can work faster than the mind, it takes a power stronger than the mind to bend perception, override emotional circuitry, and provide us with intuitive feeling instead. It takes the power of the heart."[7]

Stressed–out teachers have low HRV. Studies have shown that students taught by teachers with higher cortisol (stress) also had higher cortisol. Teachers whose hearts were regulated manage calm classrooms. The students' limbic system "reads" a teacher's emotional state. That's normal; almost everyone's heart reads the positive and negative energy of those around them. It's part of a primal survival mechanism.

However, when social structures provide safety and stability, primal instincts take a subordinate role. That allows the frontal cortices to appear "in charge." But don't mistake who is really in control. The heart may have taken a back seat, but volatile times instruct the heart to take over.

Great performers and speakers understand that audiences arrive in the grip of various emotions and distractions. That means their first order of business must be to harmonize their audience, to establish a rhythm. That aligns individual central nervous systems into a collective one. When I first learned that alignment objective, I understood why some of my workshops found incredible flow, some felt choppy, and a few included a surely troubled soul who disrupted and pulled the group down to mud level.

Classrooms that start the day with a greeting circle or another warming up exercise, are setting a CNS tone. That tells the limbic brain, "I'm included and equal." The greeting ritual creates connection, affirmation, and positive psychology. Everyone wins.

On average, every class of twenty-five students includes eight who arrive as agitated atoms. If you restructure the classroom, you can change the dynamic. Sarasota Middle School redesigned a traditional classroom layout into small teams. Page Dettmann, who was at the time the assistant superintendent, told us that students' disciplinary problems dropped by 80%. "The difference in behavior changes when you look at faces instead of the back of the head."

As Dr. Jernigan told me, "Stress breaks down your neural pathways … It's horrifying. It looks like you've been on drugs for ten years."

HRV measures stress and resilience. Chronic stress, trauma, and anxiety consume an inordinate amount of energy. They take people into depression, fatigue, irritation, and frustration.

But, what if we flip that?

In a study of over 140,000 soldiers deployed to active duty, Dr. Seligman, the father of positive psychology, and his colleagues examined those who experienced Post-Traumatic Stress Syndrome. But, they also noticed a subset of soldiers who returned stronger. Should the military test for Post-Traumatic *Strengths* Syndrome? Perhaps they should, since those soldiers exhibited profound differences in five areas:

1. They possessed *positive emotions*.
2. They found *engagement*.
3. Each had a core of close and vital *relationships*.
4. They found *meaning* in their work and lives.
5. All worked with a sense of *accomplishment*.

These five have become known by the acronym PERMA.[8] That too forms a way of educating the heart.

Coherence and Incoherence

The ability to build and sustain resilience is related to self-management and efficient energy utilization across four domains: physical, emotional, mental, and spiritual. Think of those dimensions as four tires on a car.

When all are inflated and balanced, each tire will be pliable, durable, and resilient. That enables the car to run smoothly at high speeds and easily absorb the normal bumps of the road.

1. Physical resilience brings endurance and strength.
2. Emotional resilience features self-regulation, flexibility, a positive outlook, and supportive relationships.
3. Mental resilience can focus attention, and deal with complexity and surprise.
4. Spiritual resilience aligns people around core values, sees deeper connections, shows tolerance, and offers kindness.

When one or more of those dimensions shimmy, life feels like a car out of alignment. Burnout is what happens when all four tires blow out. Dr. Jernigan says: "Burnout is a result of having fundamental life values insulted, betrayed, disregarded, for so long in your life that you no longer have a worldview that allows you to sustain daily life. It is a total collapse which is why it takes longer to recover. We have to first help that person rebuild their identity and then rebuild their world."

How Do We Start?

The best, perhaps only, place to start educating the heart is to take care of one another. True communities are comprised of people who care. You see it in their demeanor toward spouses, children, parents, neighbors, businesses, public safety officers, elderly citizens, and others. Good neighbors keep their eyes on the homes of those who are away on trips. They will gather newspapers and flyers from the yard, mow and edge, and even back in and out of a neighbor's snow-covered driveway in order to make the place look lived in.

In much the same way, Dr. Jernigan says if we have built a foundation of emotional safety, we should then keep an eye out for "signs" in and from each other. You know the signs—when a friend, family member or colleague seems increasingly tired, negative, cynical, erratic, or disappears. I am often too absorbed in my own momentum to notice a slight wobble in one of my tires. But, I have friends who will say something. They didn't do that until I asked for their help, and I gave each permission to call me out when they see the signs.

Institutions like hospitals, nursing homes, and schools do the best they can. We should be grateful for them. But, they cannot bring the detailed, nuanced, watchful care to those they try to serve. They can only bring efficiency.

It takes another human to notice the signs, such as

- When the physical clues of health and well-being suffer.
- When the worldview and sense of self wobble.
- When the medical and psychological indicators of burnout are too obvious to ignore.

That's the time to speak, the time to educate the heart.

Wrapping Up

- Children who cannot regulate their heart-brain reactions are not ready to learn; they need support to restore and rebuild that balance.
- Heart-brain impairment is commonly traced to early childhood trauma and abuse.
- SPECT brain scans identify the trauma pattern called the "ring of fire."
- Chaos in the brain sends chaos into the social surroundings.
- The chaos of others can create a contagion effect.
- The way we arrange classroom structure creates different kinds of network effects. For example, friendly or unfriendly, competitive or cooperative. You cannot logic a student out of an amygdala hijack.
- Self-regulation is the foundation for a student to be ready to learn.

Practical Reflections

1. How is my stress being unconsciously picked up by others around me?
2. How can I re-regulate myself when I feel agitated? What routines throughout the day can I use to calm my class before I add the stress of learning?
3. Do I have a wobble that I need to examine in my four key areas of coherence?

Notes

1. Ryan W. Carpenter and Timothy J. Trull, "Components of Emotion Dys-regulation in Borderline Personality Disorder: A Review." *Current Psychiatry Reports*, Jan. 2013. www.ncbi.nlm.nih.gov/pmc/articles/PMC3973423/
2. Ibid.
3. Alvin Toffler, *Future Shock* (New York: Random House, 1970).
4. Jonah Lehrer (Ed.), "The Mirror Neuron Revolution: Explaining What Makes Humans Social." *Scientific American*, www.scientificamerican.com/article/the-mirror-neuron-revolut/
5. Nicholas A. Christakis and James H. Fowler, "Social Contagion Theory: Examining Dynamic Social Networks and Human Behavior." *Statistics in Medicine*, Feb. 20, 2013. www.ncbi.nlm.nih.gov/pmc/articles/PMC3830455/
6. Deb Gorski, "Tiered Instruction and Intervention in a Response-to-Intervention Model." RTI Action Network. www.rtinetwork.org/essential/tieredinstruction/tiered-instruction-and-intervention-rti-model
7. HeartMath Institute. https://www.heartmath.org/research/science-of-the-heart/establishing-a-new-baseline/
8. Positive Psychology Center, Perma™ Theory of Well-being and Perma™ Workshops. https://ppc.sas.upenn.edu/learn-more/perma-theory-well-being-and-perma-workshops

CHAPTER 13

Community Before Curriculum

We're all just walking each other home.

—Ram Dass

When I want to get out of the house to work, I often go to Roots, our local coffee shop.

"Hello Megan, how's your day?"

She smiles, "Good. How's the book coming?"

Then we chat in that timeless adhesive of civilized life, the exchange that increases our human bond. When another patron walks in, I slowly gather my stuff and drift over to a table. I like it here; no frantic baristas churning out orders, reduced to the language of cold efficiency, "Next, can I help you?"

Lisa also likes Roots; she meets with a group of women there every Wednesday. She's been friends with some for a few decades. Later, at dinner, Lisa shares their news; stories of cancer, the pain of a child trying to find her way, the joy of graduations, the high drama of ER trips, and other real-life stuff. Lisa won't miss those gatherings.

Why is it that in the right time, space, and context, we can find a safe zone, the space and grace sufficient to connect to strangers? And, that human connection leads to the mystery of communication. And that week-after-week, heart-to-heart communication leads to caring. And, caring rolls into cooperating. And so it goes. This is the magic calculus for the most underestimated, most abundant, but least applied form of wealth: social capital. It is social capital that gives us all forbearance with one another. Social capital creates the capacity for resilience, taking risks, and doing great things. We were born to raise barns together.

When we remain strangers in our communities, workplaces, schools, places of worship, and on our own blocks, resiliency simply won't compute. No wonder the research and data say our nation is losing resilience. Our ability to rise above circumstances, challenges, and self-interests is rapidly declining. However, despite the sobering statistics, I see reasons for optimism. In our travels and research, we have discovered many outliers that are remembering and applying the formula for rebuilding the human connections. We have seen those restoring schools and communities by creating reservoirs of social capital.

The evidence is still weighted toward the prophets of doom. I am used to that after fifteen years of tackling other stuck conversations. I am consistently told why something "can't work." Or, "We tried that and it didn't work." But I still search for people and places that haven't heard that news. And, I still find them. Together, we break the norms and find that this simple formula of social capital still works miracles.

Scalable Simplicity

I stumbled upon a remarkable discovery—scalable simplicity at work— in a conversation with leaders at the Momentous Institute. I asked them, like I ask every school administrator, "What do you do for teacher self-care?" They were the first school that had an answer. When they explained, I commented, "This sounds very similar to the SEL work you do with the kids in the classrooms."

Rhonda Vincent responded that it was identical, "We can't teach what we haven't experienced. Kids know."

If scalable simplicity becomes a new lens, it becomes easy to see why something as simple as a morning circle to start class works, and will work at any scale. It's the "Mr. Rogers" formula: "I think it's very important—no matter what you may do professionally—to keep alive some of the healthy interests of your youth. Children's play is not just kids' stuff. Children's play is rather the stuff of most future inventions."[1]

Or, as I saw at a class ritual at Hamilton District Christian School in Hamilton, Ontario, "Okay, class, let's start the day and welcome your neighbor. Can someone share something that makes you grateful for our time together today?"

In this microcosm of social capital, small investments of trust, care, and being there for one another make neighbors. It is a bank account that can fund a rainy day or a vision for tomorrow. Social capital allows groups to accomplish more than they ever could on their own.

Our balance of social capital is redlining. Can we still find places that have it in abundance?

When Social Capital Is Lost

In his book, *Our Kids: The American Dream in Crisis,* Robert Putnam chronicles the tragic fate of his home-town, Clinton, Ohio, and its broader application to our nation.[2] When Putnam grew up there in the 1940s and the 1950s, Clinton was a prosperous industrial town. The community used its prosperity well by investing in parks, community services, and good schools. Clinton symbolized the American dream. But, the American dream stands on three pillars: a stable middle class, quality public education, and an economic system that rewards hard work.

In the mid-1970s, Clinton's fortunes changed. When manufacturing disappeared, so did the solid middle-class jobs with benefits. The families who could, left. Those who couldn't, settled for lower-wage jobs and stayed. But, the tax base no longer supported parks, programs, or schools. The community once provided natural bridges for interaction (like schools, churches, bowling leagues, safe and clean parks, and a vibrant downtown) between the different classes. However, with the loss of the middle class, the social bridges fell into disrepair and neighborhoods became communities of strangers. They declined into starkly contrasting zones of race and class.

From a Community of Strangers to Our Town

James and Deborah Fallows provide a second narrative, one of renewal, in their book, *Our Towns.*[3] The book is about what is going right in America. They traveled for five years, in a single-engine airplane, a total of 100,000 miles, as they visited and revisited 30 towns across America. Like Clinton, those towns fell into decline and economic dislocation. Unlike Clinton, they came back stronger and more resilient. The Fallows identified 10.5 foundation stones for renewal. I've grouped those 10 renewal features into three:

1. Restoring and building social capital.
2. Investments in quality public education.
3. Revitalizing local business.

My favorite feature in these communities is a real and vibrant downtown, not a manufactured or contrived "town square." Each of these downtowns hosts a local brewery or distillery (the half-feature), places where everyone knows your name and strangers are welcome.

Our MindShift project for this book visited three of the towns: San Bernardino, California, Greenville, South Carolina, and Holland, Michigan. My decades of association with Holland, Michigan, made it the ideal location to convene a summit for this book, and to gain a close-up view of the seeds of revitalization.

I contacted Matthew Haworth, the third-generation Chairman for Haworth, Inc., one of the three largest office furniture manufacturers in the world (and one of my former employers). When I told Matthew of our plan to bring thirty educators to Holland, he offered to host us at their headquarters. He also paved the way for our full access to the people and projects that make Holland such a great success story.

Then, I called Dan Beerens, a lifelong educator, author, speaker, and connected citizen of Holland. Dan knows the landscape, the players, the history, and how to set up behind-the-curtain tours at the schools.

Holland, Michigan: A Story of Renewal

Community connectedness is not just about warm fuzzy tales of civic triumph . . . Social capital makes us smarter, healthier, safer, richer, and better able to govern a just and stable democracy.

—Robert Putnam[4]

Holland, sometimes called the "tulip capital of America," is a manufacturing city. But, like so many industrial towns, its manufacturing base fell into decline in this century's first decade. The 2008 residential and commercial real estate collapse devastated Holland. Office furniture manufacturers suffered a hard hit. The crisis produced strong aftershocks, particularly in the schools and in the demand for mental health services.

The Haworth headquarters was little more than a concrete extension to their factory when I worked for them in 1986. At that time, they manufactured office cubicles—in brown, gray, and putty. In a classic American dream story, G.W. Haworth started the company out of his garage in 1948. He made retail displays to supplement his income as a shop teacher. Today the company has grown to more than $2 billion in annual sales with more than seventy-five hundred employees worldwide. Haworth's new headquarters is an award-winning showcase for the latest research and practice in workplace engagement, health, and well-being.

Holland's revitalized downtown draws locals and many visitors to upscale hotels, nice restaurants, coffee shops, an ice cream shop, a live theater, and several local craft beer pubs, all in walking distance from the hotels. This is not the Holland I remembered thirty years ago or even ten.

Our summit convened in December 2018. We began arriving on a clear but cold Monday afternoon. Thirty of us met across the street for dinner at the New Holland Brewery. By morning, a blanket of fresh snow lay across Holland, but the downtown streets and sidewalks were clear and dry. Of course, our guests wondered why. In 1998, industrialist Ed Prince worked with the city on an idea to install pipes from the power plant under the streets and sidewalks along 8th street. His seed capital of $225,000 was the catalyst. The experiment paid off, both practically and as a tangible symbol of Holland's ingenuity and civic spirit of cooperation. The city saves money every year in snow removal costs and it has made the downtown viable for local businesses and visitors year-round.

> *What really matters from the point of view of social capital and civic engagement is not merely nominal membership, but active and involved membership.*
>
> —*Robert Putnam*[5]

I stayed a few days after the summit to interview more people. While interviewing Brian Davis, superintendent for Holland Public Schools, he invited me to the high school's performance of *A Christmas Story*. The *evening turned into a magical showcase of community*. During the intermission, I saw Matthew Haworth and his family with other people.

"Hey, Rex, I'd like you to meet my pastor, Jon Brown."

We all joined the warmth of convivial conversation about Holland. No mistaking where their affections lie; Holland is *their town*. Like so many others, I could see how the Haworth, Davis, and Brown families consistently make deposits into the town's social capital account.

Holland High has an urban school profile with 60% of students of color and 40% Caucasian. 61% are also eligible for free or reduced lunch, doubling since 2005.

Principals, superintendents, teachers, students, and administrators from Holland District Schools, Hamilton District Schools, Holland Christian High School, Black River (a public charter), and Little Hawks preschool eagerly joined us in the summit. It was clear the leaders knew each other, had history together, and understood the unique challenges they face.

Where to Begin Building Scalable Simplicity

Social capital is built and leveraged in many ways but each expresses the value people place in one another. "The power of the gift is the connection to the giver behind the gift."[6] When we extend a hand, an offer, or just give the recipient a face to go with the financial support, something more is taking place. One reason why grants and non-profit funding have proven ineffective is that we disconnect the gift from the giver, stripping away the relationship. A dollar is a dollar but a dollar plus a friend creates a bond no transaction can accomplish on its own.

The start to scalable simplicity begins with creating a safe space for building trust. When we see success that lasts through good times and difficult seasons, we will usually see robust investments in relationships, engagement, a common vision, and a collective will at the core. Change efforts that fail are often driven by a narrow interest, top-down leadership, and frantic attempts to herd cats. Most of those processes tend to manipulate, not settle into long-term mutually beneficial relationships.

Leadership is the art of disappointing people at a rate they can tolerate.
            —*Ronald A. Heifetz*[7]

Leaders find and lead others to new places. New equals unfamiliar. Unfamiliar means risk. Risk creates fear. Fear rides the brakes. That's the same dynamic students face when they come to school not ready to learn. Pushing at a rate they cannot tolerate produces sharp fight-or-flight reactions. Ram Dass said, "We're all just walking each other home." *Home* creates its own draw. We don't drive people there; we just walk beside them. That's what builds social capital.

The first investment into social capital is building (or repairing) trust. Trust begins to emerge from the shadows when fear and skepticism recede, when the atmosphere assures psychological safety. Joseph Myers, an author, consultant, and close colleague, says trust and distrust are not opposites; they come from two separate places in the brain. According to Joseph, "Distrust guides us to safety. Trust builds relational capital."

I spend a lot of my consulting time helping teams manage large and complex construction projects. Seventy percent finish late and over budget. After years of doing this, I know the one common, "if-we-had-it-to-do-over" conclusion. "We should have spent more time in the beginning getting to know one another and learning about each other's companies." But few do it. Most of my project work exists because people were not ready to work together. The problems and resulting squabbling require my company to intervene, try to mend the damage, and then help them play catch up.

What Is Revillaging?

Robin Dunbar, anthropologist and evolutionary psychologist, noticed that at a certain size (of company, civic group, place of worship, governmental department, voluntary association, etc.), people can no longer recognize others by name. He estimated the number of people with whom anyone can hold personal relationships is somewhere between 150 and 250 people. That is known as "Dunbar's number." Beyond that number, the relational connections dissipate, and social capital shrinks.

W.L. Gore employs more than 17,000 people. But, they keep their business units at 250 or fewer people. Each group comprises an independent entity with its own balance sheet.

Lee Elementary designed a school of more than 700 students and revillaged it by dividing it into five Houses. Each house is a grade 1–5 and they live and learn in a common space, like a little red school house.

Revillaging reduces monolithic social structures down to the human scale. That scale represents the scope and speed most hospitable to personal relationships. One of the most prominent examples in American society is very large churches. Those "megachurches" inevitably form small group gatherings in order to foster healthy interpersonal relationships. Once you understand the principles of revillaging, human scale, structure, and pace, you will probably recognize that you already know or participate in such a social framework. So, how do you build that?

Step 1: Secure Stakeholder Engagement

The future is already here, just not evenly distributed.
—William Gibson

Jack Hess, Executive Director for CivicLab in Columbus, Indiana, has been my guide and mentor for the town's stored wisdom for more than a decade. Jack defines coalition building as "bringing together a diverse collective of stakeholders to solve a community's grand challenges."

The Columbus story, like many epic tales, was rooted in a problem. Columbus built a new school to respond to the rapid post-war growth of the early 1950s. But, the project turned into a costly and miserable failure. That fiasco threatened the city's largest employer, Cummins Diesel. J. Irvin Miller, the visionary CEO of Cummins, instantly saw that Cummins could not attract engineers if Columbus could not offer good schools.

Miller lived by a foundational rule, "Mediocrity is expensive; quality is cost effective." From that, he proposed that the school board hire the world's best architects to design new schools for Columbus. They agreed, and Cummins paid the architectural fees. And that is why Columbus has been ranked as one of America's premier architectural exhibitions for over a half-century.

From the wild success of the new schools, Miller extended his offer to other sectors of Columbus: a bank, churches, the county jail, a library, city buildings, park landscaping, the fire station . . . quality kept rolling across the city. America got the message that Columbus was serious about investing in the future. Diesel engineers around the world also noticed.

Miller believed in "stakeholder engagement." In other words, leaders must respect all the stakeholders in any venture, crisis, community, or grand quest. That is why "the Columbus story" created a deep and enduring reservoir of social capital. Stakeholder engagement also recognizes that *culture*, not reform, most often brings transformation. "Reform" sounds good, but it tends to bring bulldozers or spoons to dig post holes. On the other hand, culture will naturally produce engagement.[8]

Success or failure turned out to be less about individual leaders and more about the quality of how well and how willingly people work together. If we could see the Columbus model as a vision for community, we would understand some transformative "from-to" concepts:

- From top-down control to a flexible bottom-up collaboration.
- From overseeing individual actions to building tighter relationships.
- From seeking personal fulfillment to focusing on a larger and more corporate vision.
- From a belief in the plan to confidence in the process.
- From managing group actions to improving handoffs and interaction between groups.
- From being the expert to becoming the guide.
- From using relationships to build things to allowing things to build relationships.

The last point distinguishes between the Columbus approach and many process-driven strategies to stakeholder problem-solving. Other models try to build social capital as a means to an end. But, Jack sees social capital—all by itself—as the great good that Columbus hopes to achieve. The problems and the projects are simply the means to get there. In other words, are we building a school, or are we building a *community*? Just as J. Irwin Miller knew, a school can be a scaffold, from which we build or remodel a community.

Step 2: Discover the What, Why, How, and Who

The front end of a traditional school construction project might include the ISD superintendent, the school's principal, various other school officials, the District Police Chief, and the architect.

The Columbus model would start by asking, who are the people who have a true stake in the success of this new school, and how do we create value for those stakeholders?

So, besides the traditional stakeholders, the Columbus model might also include the contractors, trade partners, specialty consultants, furnishings and technology vendors, teachers, students, counselors, parents, neighbors, and other community leaders and local business leaders.

It is easy to see why each of these hold a stake in the school's success. But, it's hard to imagine how to keep that many people from becoming unwieldy, political, and expensive. However, adopting a stakeholder approach, creating social capital, building a coalition, and collective engagement turns the group into a barn-raising activity. Many hands and hearts engaged in purposeful work lighten the load. They can create a grand vision or a solution that brings pride to the community. The Columbus Coalition-Building Process follows a four-quadrant process defining what, why, how, and who:

- What are the needs and interest of the stakeholders?
- Building trust and discovering a common agenda.
- Discovering and mapping the current state.
- Developing a picture of the desired future state.
- Creating the *"from-to"* narrative.
- Finding outliers, then prototyping, piloting, and testing.
- Aligning on a course of action.
- Establishing metrics to measure progress.
- Building in a double feedback loop for learning.
- Securing and committing resources.

Step 3: Trust the Process

For several years, I worked with consulting partners who were licensed clinical Jungian psychologists. That means they saw relational patterns; they viewed individual behaviors as part of a larger system's dynamic. When we visited a client together, I felt like I was with Yoda, who could see the force, or Neo, who saw the Matrix. In the beginning, I saw individual behavior and comments as stand-alone factors. I slowly learned to see the larger context. It also helped me to break away from my well-honed and rational plans and strategies. I slowly learned to "Trust the process." And, because I did, I could also help clients do that.

Step 4: Build Safety

Google's research says the number one criterion for a high-performing team is psychological safety. In *The Five Dysfunctions of a Team*, Patrick Lencioni explains why vulnerability-based trust is the foundational necessity for everything else.[9]

Morning circles, closing circles, predictable and common rules of engagement, recognition and appreciation, properly setting expectations, and skill development are all means for building predictable and safe environments.

Step 5: Impart Self-Regulation

Because students at the Momentous Institute know how their brains operate, they understand their emotions and how to read the emotions of others. If emotions (their own or those of others) appear to be escalating, they have mutual rules of engagement to intervene. A student will take a simple glitter ball, then shake, watch, and breathe deeply as the glitter settles. That simple exercise restores emotional peace and stability. Students will even ask others to, "Go settle your glitter." Lisa and I now tell each other and our kids that!

Imagine at your next meeting, handing each person a glitter ball. Then the next time emotions flare, "Henry, settle your glitter."

If your school doesn't feel like a happy home, or you sometimes feel like a stranger there, don't ignore that symptom. If you feel your school has wandered off the human path into the land of efficiency, stop and turn back. Follow the trail back until you find where your school left the path. If cooperation is low, return to the path of caring. If caring is low, return to the habit of heart-to-heart communication. If genuine communication is low, check to see if busyness and stress have strained the human connections.

This is the magic calculus for the most abundant form of wealth: social capital. That provides the grace we need to hold together when our school or life feel like they are being pulled apart. Few can stand up alone to the curveballs and challenges that can pass through the front door any day. Social capital raises barns, but it also walks with us to court, hospitals, bar mitzvahs, weddings, and funerals.

Mountaineers know the summit—the grand pinnacle of their hard work, training, expense, and dreams—often remains hidden through most of the climb. The inability to see the goal tests everything we know, hope, trust, believe, and possess.

Some get lost or discouraged, afraid to move on up across the hostile terrain. Sometimes we cannot see the peak of purpose, nor the way back down. But, I can assure you, because I've seen it first-hand, the path up the mountain is still there. It remains hidden until a step into vulnerability leads to openness, and openness leads to trust. From there just keep following the trail markers and you will make it to the summit.

Wrapping Up

- Social capital is the most underestimated, most abundant, and least applied form of wealth.
- Social capital allows groups to accomplish what they could never do alone.
- Human scale is the key to social capital.
- When efforts grow beyond human scale they have to become efficient, and drain the social capital.
- The way the Momentous Institute prepares teachers in SEL is an example of scalable simplicity.
- Social capital is built on trust. The first step is assuming the need to repair trust.
- Trust is a decision of the pre-frontal cortex. Distrust is a reaction from the limbic system.

Practical Reflections

1. Does your school have a high or low balance of social capital?
2. What would improve psychological safety in your school and in meetings?
3. Where can you build social capital outside your school?
4. Who are some key stakeholders to include in future conversations and efforts?

Notes

1. Fred Rogers, *Life's Journeys According to Mister Rogers: Things to Remember Along the Way* (New York: Hatchett Books, 2005).
2. Robert Putnam, *Our Kids: The American Dream in Crisis* (New York: Simon & Schuster, 2015).
3. James M. Fallows and Deborah Fallows, *Our Towns: A 100,000-Mile Journey into the Heart of America* (New York: Vintage Books, 2019).
4. Robert Putnam, *Bowling Alone: The Collapse and Revival of American Community* (New York: Simon & Schuster, 2000).
5. Ibid.
6. Rex M. Miller, *Millennium Matrix: Reclaiming the Past, Reframing the Future of the Church* (San Francisco: Jossey-Bass, 2004).
7. Ronald A. Heifetz, *Leadership on the Line: Staying Alive Through the Dangers of Change* (Boston: Harvard Business School Publishing, 2017).
8. Rex Miller, et al., *Humanizing the Education Machine* (Hoboken, NJ: Wiley & Sons, Inc., 2017).
9. Patrick Lencioni, *The Five Dysfunctions of a Team* (San Francisco: Jossey-Bass, 2002).

Part 3

Putting Into Practice

CHAPTER 14

Waking the Dead: The Sleep Solution

When sleep is abundant, minds flourish. When it is deficient, they don't.
—Matthew Walker

Dan teaches first-period math. The first bell rings at 7:15 a.m., classes start at 7:30. He calls it the waking the dead hour because of how he feels and how his class performs. That first period, however, holds a clue to solving a large hidden constraint to learning. So, after coping with that zombie zone for too long, Dan decided to swing for the fence.

"Okay, stop. No math today. Let's talk about sleep."

Students looked at each other, laughed, and shifted in their chairs. Was this a sneak attack? Would he nail them for not paying attention?

But, when a few shared their stories, the floodgates opened. Students described their crushing schedules, 20-hour days, the pressure to meet the early bus, the continuous raucous roar of family arguments, TV, police sirens, and even gunshots in the night. As he listened to his students, the dots slowly and painfully connected for Dan. He saw the fog that had increasingly clouded that first period—7:30 to 8:25—over the last several years.

That's when he asked the question that had nagged him for over two years.

"Do you kids even care about math? Or do you simply need to pass and get to the next thing?" One answer triggered what would become Dan's new mission.

"I used to like numbers. But, to be honest, I don't know anymore. I thought I might go to college, but your class is a killer." Some students looked at the floor as they nodded.

That's when Dan heard himself say, "Then let's all figure out how we can make this class better."

Dan's First Experiment

Dan broached the big idea of later start times with his principal, but the idea was shot down almost before he finished. He went back to the class and together they came up with a few ideas to try. One was to turn the class into a lab environment. They were allowed to swap their desks with stool-height lab tables and sit in clusters of four. Dan thought the ability to stand and create a more social and interactive setting would help counteract the sleepiness of sitting.

Instead of lecturing to the whole class, Dan let each table work on the math concepts and applications together. Dan roamed the classroom as a coach. There was an advanced student at each table. Some had two. During the last twenty-minutes of class Dan worked with the more advanced students to help them to train their tables the next day on the next lesson. The students still at the tables worked on their homework together. Dan thought this would keep them engaged in the content and reduce the homework so they could go to bed earlier.

The class did not solve the problems of a collection of sleep-deprived students, but it did transform the energy and the shared responsibility, and social interaction gave everyone a sense of greater purpose and connection to one another. It was an experiment that was working and improving behavior and test results and was noticed by other teachers and the principal.

Dan's Second Experiment

Some of the other schools were using a blended learning format combining online work with live classroom.[1] The class already had laptops and Dan had complained in the past that they were simply expensive and glitchy textbooks. Now he could try something that would leverage more of their potential, the opportunity to take a more self-paced and outside the classroom approach. The tables remained but the format changed. The classroom felt more like a study hall. Students were able to sit at stations along the wall and work by themselves. Dan set up something like an Apple Genius bar model. Advanced students were given a Genius title for specific topics and hosted a table for students to come and work with them. Instead of the whole class having to march at the pace of the students who had the hardest time, some students zoomed through one and two years of math. And no student was left behind.

Dan was also able to get the school to sign off that online students who were ahead could count that work as attending the class and come in later for the second period. This was a great idea in concept but only a few students who had transportation could take advantage of it. Still, just getting approval was a step forward and a demonstration to the school and district of what is possible. Dan became the Chief Sleep Advocate, starting by rethinking first periods and the desperate need for rested students. If his school was going to break its vicious cycle of stagnant test scores and general disengagement, the administration, board, and community needed to understand how sleep-deprived all of us are and how that is impacting both performance and health. Dan's first period revival opened that door with great interest and a lot of questions that Dan was more than eager to tackle.

All of those new breezes stirred excitement among students. But deep metamorphosis comes slow. It continually pushes against the shadow culture of the institution. And that is as exhausting and messy as dragging a dead pig through the mud; it doesn't arrive as it might be dramatized in a half-hour TV show. Some things change while other forces and details resist.

When Change Affects the Body and Soul

Dan has taught in the same school for more than thirty years. The community has slowly but dramatically shifted. The student population is far more diverse. Student needs are more complex. He tries to fill the gap between what the school provides and what students need. Like the proverbial frog in the pot of boiling water Dan has not been aware of the toll these demands are slowly taking on his life.

Dan has gained 42 pounds, feels sluggish all day, and no longer sleeps well. He sets the alarm for 5:30 a.m. in order to be at school by 7. He rarely eats a real breakfast, but grabs a mug of black coffee and a few muffins or pastry (often a day old) in the teachers' lounge. He eats lunch at his desk and, except for a few dashes to the teachers' lounge for coffee, stays in his classroom. School dismisses at 3:30 p.m. and Dan holds a study hall and makeup hour from 4:00 p.m. to 4:45 p.m.

He will grade papers or prepare lessons for another two hours. Sometimes he stays at school to complete it, sometimes he goes home. In either case, he doesn't finish until after 9 p.m. He has little time to catch up with his wife and kids. He may have one or two beers, catch an hour of television, check his emails, and then hit bed around 11 p.m.

One recent morning, on the way to school, when Dan heard Billy Joel's *The Piano Man*, he thought, *my God, that's me. I'm just going through the motions and dying on this vine.* That was his wake-up call; that's when he started taking a deep personal inventory.

- The district's continuous changes had created a loss of purpose and probably mild depression for Dan.
- The new demands of his students were increasingly complex and stressful. And he has never received training for those deeper social and emotional needs.
- Dan is at the school and "on" from 7 a.m. to 5 p.m., a minimum of ten hours of high demands with little or no real recovery breaks.
- His full day from awakening to returning to bed is 17 hours.
- His two beers before bed disrupt his deep sleep cycle (slow wave sleep, SWS) which is the crucial time and way the brain and body go into the shop for repairs.
- At the end of the day, Dan is too tired to exercise. Now in his forties, he carries at least 40 pounds more than is healthy.
- Television and other screen time two hours before bed will keep his mind awake another two hours after hitting the sheets.
- Dan takes prescription medication to help him sleep.

I've been there; I passed through times of financial stress during the dotcom bubble and again during the 2008 real estate crash. That level of stress inflicted deep injury; I worked longer, fell into deeper anxiety, exercised less, and stopped paying much attention to my health. I became irritable and had trouble sleeping. Naturally, my family paid a price.

Dr. Amit Sood, who leads the Mayo Clinic's *Resilient Mind Program*, explains that "mindlessness," as when we shower, drive, or sit on the deck with a drink, the brain goes into negative thinking patterns 80% of the time. It replays the past or worries about the future. Our minds have a hard time staying in the present, especially when we're stressed. Imagine after a week of stress and weariness, you've got Saturday for catching up on errands and chores. With the time remaining, you find very few or brief windows of recreation or recovery. You may sleep in Sunday morning. But, often after lunch, that fogbank of Monday dread rolls in. When Dan told me he recently read that heart attacks jump 20% on Mondays, he paused and said, "I think I know why."[2]

Could Sleep Be a Silver Bullet?

Matthew Walker's book, *Why We Sleep,* contains life-altering wisdom about the power of sleep and dreams.[3] It explained why my insistence that I needed less than six hours of sleep during my thirties and forties was nonsense. But my health and energy rebounded 180 degrees as I began following Dr. Walker's advice. I am stronger and more alert today in my mid-sixties than I was in my forties.

The more I dive into this topic, the more I can see that a deeper emphasis on sleep may be the fastest and most valuable way schools could do the following:

- Immediately raise test scores.
- Improve teacher and student engagement.
- Reduce classroom behavior problems.
- Cut the diagnosis for ADHD in half.
- Reduce student traffic accidents by half.
- Reduce stress.
- Make a happier school in a week![4]
- And, adding a focus on physical fitness would strengthen and accelerate the transformation!

Based on the research and the enduring wisdom of millennia, we know sleep produces significant improvements quickly. But, shifting the education system, sports programs, parent work schedules, and the hectic nature of our lives to healthier sleep will *not* come quickly. The whole prospect is much like the old line, "The best time to plant an oak tree was 25 years ago. The second-best time is right now."

The Circadian Rhythm Shift

When he was in high school, our son Nathan just could not seem to wake up. Lisa and I often joked about "time to go wake the hibernating bear." According to Dr. Walker, that is *exactly* what we were doing! He writes, "Like an animal prematurely wrenched out of hibernation too early, the adolescent brain still needs more sleep and more time to complete the circadian cycle before it can operate efficiently, without grogginess."[5]

Imagine you or I going to bed at 10 p.m. and being forced to wake up between 3:30 and 4:00 a.m. every day. How efficient do you think you would be at work? How would that sleep pattern affect your over-all attitude?

But, that is what we're doing to our children when we force them out of bed at 6 a.m. Walker explains, "During puberty, the timing of the suprachiasmatic nucleus is shifted progressively forward," a change that is common across all adolescents. So far forward, in fact, it passes even the timing of their adult parents.[6] That explains why Dan's first-period class looks like the walking dead; their brains demand more sleep.

The Hamilton High Survey

We worked with Principal Dave Tebo and students at Hamilton High School in Holland, Michigan, for a research project for this book. We shared their research in Chapter 5. In a recent phone conversation with Dave and student project leaders, Haleigh and Luke, I asked what they had learned about the sleep habits at their school.

Haleigh spoke quickly, "We're not getting enough sleep."

Then, Luke described the common scenario for students at their school. Students get up about 5:30 to 6:00 a.m. to get to school for 7:30. Many (if involved in after-school activities or working a job) will not get home until 9 p.m. And, then they will face a heavy homework load. Through their research, they know that many students manage an 80-hour week—13 hours a day, six days a week! What would that work schedule do to *you*?

Hamilton High students must regularly decide which homework they will ignore so they can get some sleep. Do you think that might impose an unacceptable level of stress on teenagers?

We know that is nuts. But the collective demands of academic success and the blur of activity hide the outrageous price kids must pay. Making it much worse, school administrators (and parents) often send messages that bring unintended and dark consequences. Carol Dweck's

research on grit may help to restore resiliency in students, but it also gets misapplied as a hammer of guilt. One of the AP students at Hamilton, facing a grueling schedule, had to make a decision: "Study for a test, complete my homework, or sleep."

The teacher who did not receive his homework pulled out the grit hammer. The student stood his ground, "I had to make a choice and I chose to get five hours of sleep."

Remember When

I grew up during the 1960s and the 1970s, school started at 8:30 a.m. Fifty years earlier, "schools in the US started at nine a.m. As a result, 95 percent of all children woke up without an alarm clock."[7] So, why do educational systems in most of the U.S. pull students out of bed in ignorance or defiance of healthy sleep? Could that dynamic drive unhealthy, negative, and destructive behavior? Have any researchers looked into that?

Why Deep Sleep (SWS) Is Critical

Sleep is the single most effective thing we can do to reset our brain and body health each day—Mother Nature's best effort yet at contra-death.
                                                              —Matthew Walker

The protein beta amyloid gathers in sticky clumps or plaques within the brain. We now know those clumps are linked to Alzheimer's disease. In fact, Walker flatly states that dementia and cancer are related to inadequate sleep: "… sleep disturbance precedes the onset of Alzheimer's disease by several years."[8]

You can see where this is going. Sleep isn't just "nice" or "very important." It is critical. During the deep sleep cycle, the glymphatic ("glue") system grabs those toxic sticky proteins and cleanses the brain. It is "the brain's waste management system that gets rid of waste and cycles nutrients like glucose, lipids and amino acids … "[9] According to Walker, "One piece of toxic debris evacuated by the glymphatic system during sleep is amyloid protein—the poisonous element associated with Alzheimer's disease."[10]

Deep sleep drops your body temperature and your heart rate. That turns off the sympathetic nervous system long enough for the parasympathetic side to do its best work to restore the body. Deep sleep also merges memory and transfers daily input in the hippocampus (short-term memory) and moves it to the cerebral cortex (long-term memory).

A good night's sleep will also assist learning and memory retention. It is better to study and then get a good night's rest than to work late. Experiments comparing these approaches show 20–40% higher memory retention in the well-rested group.[11]

REM Sleep

The crucial rapid-eye-movement (REM) sleep cycle is most active during the early morning hours. That is when the brain dreams. Think of it as a movie director piecing yesterday's filming together and weaving it into a coherent story. Yes, those dreams can be strange and even frightening, but they are connecting the dots of unresolved tensions. Andrew Scott describes deep sleep as the stage of physical restoration and memory consolidation and REM as emotional restoration and insight generation.[12]

Infants spend most of their REM sleep absorbing all of life's stimuli and processing it into meaning. Adolescents spend up to 80% of their nights in deep sleep recovering from higher physical activity. It is generally better for all of us, especially adolescents, to go to bed earlier in order to improve both recovery and learning.

The Sleep-Deprived Brain and Risk

Deficient sleep interrupts visual perception and emotional regulation, enlarges the amygdala, and impedes the mirror neurons. That means:

- more traffic accidents;
- more risky behavior;
- more reaction to stress and tension;
- more misinterpretation of physical cues as hostile or threatening.

It means that if Dan pulls onto the highway at 6 a.m. with less than six hours of restful sleep, his brain will be as impaired as it would with a .08 alcohol content, legally drunk.

The concentric circles radiate outward; Dan's first-period students who also didn't get a good night's sleep may misinterpret Dan's drowsy demeanor as hostile or threatening. If so, he or she may shut down or act out. If one of his zombie students drives to school in the morning, they are more likely to have an accident because of impaired visual processing.

Sleep deprivation can also look like a wide range of psychological disorders—ones we medicate, like ADHD, depression, anxiety disorders, and schizophrenia. Prolonged sleep deprivation quickly leads to mental breakdowns. Dr. Walker wrote of an experiment of participants who were interrupted repeatedly during their REM cycles. By the third day, they showed signs of psychosis, paranoia, and hallucinations. Should we be concerned that early school schedules cut off the final two hours of sleep, where they experience the greatest portion of REM?

In 2016, 292,742 youth traffic accidents resulted in hospitalization and 2,344 fatalities.[13] When Minnesota's Mahtomedi School District pushed their school start times back to 8:00 a.m., traffic accidents involving 16–18-year-old drivers dropped by 70%. Wyoming found the same improvement when they rolled their class starting times to 8:55 a.m.[14]

What Are the Possibilities?

Largely because of these statistical trends, forty-five states have (as of this writing) passed legislation that allows later starting times for schools. But, only 250 school districts, out of more than 13,000, have adopted such steps. Those 250 positive outliers show what is possible. Those same districts have raised test scores significantly without resorting to hard-line tactics and pressure. When a National Institutes of Health research project studied eight schools across seven states, they concluded that "Attendance rates and graduation rates significantly improved in schools with delayed start times of 8:30 am or later. School officials need to take special notice that this investigation also raises questions about whether later start times are a mechanism for closing the achievement gap due to improved graduation rates."[15]

If the results are so clear, why have only 2% of districts tried later start times? It appears that the two biggest obstacles are morning schedules for parents and bus schedules. Others do not want to interfere with after-school sports and extracurricular activities. Those are normal pushback factors. But, if we care about student health, we must and can find creative ways around existing constraints. That means finding a few bold administrators who will approve, launch, and protect reasonable experiments.

Your Sleep Audit

At the front end of my coaching, I ask my clients the following questions (see Appendix B for more detailed information about the answers):

1. What time do you typically go to bed and wake up?
2. How much does your typical bedtime vary from night to night?
3. What time do you normally wake up?
4. Do you usually feel well rested, okay, or sluggish when you awake?
5. Do you regularly have trouble waking up in the morning?

Those questions identify optimal bedtimes, levels of consistency, and the time and quality of rest. When clients make a clear connection to those sleep factors and begin changing their behavior around sleep, they often and quickly feel transformed.

I also walk them through an audit of evening routines that prepare them for a good night's rest. That includes the details about dinner, alcohol consumption, and screen time. The latter is crucial; digital screens emit blue light waves that tell your body it is noon and shut down natural melatonin that signals the proper time to rest. Once you stop looking at your devices, including phones, it takes about two hours for your body to readjust. So, if you go to bed at 10 p.m., but watched television or check your email just prior to reclining, it will be midnight before your body moves into a restful and sleep state.

Finally, Dr. Walker asks his audiences if a pill could boost your energy, fight disease, make you smarter, increase your happiness, help you lose weight, enhance relationships, and significantly increase your resiliency, would you be interested? OK; that "pill" does exist—it is the simple, but invaluable gift of sleep. Now, imagine a school where every teacher and student arrived fully rested. Think of the possibilities! That one simple reality could dramatically transform education and our nation.

And, that is *why we sleep*. In a classical sense, we should not need this chapter. Sleep comprises a part of that great and timeless volume of what we know. Except, today, it belongs to what we *knew*. We forgot. Therefore, we are like farmers who forgot to care for their land. They stopped rotating crops, planting cover crops, resting their land, and building and maintaining buffer zones between fields. When they forgot those ancient agricultural concepts, they resorted to gorging the ground with chemicals to coax the exhausted soil into giving just a little more.

Sleep does what no other bodily function can do. We should know that. Could that be why it represents about 1/3 of our life? Wise people and cultures respect those natural boundaries. When we decide to confiscate some of that time for work and school demands, and other modern life pressures, we disrupt and destroy that essential resource. That inevitably leads to drinking too much, swallowing too many pills, and buying CPAP machines to beg a little more from our tapped-out bodies.

Wrapping Up
- Adolescent brains demand more sleep than adult brains.
- Sleep is the single most effective thing we can do to reset our brain and body health each day.
- Sleep disturbance precedes the onset of Alzheimer's disease by several years.

Practical Reflections
1. Have an in-depth class discussion about the amount and quality of sleep your students get.
2. Think of ways to engage your first period students, similar to Dan's exercises.
3. Take the sleep audit and review Appendix B.
4. Do you try to set boundaries between school and home?
5. Imagine what your next class might be like if everyone, including you, got a good night's rest.

Notes

1. "Blended Learning." Wikipedia, 11 June 2019. en.wikipedia.org/wiki/Blended_learning
2. Anahad O'Connor, "The Claim: Heart Attacks Are More Common on Mondays." *The New York Times*, Mar. 14, 2006. www.nytimes.com/2006/03/14/health/14real.html
3. Matthew P. Walker, *Why We Sleep: Unlocking the Power of Sleep and Dreams* (New York: Simon & Schuster, Inc., 2018).
4. Ibid.
5. Ibid.
6. Ibid.
7. Ibid.
8. Ibid.
9. Emily Woodruff, "Study: Deep Sleep Is Required to 'Clean' the Brain, Prevent Alzheimer's." *Being Patient*, Feb. 27, 2019. www.beingpatient.com/deep-sleep-brain/
10. Matthew Walker, *Why We Sleep.*
11. Andrew Scott, YouTube, www.youtube.com/watch?v=a3ONM_6fkRs
12. Ibid.
13. Matthew Walker, *Why We Sleep.*
14. Centers for Disease Control and Prevention. WISQARS (Web-based Injury Statistics Query and Reporting System) [Online] (Atlanta, GA: US Department of Health and Human Services, CDC, 2015). https://www.cdc.gov/injury/wisqars/index.html
15. P.M. McKeever and L. Clark, "Delayed High School Start Times Later than 8:30 am on Impact of Graduation Rates and Attendance Rates." National Sleep Foundation, NCBI, Apr. 3, 2017. doi: 10.1016/j.sleh.2017.01.002. Epub 2017 Feb. 1. https://www.ncbi.nlm.nih.gov/pubmed/28346158

CHAPTER 15

The Magic of Movement and Mini-Breaks

Those who don't make time for exercise will eventually make time for illness.

—Edward Stanley

James did well until he entered middle school. That's when he began having difficulty paying attention. Sometimes he just needed to close his eyes. Once he fell asleep. When his grades slipped, he felt embarrassed. About that same time, other students began teasing James about his weight. He wondered if he was cut out for school. He felt stuck between his family's expectations and trying to find a way to just hide, get by, or get out of school.

James was number six in a family of eight kids. He grew up with cousins, uncles and aunts, and grandparents who lived close enough to come over for Sunday dinner. Sunday activities usually started about noon, after church. James' aunts and mom handled the meal preparations. His dad and uncles gathered on the patio around the grill. James and his cousins ran around and played outside. Food, family, fun, and faith built the culture of James' life.

Weekdays were much different. Both parents left early for work. So, meals and managing the house fell into a slipshod arrangement between the eight kids. For breakfast, James usually poured a bowl of *Frosted Flakes*. The school provided his lunch. After school, he usually pulled a *Hot Pocket* from the freezer and popped it into the microwave. He did the same for dinner a couple hours later.

James was a chubby toddler; his family called him "cuddly" or "adorable." He didn't go out for sports, but spent most of his time inside with gadgets and backyard projects. At 12, he began growing bigger, faster. Then he developed hypoglyce-mia. Sadly, his parents and teachers did not know that James' body and mind were fighting with fluctuations in his blood sugar. Then, a doctor delivered the bad news: Type two diabetes. James managed the energy roller coaster and headaches with a few candy bars in his backpack.

Children spend between 50% and 70% of their time sitting while at school. Independent of physical activity levels, prolonged sitting is associated with poor health outcomes in adulthood.
—Erica Hinckson, et al.[1]

His teachers had to work harder with James as he labored under the burden of diabetes. And, in a class of twenty-five, most teachers will have up to eight students like James who battle with weight and regulating blood sugar.[2]

Since 1980, obesity rates among teens ages 12–19 have quadrupled (400x) from 5% to 20.6%.
—The State of Obesity[3]

Mrs. O

The next year was magical for James. Mrs. Ortiz, his seventh-grade STEM teacher, at 4' 11," stood eye level with most of her students. She was fun. "Mrs. O" joked with the students. A tall boy loved to stand next to her, asking the class, "Where is Mrs. O?" as he appeared to look far and wide. Then, he shrugged his shoulders and walked away. And, she always pointed two fingers toward her eyes and then back to her own. Same joke every day, but it still made everyone laugh.

Mrs. O taught math and science, but she also taught all her students some of the details on how people learn. "The brain is an energy hog and the more energy you give it, the better you'll do in school!" She had a new story every day about brain foods, sleep, exercise, breathing or ways to be happy. She also included a category called "Brain-Drains." She was on a crusade. A few years back, she too felt sluggish every day and was often wiped out by the end of school. During her annual checkup at age 40, her doctor gently talked about her weight increase. That conversation was a wake-up call. She suddenly saw it; her whole family was short and "stout." Her parents now struggled in retirement with serious chronic health issues.

Knowing she was on a similar path over the next twenty years, Mrs. O changed her diet, began walking and taking stairs, and improved enough to get off her medications. She regained that energetic playfulness that her students loved. She rediscovered the joy of teaching. And life.

Naturally, her attention shifted to her students. Every year, she had noticed more students struggling to pay attention. She sometimes joked with other teachers about her new crop of "zombies."

In the fall of 2017, a *Time Magazine* article about childhood obesity shocked her. What she experienced at age 40 was something many of her kids were going through at 14. The article's title—"More Than Half of Kids May Be Obese by 35."[4]—became another call to action. Mrs. Ortiz was heartbroken over the kids who were giving up. She became captured by a question: "How can I help them?"

She voraciously consumed books, articles, and scholarly reports. Then, one day she discovered a series of studies from Texas A&M University that presented a simple and inexpensive solution: Standing desks.

Stand or Sit?

Dr. Mark Benden tested "stand-bias" desks in classrooms. Because they are preset to standing height and must be manually changed to "sitting," they represent a classic "nudge," the behavioral psychology idea that designed environments can make it easier to do the right thing. Even better, the National Center for Biotechnological Information measured a 43% reduction in blood sugar spikes when the use of standing desks was compared to sitting.[5] That cor-responds to the improved cog-nitive performance Dr. Benden measured in classrooms.

Increased seat-time does not mean increased brain time. When we lose movement, we lose learning, retention, and making meaning.

—Kevin Baird

I drove down to College Station from my home in the Dallas-Fort Worth Metroplex to meet with Dr. Benden. Because of my work in corporate America, I was familiar with his research in workplace issues. I was very interested in his findings in schools.

When we talked, he immediately cleared up a misconception about standing work surfaces. They are not inherently more healthy; standing all day puts too much strain on your back. However, he said that a standing desk is a proxy for movement. In other words, it naturally tilts ("nudges") workers toward walking. And, that's the point, move. Frequently.

When I told him about James, he described how standing helps students who sit, "Movement increases blood flow which means more blood to the brain. Increased blood flow also regulates blood sugar. It also means the heart is working more to support the movement and that increases energy output, burning more calories."

Sally, one of James' classmates, represents a different story.

Born curious and always in motion, by second grade, she had become a distraction to her class and a constant challenge for her teachers. By middle school, one of her parents would often make a trip to school to look for the homework they knew had left home in the backpack that morning. They typically found it crumpled in Sally's desk, in her backpack, or in her locker. The work had been completed and on time.

Students sit an average of 4.5 hours in school and, combined with sitting in front of a screen, driving to school, doing homework, and eating meals, kids are sitting 85% of their waking hours.
—Henry J. Kaiser Family Foundation[6]

In seventh grade, Sally also got Mrs. O for the same STEM class. And it turned into a magical year for Sally as well. She learned a formula for success that took her through high school. Her parents also learned that Sally was normal, in the right environments. Dr. Benden's research and other studies also explain why children with ADHD perform comparably with their peers when given a standing height surface.

For example, Dr. Tracy Marks wrote, "Fidgeting and moving are a natural way to help regulate symptoms and facilitate learning in children with ADHD, and inhibiting movement in these kids makes it difficult for them to learn. Children with ADHD can't fidget and move in a non-disruptive way in a sitting desk."[7]

- *33% of children are overweight or obese.[8]*
- *10% of children have a form of ADHD.[9]*
- *18% of children suffer from anxiety or depression.[10]*
- *25% of children come from homes with economic hardship.[11]*
- *25% of children come out of homes with divorce or separation.[12]*

Every teacher has to work doubly hard with kids like Sally who have trouble focusing. They might have ADHD, suffer from anxiety, or have experienced trauma. According to the National Center for Education

Statistics, 14% of students struggle with learning disabilities.[13] That means, in a class of twenty-five, a teacher will cope with up to four students who daily grapple with these learning obstacles.

Imagine the drain on teachers who design class activities for the maximum benefit, but must also help 14% of their students who are struggling with learning challenges. Perhaps the "network effect" represents the larger drain. That disrupts or slows the entire class.

Network Effects

When I interviewed Dr. Nicholas Christakis, sociologist, physician, author, and Yale professor, he described the contagion effect in a social network. For example, a toxic employee will spread his or her attitudes over a 25-foot radius. The same dynamic spreads throughout the classroom.

Imagine a classroom with six to eight students struggling to pay attention and another three to four students trying to just sit still. Those individual students and struggles do not play out in isolation from the social dynamic. Whether those students live within a zombie state or "bounce off the walls," their contagion effect touches all students.

On the other side, happy and positive energy people influence concentric social circles of others out to three levels. Research helps us know how certain behaviors and attitudes spread, and that helps us to better understand how to design for positive effects. That's why Mrs. O's class has become one of those magnets for students. Using Dr. Christakis' work, we will explore how some administrators have designed their schools for engagement, creating a virtuous cycle of positive energy.

What if some collective movement at the start and end of class and the option for some students to use standing desks could shift that energy? What could that bring to improve the performance of the class, the general confidence level, and the stress on teachers?

Whatever Happened to Recess?

In *When: The Scientific Secrets to Perfect Timing*,[14] Daniel Pink presents research that emphasizes the need for physical breaks between concentrated periods of cognitive work. In *Deep Work: Rules for Focused Success in a Distracted World*,[15] Cal Newport explains how our minds and bodies function throughout the day in "ultradian rhythms" of recovery.

As I wrote in *The Healthy Workplace Nudge* (John Wiley & Sons, 2018),[16] ultradian rhythms represent periods of about 90 minutes of focused work, followed by a 20-minute break. And, that means a true break, not checking email or Facebook. Stand, climb flights of stairs, listen to music, walk to the park across the street. I can tell you that 90/20 work pattern allows people to accomplish in a morning what used to take all day.

Schools once emphasized recess, play times after lunch, and physical education. Those periods of physical movement provided natural breaks to recharge and to release pent-up youthful energy. But, those natural and creative outlets have been severely curtailed or eliminated to give more time for tests.

The Cost of Maximizing Classroom Time

No Child Left Behind Schools accelerated the trend of reducing physical activity and the arts, focusing instead on "discipline" and "rigor" in order to pass more tests. For example,

- Gadsden, Alabama, "schools reportedly scratched naps for kindergartners to find time for test preparation." Wynell Williams, elementary education director for the Gadsden system, placed blame for the loss on accountability measures. "If the state is holding us accountable, this is the way we have to do it. Kindergarten is not like it used to be."[17]
- Kenosha, Wisconsin, parents were shocked when the principal of the Bain School of Arts and Language announced that recess would be eliminated because the school's test scores threatened to place it on the state's watch list of schools not meeting test score standards. "If teachers want to bring their students outside, it will be only for educational purposes and will include studying," said Bain Principal Margaret Carpenter.[18]
- Orange County, Florida, canceled recess to give teachers an additional 20 minutes for test prep. "Because so much of the money is tied

to the schools' scores and their grades, everybody's pressured," said Diana Moore, president of the Orange County Classroom Teachers Association.[19]

- According to the 2016 Shape of the Nation report, just 16% of states require elementary schools to provide daily recess.[20]

Research confirms the value of physical activity and creative right-brain activities on academic performance.[21] Yet, clear data—plus what we know from experience about how movement and creative play enhance our cognitive abilities—are not enough to overcome the fear of not passing the damned tests. The "cat hair" of testing triggers the threat alarm throughout the system, overriding the less direct and less tangible benefits of exercise or creative play.

N.E.A.T.: A Simple Way to Make Big Differences

While doing this research, I discovered something that shifted my own routines, "Non-Exercise Activity Thermogenesis," or N.E.A.T.

My first reaction was that someone pulled a muscle reaching for an acronym. However, N.E.A.T's research validates our instincts, the findings from National Geographic's study on Blue Zones (communities with extraordinary longevity), and Dr. Benden's work. As Benden summarized, humans cannot counteract the damage from sitting all day by simply going to the gym for a 30-minute workout.

N.E.A.T. adds enough movement to increase heart rates and elevate body temperatures. A brisk walk, a few minutes of calisthenics, and stretching all accomplish that.

It's extremely common for individuals to put all their focus and energy on making it to the gym for an intense hour of training without much focus on the remaining 23 hours of their day. No matter how hard these individuals try, it is nearly impossible to out-train a sedentary lifestyle—period!
        —Amanda O'Brien[22]

For example, through N.E.A.T., I started parking at the far end of a parking lot, taking stairs instead of an escalator, carrying my roller bag, taking walking breaks, walking as I lead workshops (especially while people are working on assignments), and jogging to the store instead of driving. Over the course of a day, they all add up to more than you would imagine. Amanda O'Brien supplies a helpful perspective: ". . . assuming you train at a moderate intensity for an hour . . . your workouts only consist of 10% of your daily energy expenditure, whereas Non-Exercise Activity Thermogenesis accounts for a whopping 20%."[23]

When Fort Worth adopted the Blue Zones program, Mayor Betsy Price told me about the changes they made to encourage walking and spending more time outside. For example, in the Crowley School district, concerns for child safety had gradually reduced the number of kids walking or biking to school. So, a Blue Zone initiative created "The Walking School Bus," parents and adult volunteers walking small groups of kids to school and home again. That adds up to five miles a week of walking exercise for the children and the adults.

Obviously, we don't lack the opportunities to *move* throughout the day. We just need to collectively and creatively think about it, discover some examples, and experiment.

Reminder from Little Hawks

No child should sit for five hours in uncomfortable chairs to absorb information. That's why companies spend $600–$1500 for adjustable ergonomic chairs! I can tell you, that if corporate America spends that kind of money, comfort is very important!

Although Holland, Michigan's Little Hawks program is pre-school, they can teach K–12 schools so much. The Little Hawks building and outdoor activity area nudge into the edge of a forest. Most of the activities in the students' day keep them outside—in all weathers. Their facility, methods, and teacher-student connections are profoundly organic. Our team saw their teachers coach and teach, but they also smile and laugh with the kids. That is what parasympathetic learning looks and feels like. We all asked, "Why can't school be more like this?" The fact of the matter is that any school can be more like Little Hawks at any grade level.

We have seen so many schools create similarly engaging experiences, and all of them—Sarasota Middle School, Momentous Institute, Canyon View High School, RISE, DaVinci, Bulldog Tech, Kostoryz, and dozens of others—deploy active learning. Humans naturally move, explore, play, interact, make noise, test, break things, build, and solve problems.

Most people know (even intuitively) that physical activity:

- Releases pent up energy (today, we also know it helps students with ADHD).
- Improves group dynamics (including classrooms).
- Reduces stress (by flushing out cortisol build-up).
- Increases a sense of joy.
- Creates social interaction (by heightening serotonin).
- Increases energy and stamina.
- Improves blood flow and concentration.
- Offers cognitive recovery time.

These are a few simple reminders that what we know and have known produces significant cumulative benefits. Imagine what adding these might do to reduce stress and improve classroom and school performance.

Wrapping Up

- Provide standing height surfaces for students who need help to pay attention. That will also reduce the demand and stress on the teachers.
- Give students physical mini-breaks to relieve the stress of the cognitive load and improve their engagement.
- Teachers should take personal mini-breaks for the same purpose.
- If you can't find time for regular exercise, incorporate small changes (like using stairs instead of elevators) to increase your physical activity. Small increases of movement throughout the day add up to double the benefit of 30 minutes of exercise once a day.

Practical Reflections

1. What are some ideas for burning up the pent-up energy in your students before you start lessons?
2. What creative ways does your school use to encourage moving more?
3. When do you have your highest energy? When do you experience energy dips? How can you better manage dips without caffeine or sugar?
4. How can you take advantage of N.E.A.T. to increase your daily movement?

Notes

1. Erica Hinckson, Jo Salmon, et al. "Standing Classrooms: Research and Lessons Learned from Around the World." *Sports Medicine* vol. 46 (2015). 10.1007/s40279-015-0436-2
2. Centers for Disease Control and Prevention, "Childhood Obesity Facts: Overweight & Obesity." www.cdc.gov/obesity/data/childhood.html
3. The State of Obesity, "Childhood Obesity Trends." www.stateofobesity.org/childhood-obesity-trends/
4. Jamie Ducharme, "Obesity in America: More Than Half of Kids May Be Obese by 35." *Time*, Nov. 29, 2017. time.com/5040902/childhood-obesity-in-america/
5. John P. Buckley, et al., "Standing-Based Office Work Shows Encouraging Signs of Attenuating Post-Prandial Glycaemic Excursion." *Occupational and Environmental Medicine*, Feb. 2014. www.ncbi.nlm.nih.gov/pubmed/24297826
6. Henry J. Kaiser Family Foundation, "Generation M2: Media in the Lives of 8- to 18-Year-Olds," Jan. 20, 2010. www.kff.org/other/event/generation-m2-media-in-the-lives-of/ (accessed Mar. 2, 2015).
7. Tracy Marks, "ADHD, Not Just for Kids." www.markspsychiatry.com/adhd-not-just-for-kids/
8. American Heart Association, "BMI in Children." www.heart.org/en/healthy-living/healthy-eating/losing-weight/bmi-in-children
9. Angelica LaVito, "About 10 Percent of US Children Are Diagnosed with ADHD." *CNBC*, Aug. 31, 2018. www.cnbc.com/2018/08/31/adhd-diagnosed-in-about-10-percent-of-us-10children-study-finds.html

10. ADAA (Anxiety and Depression Association of America), "Facts & Statistics." adaa.org/about-adaa/press-room/facts-statistics
11. https://www.childtrends.org/indicators/adverse-experiences
12. Ibid.
13. https://nces.ed.gov/programs/coe/indicator_cgg.asp
14. Daniel Pink, *When: The Scientific Secrets to Perfect Timing* (New York: Riverhead Books, 2018).
15. Cal Newport, *Deep Work: Rules for Focused Success in a Distracted World* (New York: Grand Central, 2016).
16. Rex M. Miller, et al., *The Healthy Workplace Nudge* (Hoboken, NJ: John Wiley & Sons, 2018).
17. "No Time for Recess, No Need for Nap." www.fairtest.org/no-time-recess-no-need-nap.
18. Ibid.
19. Krista Brunson, et al., "Should Elementary Schools Have Recess? Some Parents Fight for Break." *TODAY*, Jan. 14, 2015. www.today.com/parents/should-elementary-schools-have-recess-some-florida-parents-fight-break-1D80423842
20. Katie Reilly, "Is Recess Important for Kids? Here's What the Research Says." *Time*, Oct. 23, 2017. time.com/4982061/recess-benefits-research-debate/
21. Ibid.
22. Amanda O'Brien, "The Power of Walking," Central Athlete blog. www.centralathlete.com/blog/the-power-of-walking-1
23. Ibid.

CHAPTER 16

Physical Education:
The Gathering Storm

To keep the body in good health is a duty... otherwise we shall not be able to keep the mind strong and clear.

—Buddha

Like most Americans, I have long assumed a corrupt collaboration of villains—big insurance, big pharma, other special interests, government inefficiencies, and thousands of players gaming the system—is what has driven the rise in medical costs.

In December 2018, a *Forbes* article about the healthcare industry confirmed my conclusions.[1] It profiled several villains behind everything wrong with healthcare in America. The article was very good. And very wrong. It and I totally missed the true villain. So do many people and cultural centers. We all tend to embrace a story similar to the narrative of low-level drug dealers caught in the act, but ignore the kingpin behind them all.

So, what is the true villain behind our healthcare crisis?

First, let me introduce you to Dr. Michael Roizen, who has been the Chief Wellness Officer (CWO) for the Cleveland Clinic since 2007. In that role, Dr. Roizen helped the Cleveland Clinic to become one of the few organizations on the planet that have reduced the level of chronic disease among its employees. With that, they also reduced the hospital's own health costs.

The Real Villain

Roizen knows, and helped me understand, that *chronic disease* is the kingpin, the "Godfather" we face. This master villain is expanding its nefarious grip at an annual compounded rate that is climbing faster than corporate revenue growth or the economy.

Before he arrived at the Cleveland Clinic, their employees reflected the same levels of chronic disease as the rest of the nation. Toby Cosgrove, Cleveland Clinic's president, understood the implications and drew a line in the sand. In 2005, he banned smoking on the campus. That was just the beginning. In 2007, they stopped hiring doctors who smoked. His logic was clear and so was the burning platform. If the Cleveland Clinic could not reverse the trend of chronic diseases, how could they— one of the most respected medical institutions in the world—achieve the credibility necessary to help others?

This epic mission was perfect for a character like Dr. Roizen. Changing the habits of patients is the biggest obstacle doctors face when treating chronic disease. Given a *Change or Die* option, only one in nine patients will change.[2] Dr. Roizen experienced the same frustrations. Patients ignored simple treatments that would save their lives. He got tired of saying, "Just take the blood pressure medicine so I won't have to perform open heart surgery on you." That didn't work.

So, he tried a new approach on a new patient: "You are 47 and have the body of a 52-year-old. How would you like to feel like you were in your early forties?"

That simple reframing brought a transforming effect to that patient. So much so that the patient (a wealthy and entrepreneurial executive) wrote a check to Dr. Roizen to develop and expand that "living younger" mind shift for patient care. That check helped underwrite the development of the *Real Age* assessment and the "living younger" process.

As hard as it is to get a few patients to change their lifestyles for some distant future promise of health, imagine the audacity to think you can get one hundred thousand employees to change. That is exactly what Toby Cosgrove's leadership and Dr. Roizen's strategy provided—a roadmap for changing the nation's health.

That roadmap can also work in our schools. Now is the time to begin.

Houston, We've Got a Problem

Watching a chronic disease play out, knowing its inevitable path, and seeing it creep into our own families and friends is horrible and tragic. That should provide enough motivation to launch and sustain a great movement around reversing that trend. But it's not.

To help me understand the villain we face, Dr. Roizen opened a fire hydrant of statistics, projections, and scenarios that detailed a dark future. I admit that six hours of listening to his very credible doomsday story shook me. But, the fact that the Cleveland Clinic did it also gives me hope. We will unpack the details as we move through this book.

How Did We Get Here?

Since the time Dr. Roizen first saw the gathering storm of chronic disease, he has worked to slow and reverse the trend in the adult population. Now, he is equally concerned over the same trend in our kids. Chronic diseases in younger people are rising at rates similar to older Americans. The three primary causes are: (1) eating too much of the wrong kinds of foods; (2) a lack of exercise or even movement; and (3) unmanaged stress.

He told me, "We know exactly when this rise of chronic disease started, 1983. We ate 2,300 calories, plus or minus 60 calories per day from 1858 to 1983. We reached 400 extra calories per person per day by 2000. The problem now is a concurrent *drop in physical activity*. Fifty percent of Americans—women, men, employed, unemployed, Hispanic, Asian, whatever—do less than 10 minutes of physical activity any day of the week. Our norms are screwed up. *Obesity is now the norm*."[3]

I was that guy! Four hundred extra calories represent about 1.5 pounds of weight gain per year. When I reached my mid-thirties, I had gained more than 35 pounds. And, I was experiencing early signs of a bad road ahead, including constant and unshakable fatigue and occasional

Fifty percent of Americans—women, men, employed, unemployed, Hispanic, Asian, whatever—do less than 10 minutes of physical activity any day of the week. Our norms are screwed up. Obesity is now the norm.

(and painful) gall stone attacks. At 35, I hit 185 pounds. If I had stayed on that path, I would register 210 pounds by age 51. My wake-up call came early; at 37, I ended up on the operating table. That started a turn-about for my health.

Obesity is a national norm. That is more than sad; it brings a serious threat to our future. More than 70% of the U.S. population is overweight, and we recently surpassed 50% in obesity. The real problem is not the weight, but the way it throws our metabolic systems off balance and extends a warm invitation to chronic diseases.

In 1984, the United States spent $405 billion dollars on health costs, about 10% of GDP. By the end of 2018, we surpassed $3.5 trillion dollars and *18% of GDP.*[4] It is doubling every ten years! Eighty percent of this cost treats chronic disease and is rising at a compounded 7% annual rate.[5]

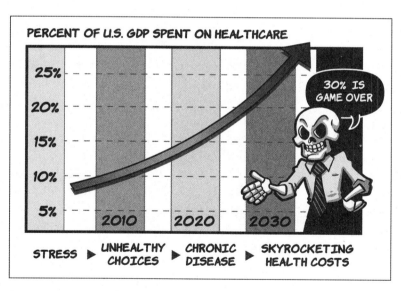

Dr. Roizen continued his vivid description of the storm, "Somewhere between now and 2030, health costs will reach more than $7 trillion and surpass 30% of GDP. If we don't reverse this trend over the next ten years, it will be game over!" He understands that the cost burden may introduce the following disaster scenarios:

- Force many industries out of business or send them overseas.
- Require rationing of health services.

- Create civil disruption.
- Make taxes jump more than 50%.

I asked him to explain this last piece. He quickly pulled a slide deck with a chart of federal spending onto his computer screen. At the end of 2017, federal expenditures were 21% of GDP and split 50/50 between healthcare and non-healthcare expenses. With health costs growing at a pace to double in the next ten years, the federal piece of that equation will also double. Besides the added personnel costs of medical expenses and health insurance, taxes will have to increase by half just to cover the federal burden.

Dr. Mark Benden adds an important footnote to that scenario for educators. Childhood obesity and diabetes used to be rare. They no longer are. Twenty percent of high school students will graduate overweight or obese. That number doubles by the end of college. Dr. Benden projected the new calculus for employers hiring Millennial and Gen-Z workers.

"You and I were 150 pounds when we graduated from college. We were in good shape, and good to go. After a few healthy (and low-cost) decades, our employers may have to deal with some of our health problems in our seventies.

"But, with many college graduates today already coping with obesity, their companies will face the employee health problems much earlier. They will have to deal with employees in their *forties,* facing twenty-five years of seriously declining health and rapidly increasing costs. If you come out of college at 220 pounds and throw another 40 pounds on by retirement, 260 pounds is a whole different dimension."

Mark talked about medicine now reaching a point where we measure Quality of Life Years (QALY). Like a Kelly Bluebook valuation for life, you look at the age and then discount it based on miles and damage. 1 QALY is equivalent to a year of perfect health. It is an economic tool to help compare the cost of medical intervention with the remaining years the intervention is projected to add. In light of Dr. Roizen's doomsday scenario, we are surely headed for inevitable and severe health rationing. And, as chilling as it sounds, our economic survival will make life and death decisions, and make them quickly and efficiently.[6]

How Physical Fitness Became a Strategic Initiative to National Security

Physical education (PE) was once considered part of an essential three-legged stool for education: academic studies, fitness, and character.[7] At the end of World War II, our new prosperity, the shift to a service economy, and growing college enrollment shifted educational priorities toward academic learning.

Just five years after the war ended, a new conflict exposed that shift and our vulnerability. In June 1950, the North Korean People's Army (NKPA) crossed the 38th Parallel and launched a surprise attack on South Korea. The South Koreans were unprepared, ill-equipped, and overpowered in just three days. After the UN denounced the attack, the United States entered the fray. But, the first battle exposed a distressing weakness. US troops could no longer physically meet the challenge of conflict.

An after-war assessment further concluded, "American troops struggled in the Korean War, and military analysts traced many of the conflict's causalities to a lack of physical hardihood and preparation for the rigors of battle."[8]

In response to those defeats, President Eisenhower created the Council of Youth Fitness in July 1956. The council recognized that the nation's shift from an agrarian and labor-centered economy to a consumer economy now limited many of the natural physical activities people grew up with. Schools became the focal point for the new strategy. In addition to physical education (PE), the council also provided suggestions that would help adults and families to become more active. They look a lot like those I provided in Chapter 15 in adopting N.E.A.T.

1. Take your dog for a walk.
2. Start up a playground kickball game.
3. Join a sports team.
4. Go to the park with a friend.
5. Help your parents with yard work.
6. Play tag with kids in your neighborhood.
7. Ride your bike to school.
8. Walk to the store for your mom.
9. See how many jumping jacks you can do.
10. Race a friend to the end of the block.

As president-elect, JFK signaled a new era when he wrote:

Our growing softness, our increasing lack of physical fitness, is a menace to our security. Physical fitness is not only one of the most important keys to a healthy body, it is the basis of dynamic and creative intellectual activity. The relationship between the soundness of the body and the activities of the mind is subtle and complex. Much is not yet understood. But we do know what the Greeks knew: that intelligence and skill can only function at the peak of their capacity when the body is healthy and strong; that hardy spirits and tough minds usually inhabit sound bodies.[9]

As president, he elevated the Council of Youth Fitness program and renamed it the President's Council on Physical Fitness. His attempt to revive the triune harmony of body, mind, and character training led to a surge of nationwide adoption of PE. About 4000 schools took on an even more rigorous model. None exemplified Kennedy's ideal better than La Sierra High School in Carmichael, California.[10] Those programs have all but vanished except for a few schools like Prescott Junior High in Modesto, California.[11]

A documentary, *The Motivation Factor* (Doug Orchard Films, 2017),[12] showcases the unprecedented mass mobilization to physical fitness during the 1960s through schools. I remember assembling in the gym and marching to the *Chicken Fat* record during elementary school PE. It was a concentrated and coordinated national effort on a scale hard to imagine today.

"Chicken Fat" was produced in a three-minute, radio-friendly version and a six-minute version to accompany schoolchildren during workout routines. The song didn't get much airplay, but the chorus of "go, you chicken fat, go!" became ingrained in the memories of tens of thousands of children doing sit-ups in school gyms around the country.
—JFK Library[13]

Every able-bodied student took part in PE. Every day. My school kept a log for each student, tracking the number of push-ups, pull-ups, jump distance, 60-yard dash time, etc. The program rewarded improvement with badges and ranks for achieving benchmarks. Level one included 10 pull-ups; I tried it recently and got to three.

The research is clear on the positive benefits of physical education.[14] The brain consumes, on average, 25% of our calories. If the body does not efficiently send blood to the brain (or if that fuel is unhealthy and compromised), the brain will fatigue faster or operates sluggishly to conserve energy. Since becoming focused on my own energy and recovery patterns, I've experienced the same thing. When I first started tracking my level of recovery, I was frequently in the redline category. I had assumed a slow start in the morning and dips of energy during the day were normal, before I started to see the numbers. But, because the feedback allowed me to adjust, my recovery and energy levels steadily moved into the normal range with an occasional peak energy day. I now have more peak days than normal and an occasional redline day. More importantly, I can now feel the difference.

The Perfect Storm

Because we seem to have forgotten JFK's message that "intelligence and skill can only function at the peak of their capacity when the body is healthy and strong,"[15] education has become more intensely focused on one thing—test scores. Could a "perfect storm" of early 1980s factors explain why?

- Physical Education's decline in K–12 schools started about 1984.
- Our nation's increase in caloric intake happened at about the same time.
- The 1981 kidnapping and murder of 6-year-old Adam Walsh shifted the social and physical activities of children. Fear "... created a nation of petrified kids and paranoid parents. . ."[16]
- In 1983, the Reagan Administration's report, *A Nation at Risk,* drove a new agenda for singularly emphasizing academic performance that has continued in different versions through each successive administration.[17]

Growing Up in the Era of the President's Council on Physical Fitness

"Mom, I'll be home for dinner!"

That short announcement and the screen door slamming shut marked the start of a normal summer morning for me. I grew up in

Arlington Heights, Illinois. Pioneer Park was just a half-mile straight down our street. I rode my red Schwinn there and everywhere. During the summer, mom made sure she signed us up for every activity available. I left the house with everything I needed for the whole day—my tennis racquet, baseball glove, swim trunks, towel, and a sack lunch with an apple for an afternoon snack. Swimming lessons started at 9 a.m., followed by handicraft, model making, or tumbling class at 10:30. After lunch, I took tennis lessons for a few hours, ate the apple, and joined baseball practice at 3 p.m. I'd ride home in time for dinner at 6.

During the school year, I also rode my bike or walked to school. We had recess mid-morning, if I finished lunch early, I could play outside. I had PE three-days a week. By Junior High, we competed in running, jumping, push-ups, sit-ups, and pull-ups. In high school, the regimen of physical fitness continued but added track and field or gymnastics. The only way to get out of PE in high school was to play a sport. I signed up for a sport all year round. We rode our bikes and played outside after school or joined organized athletic activities until dinner. Here's my point; movement and playing *outdoors* fit our natural rhythm of life and school.

Why We Need PE in School More than Ever

A lot has changed since those days of living on my bike, or in Pioneer Park, or on basketball and tennis courts. And, a lot has changed since I played organized baseball or tennis with a $25 racquet and strings and a $10 pair of Converse Jack Purcell's.

We will never go back to those simpler times. However, the need to stay healthy remains. Staying active and healthy is more urgent today. The rhythms of life no longer support the natural flow of physical activity. So, what was once routine and seamless, now requires work and planning. I discovered that hard work when we raised our kids. I quickly learned it was no longer easy or considered safe to walk or ride a bike to the park. To play a sport, it took a lot more than an off-the-shelf tennis racquet and a pair of $10 all-purpose shoes.

Today, other competing factors limit physical activity and playing outdoors. Our culture has moved indoors. In fact, according to the Environmental Protection Agency (EPA), we now live 96% of our lives in artificial environments (mostly buildings and transportation modes). As often lamented, time in front of screens has severely constricted living an active and outdoors life.

Bold Leadership for Physical Fitness

Dr. Roizen says that rallying leaders to the national threat will require something similar in scope and audacity to a Marshall Plan.[18] President Kennedy's challenge created that kind of unifying effort and lasted for almost twenty-five years. Prescott Junior High in Modesto, California, reflects the JFK-style response. Prescott's program elevates rigorous physical fitness and character development in step with academics. The school shows what is still possible with bold leadership. But would such a national school movement even be possible today?

Toby Cosgrove, like President Kennedy, understood the threat. In addition, he and Dr. Roizen also saw the holistic benefit of healthy and vital employees and citizens. But the contemporary cultural environment requires a different model for marshaling resources. We live in an Internet world; good ideas spread virally and can be unleashed locally by hundreds and maybe thousands of people like Cosgrove or Roizen. They just need a reason why and a set of web links to resources that will release the power. We and others have provided "the why." Consider these two Internet approaches that are working to give traction to the why and doing it very well.

GoNoodle[19]

GoNoodle.com presents a modern version of the "Chicken Fat" record. They sent a few million copies of "Chicken Fat" to schools across the country, but "Trolls: Can't Stop the Feeling" soared past 60 million views in the summer of 2019. The GoNoodle YouTube site has close to 600,000 subscribers.

The Blue Zones Challenge for Teachers[20]

"Blue Zones" was a National Geographic project that identified eight communities across the globe with significantly lower rates of chronic disease and higher numbers of centenarians. The "Blue Zones Challenge for Teachers" is a holistic strategy to create healthy cultures at community, organizational, and school levels.

The teacher challenge shoots straight: "For the first time in living history our children are expected to live shorter lives than their parents. The culprit: childhood obesity."

The Blue Zone organization will only work with organizations committed to their holistic approach. They provide the training and support to help schools implement the programs and transition through the culture change.

A New Generation of Physical Fitness

District 203 in Naperville, Illinois, has reimagined physical education as a cultivation of lifelong fitness, beginning in kindergarten. Their program takes a much different approach than the competitive design of PE so prevalent in the 1950s and the 1960s. The old way measured push-ups, pull-ups, sit-ups, high jumps, long jumps, and running. Sports were designed as competitive activities, not a practice for lifelong fitness.

District 203's description of its goals and values reflect President Kennedy's vision, but established in today's context and supported by current knowledge. Here is how they envision physical education:

The Physical Education Department, as well as Naperville School District 203, has made a commitment to prepare students to live healthy, productive and physically active lives for the 21st Century.

- *Physical education will provide every student with a variety of challenges that will contribute to the development and maintenance of their physical, cognitive, and affective well-being.*

- *Students will be provided with the foundation for making informed decisions that will empower them to achieve and maintain a healthy lifestyle.*
- *Physical Education is a lifelong process, which is the primary responsibility of the student, shared by home, district and community.*

Physical Education Curriculum Beliefs

- *The following strands must be interwoven into the K-12 Physical Education curriculum: movement skills strand; fitness education strand; team building strand; cognitive/literacy strand and technology strand.*
- *Quality daily Physical Education is essential, Kindergarten-12.*
- *Delivery of quality instruction requires certified physical educators.[21]*

Schools moving in this new direction are also rethinking their facilities. The best new gymnasiums have been designed more like new recreation and fitness centers.

A New Commitment to Health

Even though we understand more about the relationship between a healthy body and a sharp mind, we more often think of it in connection to students. But, of course, it also relates to teachers. As I saw at the Next Jump Academy, too many teachers have simply adapted to living with health deficits and feeling poorly.

That condition is relatively new in American culture. Until the 1980s, physical education (PE) was highly valued and protected; educating the whole child included the body. Thankfully, today, public awareness seems to be shifting back to a recognition of the need for healthy and active students. But, that need is just as great for teachers.

The few tools we highlighted in this chapter provide a small sampling of the resources for expanding health. However, despite the increasing quality and accessibility of more sophisticated instruments, change does not come easily or quickly. I know this; as a consultant, coach, and futurist, I've worked with hundreds of organizations and leaders struggling with change. It almost never goes as planned or desired. Those who succeed always seem to walk in the Cleveland Clinic kind of clarity and focus.

Without that singular, unrelenting, "full metal jacket" commitment, leaders won't be able to create the right strategy, develop the discipline, and maintain the persistence needed to shift the values, attitudes, habits, and behaviors. Whatever they do will be insufficient. And that will ultimately collapse and wash back into the sea as one more well-intentioned initiative made of sand.

Wrapping Up

- The link between a sound body and sound mind is part of ancient wisdom.
- U.S. education was once a three-legged stool that included academics, character training, and fitness.
- A focus on test performance has reduced or removed physical education.
- Twenty percent of high school graduates will be overweight or obese. That doubles to 40% of college graduates.
- Obesity leads to chronic disease. Fifty percent of the population suffers some form of chronic disease. And that represents 80% of health costs.
- Exercise improves blood flow, and that is essential to proper brain function.
- We spend 96% of our lives inside a physical environment.

Practical Reflections

1. How much time during the week do you get physical exercise?
2. If your school has cut PE, could this be a topic for discussion?
3. Should able-bodied fitness be required as part of a complete education?
4. What are the biggest constraints to including fitness as core curriculum? How can you address those constraints?

Notes

1. Dr. Robert Pearl, "Shame, Scandal Plague Healthcare Providers in 2018." *Forbes*, Dec. 11, 2018. www.forbes.com/sites/robertpearl/2018/12/10/shame-scandal/#247fd55b6807

2. Alan Deutschman, *Change or Die: The Three Keys to Change at Work and in Life* (New York: HarperCollins, 2008).

3. Rex M. Miller, et al., *The Healthy Workplace Nudge: How Healthy People, Cultures, and Buildings Lead to High Performance* (Hoboken, NJ: John Wiley & Sons, Inc., 2018).

4. Rabah Kamal and Cynthia Cox, "How Has U.S. Spending on Healthcare Changed over Time?" Peterson-Kaiser Health System Tracker, Dec. 10, 2018. www.healthsystemtracker.org/chart-collection/u-s-spending-healthcare-changed-time/#item-health-services-spending-growth-slowed-a-bit-in-recent-quarters_2018

5. Rex M. Miller, et al., *The Healthy Workplace Nudge*.

6. Ibid.

7. *The Motivation Factor*, Doug Orchard Films, 2017, motivationmovie.com

8. Brett McKay and Kate McKay, "The History of the Army's PT Test." *The Art of Manliness*, Nov. 29, 2018. www.artofmanliness.com/articles/history-of-the-armys-pt-test/.

9. "Sport at the New Frontier: The Soft American," *Sports Illustrated*, Dec. 26, vol. 13, no. 26, 1960, pp. 14–17.

10. *The Motivation Factor*.

11. Jake Rossen, "This 1960s High School Gym Class Would Ruin You." *Mental Floss*, Apr. 13, 2015. mentalfloss.com/article/62991/1960s-high-school-gym-class-would-ruin-you

12. Nan Austin, "Prescott Junior High PE Program Stars in Documentary." *Modbee*, Modesto Bee, May 27, 2017. www.modbee.com/news/local/education/article153089529.html

13. JFK Library, "The Federal Government Takes on Physical Fitness." www.jfklibrary.org/learn/about-jfk/jfk-in-history/physical-fitness

14. "Exercise and the Brain: How Fitness Impacts Learning." *Hey Teach!*, Jan. 16, 2018. www.wgu.edu/heyteach/article/exercise-and-brain-how-fitness-impacts-learning1801.html

15. JFK Library, "The Federal Government Takes on Physical Fitness."

16. Olivia B. Waxman, "Adam Walsh Murder: The Missing Child Who Changed America." *Time*, Aug. 10, 2016. time.com/4437205/adam-walsh-murder/

17. National Commission on Excellence in Education, *A Nation at Risk* (Washington, DC: U.S. Department of Education, 1983).

18. The massive—$15 billion—U.S. plan to rebuild cities, industry, and infrastructure in Western Europe after World War II.

19. www.gonoodle.com

20. "Blue Zones Challenge for Teachers." Blue Zones. www.bluezones.com/services/education/blue-zones-challenge/teachers

21. Naperville, District 203, "Curriculum & Instruction/Physical Education Overview K-12." www.naperville203.org/Page/4193

CHAPTER 17

How Small Changes Make Big Impacts

The power of the aesthetics of joy is that they speak directly to our unconscious minds, bringing out the best in us without our even being aware of it.

—Ingrid Fetell Lee[1]

Budgets for inner-city schools are always tight. So, maintenance and repairs become the inevitable target areas for cutbacks. The National Center for Education Statistics explains why that matters; the center estimates that over 50% of schools lack proper upkeep.[2] And, because of that, 58% of students attend schools rated in fair or poor condition.[3]

But what is the real cost? Most students spend about 14,000 hours in school from kindergarten through twelfth grade. If you spent the next 14,000 hours of your life in a leaky, too cold, too hot, dirty, and depressing environment, how would it affect your attitude, performance, or physical and mental health?

America's commercial interests know that facilities are crucial to the desired outcomes. I saw that up close in forty years of working with architects, designers, workplace strategists, and contractors helping companies create the best environments possible. Because they knew they *had* to do that to attract, support, and engage employees, they spent staggering amounts of money to make sure the building was fully equipped to play its requisite role.

A well-designed environment uplifts, inspires, energizes, and refreshes those who work there. That's why good design will always be cost-effective. Education can learn from the world of commercial real estate. The cost of design and construction of buildings has traditionally been regarded as "sunk costs"—those costs that can never be recovered. But, over the past couple of decades, more of that industry has begun to think of the cost of buildings, not as unrecoverable costs, but more like compound interest. As I wrote in *Change Your Space, Change Your Culture*, "If we could see it [the building] as the way to shape culture, we might begin to understand that it grants a great return on investment."[4]

Good design announces who we are, what we do, what we expect, how we do things, and how we relate to one another. That's why good design is lucid, even eloquent. I've seen wonderfully reimagined cinderblock buildings develop articulate voices throughout their business, medical, or educational communities. I know an auto paint and body shop that was renovated into a well-designed school. Its voice is heard across the nation.

As most of us know, education lags far behind business and industry in recognizing the connection between buildings and those who work in them. But, education often remains powerless to break out of their prisons. Let's look at several simple, low-cost, and very creative approaches, small changes that brought major renewal to schools.

A Voice of Hope: North Rowan High School, Spencer, NC

Meredith Williams came home to the town where she grew up, Spencer, NC. When she took the principal's position at North Rowan High School in 2016, the school ranked at the bottom in state performance indices. The official statistics say 75% of Rowan's students receive free and reduced lunches. Meredith says it's higher.

She set up her office directly outside the cafeteria to be more connected to the students. Her window looked directly across the street at her childhood home.

"I grew up where my parents still live and I knew I had come home. And my job here … was to improve the system for everyone.

"When I arrived, it felt like a hopeless situation. Everyone seemed to expect and nurture failure. The physical plant was in terrible condition. The front doors were falling off the hinges. They wouldn't lock. Trash cans sat in the halls to catch leaks, even when it wasn't raining. We had high teacher turnover, low attendance, and serious discipline problems. Many would have described Rowan High School as a 'dump;' naturally, the attitudes, performance lived down to what the environment announced."

The chance to break those patterns came in two fortuitous developments. The first came through legislation that provided troubled districts a temporary reprieve from test scores (similar to charter schools). Meredith said, "That gave us a chance to rethink our students' experience."

The second catalyst was support to turn a classroom into a ninth-grade design lab. OFS Furniture, Green Standards/Wells Fargo, Interface flooring, CF Stinson textiles, and Buzzispace donated furniture, reducing the actual cash expenditure to just $7000.

Meredith saw an astonishing transformation when the kids walked into their fully furnished, transformed, and oh-so-cool design lab. The room made it clear that the lab was a place to explore, experiment, create, and make. Together.

Meredith told me, "The design lab let me see that students are taught by more than the teacher. They are also taught by their environment. I saw why it was important that the environment corresponds to the culture that we were trying to create."

Living in a dump is stressful. It is dehumanizing. Such an environment says those who work there are not valued, that what people do there is not important. And those messages soon translate into doubt that things will ever change. But the physical plant changes—the temporary reprieve from test scores and the design lab—became the catalysts, the down payment, to prove those kids were worth it. They could live up to higher expectations.

Those two changes produced a ripple effect throughout the rest of the school. Rowan High has kept rolling; new renovations include a tenth-grade design lab and converting an area in the cafeteria to a Barnes & Noble–like study lounge.

Societies have always been shaped more by the nature of the media by which men communicate than by the content of the communication.

—Marshall McLuhan

Meredith summed it up well, "When we moved away from enforcing rules of compliance and created an environment of kids learning because they wanted to, we cut our discipline referrals by 50%. And, we cut our out-of-school suspensions by 22% in the first year."

Lessons for Healing Children

If one wishes to stimulate care, one must become involved in the real work of a place.

—David B. Schwartz

When I walk into hospitals, my inner brain activates before I even walk through the door. My heart rate increases and my breathing quickens. I enter the place concerned and vulnerable, but confronted by the sterile efficiency of most hospitals, my emotions have no place to go. So, they go inward. But children's hospitals feel so very different from the moment you enter. Their environments are emotionally intelligent.

When I first walked through the Mayo Clinic Children's Center, as part of a group of architects and wellness experts, I immediately noticed the creative use of color and design. The space made all of us feel loose, free, playful, curious, and engaging. We lost a few members who wandered off to explore. We were having fun in a very serious and sometimes sad place.

That was the intent. Design purposely released play, curiosity, freedom, and fun. Why? Because kids who are patients, and their families, walk in worried. So, the space must do some quick and heavy lifting to create peace and happiness.

These were not random acts of "happy" colors. The Mayo Children's Center design was the product of a healthcare practice called Evidence-Based Medicine (EBM). The movement started in the 1970s but found traction through a 1984 study observing a link to faster recoveries for patients who had a window view of nature.[5]

Mayo's Children Center applied an offshoot of EBM, Evidence-Based Design (EBD), to leverage the healing power of the environment.[6] It's easy to see why EBD is more extensively used in children's hospitals than adult care facilities. Children, as patients, are more vulnerable and dependent. So, Mayo's environment tells those children, "You are safe and cared for."

The purposeful use of colors creates a friendly, calming, and inviting environment; they relieve fears, foster hope, and create delight. So, naturally, those emotions improve healing. Guess what; these emotions improve learning too. And that improvement comes through a small investment in material, and the guidance of a good designer.

Publicolor: "Injecting Joy in Lifeless Places"

We use color therapeutically. We use color to change attitudes and change behavior ... It comes from the premise that if you change the environment, you change the way people are in that environment ...
—Ruth Lande Schuman, founder of Publicolor

Ruth Lande Schuman, a former industrial designer who fully understood the psychological effect of design and environments, did not like seeing public schools that failed to foster creative thinking and learning. She was also appalled that those conditions fell disproportionately on New York City's most vulnerable students and neighborhoods. Although she had little money, she had one big idea—paint a school as a way to introduce beauty, and restore pride and hope. And, that was the birthing room for her company, Publicolor.

When Ruth launched her first project in 1994, her model was simple: (1) engage students in a project-based learning process painting their school; (2) teach each team in simple design and use of color; (3) find a few partners like Tarkett and Suzanne Tick Design for design support and materials; and (4) involve the community and bring beauty, one school at a time. That project became Publicolor.[7] Since its start, Publicolor has painted over 450 schools and evolved into a multi-year leadership development program. Today, 95% of students who go through the program graduate. New York City's average is 68%.

Jonathan Stanley, National Vice President, Education Sales for Tarkett, took me to meet Ruth. He has worked closely with her on several projects. After my visit, we arranged a field trip for students in the Summer Design Studio Program. This group was working on creating healthy and motivating environments. We took them to Delos, the founders of the WELL Building Standard. They had just moved into their new headquarters in Manhattan's Chelsea neighborhood.

Delos' office was designed to showcase the most advanced technology for lighting, acoustics, and air quality. The building is a research and education tool. Every element in the space—living walls, working garden, sit-to-stand desks, an organic food kitchen—tells a story.

The tour clearly and greatly expanded their vision and stimulated deeper conversations. However, despite the dazzling, advanced technology, the students seemed more focused on the human side of what it would be like to work in such an environment.

For example, one student said, "I can't believe the fresh fruit just sitting out here, and it's free to eat!" Some of the students loved the freedom to go outside to the garden patio and look across the Manhattan skyline. Others were impressed that the people in the office had the freedom to work on projects with whoever and wherever they chose. The students most enjoyed the simple things, ordinary things, human things. Naturally, they were also inspired by ideas they could take back to help their schools get "Publicolored."

A Small Nudge in the Right Direction

A general "law of least effort" applies to cognitive as well as physical exertion.

—Daniel Kahneman

You enjoy as much food, family, and friends as you can handle in the Christmas season. When January turns the calendar, you think, "Hmmm, guess I need to lose a few pounds; I'll behave myself for the next few months."

And you do. You eat more salads, smaller portions of lean protein, and cut out the alcohol, hoping to shed some weight and rebuild a little self-respect. But, the first Friday night in January, your spouse is out of town, and old friends invite you to go out for dinner. You think, "Gee, I need to get out. I should be okay, I'll take it easy and order a Caesar salad with salmon, no croutons and light dressing. Oh, and just one glass of wine and no dessert."

Your friends pick one of your favorite restaurants. You especially love their steaks. But, you stick with the plan and order your salad and one glass of wine. Then, you and your friends get wrapped up in deep conversation about the holidays, family, and some hilarious episodes with relatives. Your diligent waitress makes sure your wine glasses remain full. After an hour you realize you have been sipping all evening.

Later, the waitress returns with a full tray of their specialty desserts. You blew it on the wine, but you *will not* order dessert. And, you win; you don't order dessert. But, two of your friends order that famous molten chocolate cake with vanilla bean ice cream! The ever helpful waitress brings spoons for everyone. You spent the evening living in the moment, absorbed in the camaraderie of old friends, and surrounded by food and drink. You fell into temptation. You were nudged.

What is a Nudge?

The human brain is more easily influenced than we think. Because the brain is a calorie hog, it must ration its use. So, the easy and mindless stuff—showering, driving to the store, casual conversations, watching screens, email, eating—can typically be handled on autopilot. We *think fast* and in the moment. This low-demand activity represents about 80% of our brain's work.

The brain reserves its remaining energy for deep reflection, emotional intimacy, important phone calls, potential threats, and preparing tax returns. This thinking requires more time to weigh options, consider consequences, take extra care, or just be fully present. That same kind of demanding mental work is what wears teachers down and can drain their tank within the first hour of school. A simple technique that economists call a "nudge" offloads high-demand mental work to our autopilot.

In a previous book I wrote, "A nudge makes the right thing easy. It tips the better choice into the 'automatic' realm." A fuel efficiency gauge near the speedometer is a nudge toward slower and gentler driving. Displaying bottled water and healthy juices at convenient reach (and hiding soft drinks) nudges people toward healthier consumption. Those kinds of cultural nudges flow out of behavioral economics. The positive reinforcement or the gentle suggestion shifts people toward greater safety, better health, economic improvement, and other individual and group benefits.

"Before he won the 2017 Nobel Prize in economics, Richard Thaler was most known for changing our nation's approach to 401Ks. In 2006, his research persuaded Congress to change 401K enrollment from an opt-in structure to an opt-out. That difference, that little nudge, increased 401K participation from 30% to 90%."[8]

How Do We Make Our Choices?

Traditional economics examines how culture and tradition influence economic practice and policy. That includes a close look at how humans make risk-reward decisions. It is built on the assumption humans are rational beings. It works like this.

I assume if I offer you sufficient information and adequate incentives, you will make good choices. But it doesn't actually work that way in real life. That's why change management seldom works. No one follows (or reads) the policies, procedures, or benefits.

If you've ever led a change initiative or run a complex project, how much stress did you encounter herding cats and babysitting? How many times did you say things like, "Why can't someone, anyone, just follow the damned instructions?" Amos Tversky and Daniel Kahneman, the fathers of behavioral economics, concluded that to cope or survive, we develop gut responses, paths of least resistance, and rules of thumb to conserve calories.

We may have been taught humans are rational decision-makers. The evidence says otherwise. Lisa and I (and most parents) assumed our children were rational beings, would follow the rules, and take initiative. Well… they didn't. I can imagine every teacher who is reading this just sat up, mumbling, "You got that right; I've got a class full of those kids."

Daniel Ariely, another renowned behavioral economist, says we are irrational beings, however, we are predictably irrational. That insight forms the basis of choice design. That is, we design subtle nudges into physical structures, nutrition, various policies, computer programs, automobiles, financial management, etc. Our society has learned how to make the "right" choice easy, involuntary. As Daniel Kahneman, the co-creator of behavioral economics, said during a recent podcast, "… instead of asking, 'How can I get him or her to do it?,' start with a question of, 'Why isn't she doing it already?'"[9]

Choice design carries the magic to transform behavior in classrooms and schools by using nudges, social dynamics, and culture. Think of social dynamics as a group version of nudges and culture as an organizational, collective form of nudge. But, if behavior change is the goal, we have to flip our thinking from logical left-brain rationale, demands, protocols, procedures. We have to do as Kahneman suggested, first ask what gets in the way of the good choice, remove the constraint, and then create an easier but better option. To help people choose well, we must create a path of least resistance.

> *Our environment can provide continuous "nudges" which impact our behavior, our brains, our mindset.*
>
> *—Kevin Baird*

The Six Pillars to Effective Nudges

So, how can nudge thinking tilt schools toward healthier and happier experiences for teachers and students? Let's consider six pillars for bringing effective change:

1. **Default**: *Make the desired or healthy choice the default option.* Maple Valley, Washington's Tahoma High School features an open lobby with high ceilings, natural light, and beautiful main central stair that creates a central social space. It functions as a crossroads, a mixing bowl, and a connecting place.

   The new STEM classrooms at Sarasota, Florida's Middle School removed student laptops and designed half-round tables using only one monitor. Those changes supported the school's new team-based learning model. Instead of students working independently the half-round tables nudged students to work together.

2. **Appeal**: *Give the nudge a solid appeal.* The Media Center at Richard J. Lee Elementary in Coppell, Texas, sits elevated in the middle of the facility. It is surrounded by beautiful terraced wood steps that double as seating. The center acts as an agora for the entire school. It is the default choice for doing homework, reading, or social interaction.

3. **Intuitive**: *A nudge is intuitively clear.* It signals permission and invitation. Architects call that "legible design." For example, some schools are expanding the use of cafeterias (including booths) to encourage small groups to work together.

   Camas (Washington) Discovery High School includes writable walls. Because of the walls' existence, they give permission for any student to use them. Every vertical surface at Lee Elementary is a writable surface, including the glass guard rails along the atrium of the space.

4. **Simple**: *Less is more.* A few good choices are better than many. Classrooms at Canyon View High School as well as Lee Elementary have simple mobile adjustable tables and chairs. They are easy to move and reconfigure. At the start of each class, that is exactly what they do; they configure the room the way they want to learn that day.

5. **Feedback**: *Giving people immediate positive feedback reinforces behavior.* Removing traditional visual barriers between classrooms and increasing

common space at Canyon View and Lee Elementary create a real-time feedback culture. Teachers can see students, even those from other classes, and students can see teachers. These frequent and fluid touch points act as social calibration nudges.

6. **Norms**: *Leaders produce the positive behaviors they desire by modeling, recognizing, measuring, and rewarding.* These include a shift from playing the expert role to a guide. One principal described her "challenge-based" model to me. When some female students approached her complaining about the boys monopolizing the soccer field during recess, she said, "Then, will you work on that and give me some recommendations?" The girls designed a scheduling system the school implemented. And, the principal's attitude and tone formed a new norm, a standard, that let students know that was their school too. That norm nudged them to find a solution.

Gardens: A Forgotten Teacher of Wisdom and Truth

A garden is a grand teacher. It teaches patience and careful watchfulness; it teaches industry and thrift; above all it teaches entire trust.
—Gertrude Jekyll

In July 2018, our research for this book led our MindShift group to *A Place Called Home* (APCH) in Los Angeles. From its 1993 beginning, APCH saw its mission as a means "to provide the gang-affected youth of South Los Angeles with a safe haven away from the life-threatening dangers and temptations of the streets."[10]

That mission includes K-12 education for high-risk young people in (and beyond) their 90011 zip code. We spent much of our time in RISE, a high school, facilitated within APCH. Among its other extraordinary achievements, RISE created a small community garden that transformed the students, helped the families that participated, and spread to the neighboring church and police facility. The garden also became a catalyst for community and revillaging a gang zone.

Because RISE sits in the middle of the food desert of South Central LA, they planted a small vegetable garden that became a change agent for the community. That one pebble of wholeness, dropped in that pond, rippled in concentric circles throughout a broken system.

Recall your delight in walking through a lush garden, touching and tasting what grew out of the soil. Imagine that delight in kids who live in a dystopian concrete habitat. Students learned about biology, botany, and agriculture. Some of the produce feeds the students through the cafeteria. They also learned the ancient rhythms of agrarian life, including the healthy pride of reaping the investment of their work. They learned a valuable civic lesson on reciprocity and contributing to the welfare of the community.

When parents became curious, the school invited them to work in the garden with their kids and to take the fruit of their labors home. Everyone, students, parents, and others in the community touched wholeness as a natural, outward, nourishing, and healing force of life.

A neighboring church, inspired by the RISE garden, created a community garden, a much larger one, on their property. The roots of community began to spread; the local police station converted part of its property into another garden.

Do you think such creative excellence and community renewal may have contributed to APCH high school's 95% rate and 80% matriculation to college?

The Green Bronx Machine: "Planting Seeds, Harvesting Hope"

Stephen Ritz, a teacher in School 55 in the South Bronx, stashed a box of daffodil bulbs behind his classroom radiator to keep them from becoming projectiles in the hands of disruptive students. But, he forgot about them. Six weeks later, when an enraged girl pushed a boy against the radiator, the boy, desperate for some tool of defense, reached behind the radiator and pulled out ... a bouquet of daffodils. Radiator steam had forced them into full bloom. The boy quickly whirled and presented the bouquet to the girl as a peace offering. That spontaneous act inspired a small and serendipitous movement in School 55. No plan, no thought of changing lives, no viral video; boys just began giving flowers to girls. That moment brought a true epiphany to Ritz.

Ritz "turned the moment into a green curriculum, a movement that would change his life and the lives of countless others. He incorporated vegetable gardens into sections of the South Bronx, on school grounds and on top of a building, organized the Green Teens, and then founded the Green Bronx Machine, a federally registered and approved nonprofit organization with 501(c)(3) status that seeks to be an engine of community change by fully integrating indoor vegetable gardening and green curriculum into a K-12+ model. This model is being used in 5,000 schools across the United States and in Canada, Dubai, and other countries.

"Ritz's students now have near-perfect attendance and graduation rates, they have significantly raised their passing rates on state exams and he has helped create 2,200 local jobs by changing mindsets about food, wellness, and obesity in the middle of the largest tract of public housing in the South Bronx."[11]

Ritz hears the voice of his building booming throughout his community: "We have thousands of residents out there looking at us from the projects. And our classroom is glowing in the middle of the night, and they're saying, 'What's going on in there?' He also understands the core magic in his astounding project, "When you teach kids about nature, they learn to nurture. And, when kids learn to nurture, we as a society embrace our better nature."[12]

What Does This Mean?

To sum it all up, buildings have a voice, a say in the learning for the teacher and the student. A well-designed and built environment will cause one crystalline sound to penetrate the surrounding community. Before we ever walk into the building, what we heard from the building will set our emotional thermostats with one of two settings: it's safe or a threat. Any environment that feels institutional sets our warning systems in motion. But, human environments that make us feel warm, welcomed, and secure will make us feel at home. Students instinctively know that.

It's time for school boards and districts to pay attention. Small and inexpensive changes can bring great and enduring change. You can keep repairing, tightening the screws of discipline, killing dreams, and fostering failure, or you can spend a little time and money to build transforming environments.

Wrapping Up

- Students will spend up to 14,000 hours in a school from kindergarten through twelfth grade.
- A well-designed environment inspires and energizes.
- Good design is always cost-effective.
- Students are also taught by their environments.
- Living in a dump is stressful.
- The purposeful use of colors creates a friendly, calming, and inviting environment.
- A nudge tips choice into an "automatic" realm.
- Choice design makes the right thing easy.
- Instead of asking "How can I get him or her to do it?," start with a question of, "Why isn't she doing it already?" And ask, "How can I remove the constraints?"
- Conduct a nudge audit. Identify subtle nudges that encourage unhealthy behavior or healthy behavior.

Practical Reflections

1. What message and feeling do our facilities and classrooms communicate?
2. What are some easy improvements that might become a catalyst for bigger change?
3. How can you partner with your community to help improve your facility?
4. How can you apply nudge thinking to encourage healthier behaviors?

Notes

1. Ingrid Fetell Lee, *Joyful: The Surprising Power of Ordinary Things to Create Extraordinary Happiness* (Boston: Little Brown, 2020).
2. National Center for Education Statistics, "The NCES Fast Facts Tool Provides Quick Answers to Many Education Questions (National Center for Education Statistics)." NCES Home Page, a part of the U.S. Department of Education. nces.ed.gov/fastfacts/display.asp?id=94
3. Spotlights, "The Condition of Education, 2013." Spotlights: The Status of Rural Education–Indicator, May 2013. nces.ed.gov/programs/coe/indicatortla.asp
4. Rex M. Miller, *Change Your Space, Change Your Culture* (Hoboken, NJ: Wiley, 2014).
5. Roger S. Ulrich, et al., "A Review of the Research Literature on Evidence-Based Healthcare Design." *HERD: Health Environments Research & Design Journal*, Apr. 1, 2008, pp. 61–125. doi/10.1177/193758670800100306.
6. Ferhat D. Zengul and Stephen J. O'Connor, "A Review of Evidence Based Design in Healthcare from a Resource-Based Perspective: Semantic Scholar." *Journal of Management Policy and Practice*, vol. 14, no. 2 (2013). www.semanticscholar.org/paper/A-Review-of-Evidence-Based-Design-in-Healthcare-Zengul-O'connor/9a3ad1acdb3c1dc6c3a7ebef41c6d9eaf-9ba8c00
7. Publicolor, "About Publicolor, New York." www.publicolor.org/about
8. Rex M. Miller, et al., *The Healthy Workplace Nudge: How Healthy People, Cultures, and Buildings Lead to High Performance* (Hoboken, NJ: John Wiley & Sons, Inc., 2018).
9. Stephen J. Dubner, "How to Launch a Behavior-Change Revolution." *Freakonomics*, podcast, Oct. 29, 2017. freakonomics.com/podcast/launch-behavior-change-revolution/
10. APCH. https://apch.org/who-we-are/
11. Tom Oder, "How a Bronx Teacher Started a Green Classroom Revolution That's Spreading across the U.S." MNN, Mother Nature Network, Sept. 6, 2017. www.mnn.com/your-home/organic-farming-gardening/stories/stephen-ritz-green-classroom-revolution-bronx-power-plant-book.
12. "Stephen Ritz, Founder of the Green Bronx Machine: His Story." YouTube, May 26, 2016. www.youtube.com/watch?v=9Dt0odlFzmQ

CHAPTER 18

Leading Change: From Compliance to Ownership

If you're not making a mistake, it's a mistake.

—Miles Davis

Mike, one of my coaching clients, the president of a large regional distribution company, recently told me of one summer intern's analysis of their market data. He said, "Rex, as I listened to him, I wondered how a 19-year-old, who doesn't know our business, spotted and articulated our Achilles' heel in the market and offered a darn good strategy. I also wondered why we missed it and what else we may be missing. I know this business inside and out, but it has gotten so complex and changes so rapidly. If I continue to try to *run* things, I won't have time to hear an idea from an intern who will only be here for a summer. Complexity is forcing me out of my get-it-done mindset. I've got to think more, process, and then connect the dots more than I've imagined."

That same week, I had breakfast with Reed, another company president. Reed's company has succeeded because of what author Les McKeown calls, the leader's "golden gut," a combination of knowledge + experience + insight + execution. I've been trying to help him shift his role and mindset from being the boss (the decider) to the leader (chief facilitator).

A few weeks ago, their phone system went down. Knowing that customers' inability to get phone support could suffocate his business, he plunged in and bought 30 cell phones for the customer service agents. Once the crisis was over, he gathered the management team to ask, "How the hell did this happen?" A combination of old technology, demand that exceeded capacity, and a lack of role clarity gave everyone an excuse for why they did not take "ownership." Everyone on the team knew it was a problem in the making, except the president. He did what many bosses do. He reamed them out, shamed them for not taking ownership, and threatened to hold people accountable in the future.

He told me, "I had to become the big frog in the room." In other words, only he has the golden gut to run the company. When he saw the look on my face, he said, "What was I supposed to do, let my company go out of business?"

Once again, I tried to help him see, "Every time you do that, you reinforce that no one, except you, dares make an important decision. If they do, your golden gut will override it or you will turn into the big frog if it doesn't go well."

"I know, I know… I'm changing. It's been fourteen days since I did the big frog and I think they are starting to get the message."

I smiled, "Let's wait until the next crisis before trying to convince me you have exchanged your boss status for facilitator-in-chief."

Moving to Jazz

According to Frank Barrett, jazz musician and business author, today's leaders must unlearn a lot, "… because the enemy to jazz improvisation is your own routines and habits and success traps. There's a temptation to play what you've done well in the past because you're on the spot having to make something up in front of an audience. And it's in public, and you can't take it back, much like executives have to take action, and they can't take it back. It's in public. It's a commitment."[1]

These two business leaders, Mike and Reed, demonstrate the difficulty in moving from rehearsed and tightly arranged music to learning the improvisational nature of jazz. It is more than learning new principles or methods. It is rewiring assumptions and habits developed over time and under fire. That change requires extensive rewiring.

Today's leadership mindset does not revolve around the old and cold calculus of "problem solving." Leaders must be larger, more generous, more flexible, and more interactive with all the players. Insight and "solutions" may come from anywhere, even a 19-year-old intern. Imagination soars far beyond tactics and strategy.

In the same interview, Frank Barrett said, "… if you're just in a problem-solving mindset, your imagination is going to be shrunk. The interpretive possibilities of action will be smaller. You have to have a mindset that says yes to the possibility that something new and interesting and creative can emerge."

The Worlds of PUSH and PULL

Today's leaders face a choice between what John Hagel and John Seely Brown call PUSH and PULL.[2] PUSH is a linear and planned approach, plodding through a checklist. PUSH assumes that leaders or experts have all the answers and that success results from tight and detailed planning. PUSH leaders see themselves as conducting a well-rehearsed orchestra.

PULL is like playing in a jazz band. A PULL leader improvises, challenges assumptions, and invites other stakeholders to play in the band.

In order for PUSH to work, events over time must remain relatively stable and predictable in order to create standardized efficiency. That also describes today's educational challenge. If students go down the assembly line, acquiring the features (skills) in the proper order and timeline, they will come out the other end ready for college and life. We give them an inspection sticker called a diploma. That used to work.

Today's world of education, however, must cope with the same dilemma many manufacturing companies face. PUSH handles highly complicated functions like building car engines or operating an office building's electrical-mechanical system. However, the business side of manufacturing is anything but predictable. What happens when a business (or an institution like a school), which

Push operates on a key assumption— that it is possible to forecast demand. Based on this assumption, push works mightily to ensure that the right people and resources are delivered at the right place and the right time to serve the expected demand.

—John Hagel[3]

was built on economies of scale that require a year or longer to build capacity, suddenly confronts innovation or tariffs that change the learned parameters overnight? It is like driving down the highway at 70 miles per hour and suddenly throwing the transmission into reverse.

PULL operates in a networked system of real-time demand. When a need arises, we reach out to a network of resources and pull them in. We don't have to own, inventory, or manage those resources.

Cab companies, for example, operate as PUSH businesses. They predict demand, buy an inventory of cabs, hire drivers, and dispatchers, and contract with insurance carriers, accounting services, and maintenance facilities to meet that demand. Cab companies limit the number of drivers in a balancing act between supply and demand. At one time it cost about $1 million to become a cab driver in New York. Although cab drivers can sell their medallion or pass it to a family member, today that investment is essentially worthless.

Why?

Uber and Lyft chose the PULL model. Almost anyone can drive for Uber. No investment. Their app replaces all the cab infrastructure listed above. Rideshare is a simple, frictionless, on-demand service that is 30–50% less expensive than cabs. Many other services we now routinely use—Amazon, Netflix, Airbnb, Door Dash, etc.—replaced businesses stuck in a PUSH model.

In education, administrators face a similar shift. If they remain the clearinghouse and the "deciders" from the old order, they become the bottlenecks; they perpetuate a compliance mindset that struggles to PUSH. But, they can also choose a PULL approach, defining and designing the outcomes needed, creating small coalitions empowered to do real work, and then walking away and letting them solve it. A PUSH system is built on organizational charts, job descriptions, and silos. It requires approvals and budgets to start action. But, it can grind to a halt if one department needs help from another. A PULL model comprises a network of people and knowledge. When a need arises, anyone, anywhere in the organization can choose to contribute.

PUSH typically produces a code of compliance. PULL builds an ownership culture. This distinction is vividly displayed throughout the business world. And it is just as relevant within (although less visible to) the educational world. Let's look at how that story is playing out in Mesquite, Texas.

The Journey from Compliance to Ownership

Dr. David Vroonland, the Superintendent of the Mesquite ISD, served as part of our team on *Humanizing the Education Machine*. His contributions were so valuable that I interviewed him for this project. What he is doing in Mesquite captures a pivotal plank of this book.

David was born to a single mom and grew up in poverty in Waterloo, Iowa, in foster homes. He lived with up to twenty other children at times. At age 10, he was adopted by the Vroonland family in Cedar Rapids.

He remembers, "Taking two paper grocery bags, filled with my stuff, and sitting in the back seat of the car alone, and being driven from Waterloo to Cedar Rapids. New room, new house, new family, new name, new school, new friends, new church; everything new at 10."

To his surprise, he found that his school fully accepted, affirmed, and engaged him. Education gave him horizons. By the time he was 18, he knew he would be a lawyer, minister, or teacher, all "in the pathway to serve." He chose education because he felt he would have the most impact there.

After teaching and coaching across America and in Japan, he served as the Assistant Superintendent of the Allen, Texas, ISD, and then as Superintendent for the Frenship ISD in Lubbock. He admits to being very comfortable at Frenship. But, as he moved toward retirement, he realized he wanted to work in an urban setting. Then, the Mesquite ISD called. After a series of interviews, they offered him the Superintendent role; he was their first outside hire in fifty years. He says, "They were perfect; they represented the unique opportunity to fulfill my design. The student population was 76% free and reduced meals; the ethnic mix was 57% Hispanic, 25% African-American, and 13% Caucasian."

He sees Mesquite as reflecting his blue-collar, foster home roots; he says, "This is Waterloo; this is Cedar Rapids. My reception has been incredible. I did not come here to bring strategy. Instead, I brought a vision, and I connected that vision to my story, and that resonated with the people. I literally walked all 47 campuses and presented to all staff for the first eight days."

He has not forgotten the other foster children he grew up with. He works every day in the confidence that, "Especially for children who have experienced trauma, schools can serve as agents of hope and encouragement."

The Ownership Model of Education

Vroonland believes the American Dream cannot work without a public education system. As a proponent of an "ownership model" for public education, many see him as an innovator. And, he works hard to build an ownership culture within his district. He calls it "moving from obedience to ownership." He wants to "create a new narrative for public ed."[4]

When he arrived in Mesquite, he walked into a compliance-based system. "Everything went through central office," he says. "Principals couldn't make decisions without going through the central office.

"Well, the high school principals took me to lunch the first day. They asked me what I thought about 'Walkthroughs.'[5] These principals were required to do 25 a week and then turn them in each Friday.

"So, I asked, 'Turn them in to who?'"

"Central office."

"I bet you're doing a boatload of them on Friday." They smiled and nodded.

"And, I'm betting no one's reading them." No one smiled, but all nodded.

"So, let's address their value. Let's talk about what we value, and what we value in Walkthroughs."

And, that is how the new superintendent transformed the principals into a new conversation. They saw that Walkthroughs added some value. But, that was the first conversation that reframed the compliance mentality. It shifted the energy to discovering the value behind the Walkthroughs instead of checking them off a list.

That next year Vroonland junked the district Walkthroughs altogether, and replaced them with campus-developed and campus-owned Walkthroughs. As he says, "It's foolish to focus on compliance rather than values.

I had to redirect the cultural gravity that defaults to compliance. That includes the default to data without asking the value in or behind that data."

He quickly saw how compliance systems lose sight of value; they have no "people equation." People lose any sense of what the system is about. Overcoming the system becomes a persistent daily effort.

Moving from compliance-based systems to an owner-ship culture requires a big shift. He found that even the term, "ownership culture," carried a dramatic impact. It shifted thinking and behavior; deeply and rapidly and without major resistance. How did they bring such a profound change without major pushback? David believes it was because he focused on the values, not plans. He articulated vision and allowed the principals and other leaders to develop the plans for giving traction to the vision.

> *Do we measure what we value? Are we valuing what we measure?*

The Distributive Leadership Model

He recalls, "The shift that happened in Mesquite only happens by investing in and emphasizing leadership development.

"We first developed a Distributive Leadership Model. We realigned responsibility to the points where decisions must occur. While I am the spokesperson for the district, the leadership needs to occur down in the system.

"I persistently explain my role to our leaders to remind them of their role. Our mission is not debatable. If all third graders must achieve grade-level reading and we've got three years to get that done, that's not up for discussion. *How* we get there *will be* discussed. I don't provide the how. If I do, then people feel like they're victims of my plan. I engage our employees in design. And, I help their design work to prevent them from falling into a victim mindset. You've got to let people do the work of discovery to understand the nature of the problems first.

"Since we've employed this strategy, we've seen significant improvement in all grades. And, there is no compliance tool! We call it 'framework thinking.' We build frameworks of operation and allow flexibility within that framework so people can have the freedom to use their judgment."

Thinking Creatively *Inside* the Box

We all talk about "outside the box" approaches. And that idea can be helpful in reaching for a new awareness. But, we must also identify our constraints, the realities of the box. The box is real. Specific parameters will always define the operational conditions. Vroonland explains that further, "Look; I can't change the fact that a kid has one parent. I can't change the fact that some parents don't pay attention to their kids. Those are facts. But, we have a lot of room to do creative work inside that framework. Each campus in our district operates within the frameworks, based on the needs of the child.

"I can't come in and design a solution for kindergartens at my 33 elementary schools and believe that my solution will solve their problems. The child showing up every day in one class isn't the same child in another school. The teacher must have the ability to be innovative, that ability to be nimble and responsive to the needs of the child standing in front of them at any moment; you can't design that from my office.

"Now, when I walk the campus, teachers will come up to me and start talking about where their children are on grade-level reading. Why is that important to me? Because they're owning it. They're excited because it's their baby.

"A teacher came up to me recently and said she's been teaching 15 years, has never worked harder than she's working now, and has never been happier! As she talked, I realized that working under compliance systems is actually fairly easy; all you have to do is follow the rules. However, when you have to be the designer and owner, it's more responsibility, more difficult, but it's more rewarding!"

"You Have to Be Fearless"

I asked David how an ownership culture works in an accountability culture.

"Well, you have to be fearless. The system you create sets the tone. A fear-based system is based on avoidance of failure. But, imagine what it would be like to stop operating in fear and instead focus on learning and improving. Being accountable, and education's *accountability culture* are two different things. One definition of accountable is 'answerability.' You have to answer to proper authorities and stakeholders why you did certain things. But, the accountability world of education often creates the opposite. We've seen it time and time again. The fear of the consequences for not achieving these artificial measures of achievement leads to playing it safe or gaming the system.

"We require a teacher to take 25–30 very different kids, coming in at different levels of capability, readiness, learning differences, and maturity. And, that teacher is required to have them all prepared to pass required tests at the same time. To do that, many schools require teachers to cover the same subjects, for the same grades, on the same day, in the same way. This misguided attempt to create consistency and account for having covered the required content creates a system that perverts its mission of educating children. This is the same issue and the same conversation I had regarding Walkthroughs.

"By removing the pressure of accountability and replacing it with a sense of ownership, we remove fear. More than that, we actually instill a sense of adventure and the opportunity to do great work and make a difference in kids' lives. We have the high honor to be fearless, to get beyond 'We can't, we've never, they won't.'"

When you look at superintendents like Dr. Vroonland, who come into districts as innovators, they must change the existing culture or nothing will change. Their ideas and visions may sound wonderful, hopeful, and inspiring. But they will quickly wash away like sandcastles without a culture change.

The Chick-fil-A Model

David told me that Apple and Google have talked with him about designing an innovation system that franchises its schools. I asked him to explain.

"I used to think franchising was a terrible idea for public schools, but now if you look at a company like Chick-fil-A as a franchise, they provide clear parameters that every store follows, but they also allow local autonomy to tailor the service to their community. In an innovative system, you've got to have the ability to be responsive and nimble. But, at the same time, understand the values and boundaries in which you operate."

David continued, "Five schools will be our pilot projects; a high school, middle school, and three elementary schools will take part in the design work. This will take at least three years.

"If this were a compliance-based structure, the process would be simple, top-down communication. But, in an ownership culture, there's got to be a lot of conversation around values and operational conditions. People have to have clarity of understanding. But when we get this in place, I can see teachers' ability to respond to the needs of the kids will be far beyond anything we've ever seen. That's the thing about ownership. Compliance moves you to the point of the expected outcome. Ownership moves you to a point of excellence."

What Does That "Point of Excellence" Look Like?

David kept rolling, "A lot of little things create a broader ecosystem of ownership. For example, we're training our entire board to roll out our own local accreditation tool."

"Your board will accredit schools?" I asked.

"Yes, and there's not a single piece of compliance inside the accreditation tool. It's all based on a school's ability to move toward excellence in the things its community values. It's more than just getting 80 on a test; that's not the point. There is no meaning behind a number. You don't want to hear that as a parent; I don't want to hear that as a parent.

"But, look at the possibilities for a new way. Since my son Matthew had already moved beyond the content in his physics class, his teacher gave him an opportunity to connect his physics with the work he was doing in his architecture class. He loved it and thrived! As a senior, he was even given the opportunity to design a learning space for Mesquite High School. They just completed it. That's the way we need to think."

I could see David takes excellence in education seriously. In fact, he told me Mesquite is getting ready to build a CHOICE high school.

"What is that?"

"Our CHOICE high school will have four schools in it: Technology, Engineering, Health Science, and Construction Science. And, we're going to try to align them to a university. I want students to get a deep portfolio of experience that makes them very competitive right out of high school for a $70,000 job.

"Another point about excellence; it's about developing a culture that focuses *on the child*. That is what teachers want to do. It's not like I'm appealing to something foreign to them. That's why they became teachers. I'm giving them what they want. Now they will also carry more responsibility and more planning; these are things that come along with ownership culture. These things are part of being truly valued as an educator.

"When you are moving towards excellence, it's important for leaders to remove the obstacles, and that has been our first step. Our second step was to focus on leader capacity. We have done that for two years and I was the trainer. We built systems to support the autonomy and ownership we were teaching. We also have four Executive Directors for Leadership Development. Their sole job is to spend at least 75% of their day on every campus working with administrators, forwarding the vision of the district, and helping them forward in their efforts."

Finally, I asked, "From where you sit, David, why do you think compliance systems came into being in education?"

"Because we fundamentally do not trust leaders or teachers. It is easier to create compliance structures and run them out of a central office to maximize efficiency. The companies that really focus on efficiency models are failing and they're failing fast. They have to double down on the creative side of the ledger to break out of the law of diminishing returns inherent with any efficiency system. But, in education, it does not matter if we get to the end of the year faster and cheaper if our students lose ground, become less engaged, and find themselves unprepared for their next phase of life.

"We must invest in the capacity development of people. We're in a people business."

New Leaders Manage the Emotional Journey of Their Organizations

The transition from compliance to ownership constitutes a change in identity, values, habits, and behaviors. These are non-cognitive skills, emotional in nature. Building this new capacity in an organization known for, measured by, and secure in compliance has been described as building your plane while flying it. It is a necessary transition for public education to remain relevant as the cornerstone to our democracy and setting students on a life path to pursue happiness.

David Vroonland understood his primary role was to manage and pace the emotional transition of the organization by listening, coaching, and experimenting together. He knows what all good leaders know, that organizations have collective nervous systems. They manifest fight or flight when confused or feel threatened. The organizational glitter ball equivalent in a collective amygdala hijack is a culture of instinctive empathetic listening, support, and coaching. The glitter may not completely settle the first time, the second, or third. The glitter settles when the mental decision to trust surpasses the emotional instinct to distrust.

It's always a sign of a good culture when a leader can talk candidly, without reaction, in an open and broad dialogue. The right dialogue leads to exploration, to ideation, to a willingness to try something. If that looks similar to the learning flywheel in Chapter 2, it is. The environment children need for engaged learning is the same one adults need. David Vroonland understands this is how leaders today lead change. Organizations change at the rate of their emotional readiness.

Wrapping Up

- PUSH leadership assumes leaders solve problems and drive to success. PULL leaders improvise, challenge assumptions, and invite other stakeholders to "play in the band."
- PUSH typically produces a code of compliance. PULL builds an ownership culture.
- Dr. Vroonland said he "articulated vision and allowed the principals and other leaders to develop the plans for giving traction to the vision."
- True accountability takes ownership. But, compliance cultures lead to playing it safe or gaming the system.
- Organizations have collective nervous systems. They manifest "fight or flight" when they are confused or feel threatened.

Practical Reflections

1. Frank Barrett said, "… the enemy to jazz improvisation is your own routines and habits and success traps." Is he correct? Does that speak to you about your own leadership style?
2. Dr. Vroonland shifted the energy in his school district away from checklists and toward the bedrock values down below the checklists. Can you see examples within your own world?
3. Dr. Vroonland also said teachers must have the ability to be innovative, "that ability to be nimble and responsive to the needs of the child standing in front of them at any moment." Would such a system help (or constrain) your job?

Notes

1. Jeff Kehoe, "What Leaders Can Learn from Jazz." *Harvard Business Review*, Mar. 30, 2015. hbr.org/2012/08/what-leaders-can-learn-from-ja
2. John Hagel and John Seely Brown, *The Power of Pull: How Small Moves, Smartly Made, Can Set Big Things in Motion* (New York: Basic Books, 2012).
3. Ibid.
4. David Vroonland, interview by Shannon Buerk, May 1, 2018, *Culture Catalysts with Shannon Buerk*, Engage2Learn.org, May 1, 2018.
5. A walkthrough is an administrative concept that takes principals and other administrators on quick tours through classrooms. They are not designed for formal teacher evaluation, but rather quick snapshots of practices and policies. Then, naturally, the "walkers" write reports.

CHAPTER 19

What Teachers Really Need to Help Students Thrive

Every school is embedded within an existing community that connects hundreds of families through their children. The strength of these connections depends upon a sense of partnership resting on a shared commitment to education. In a safe community with strong families that value education, a competent teacher can do a good job. In a dangerous community with few resources, fragmented families, and an indifference to education, a successful teacher has to be a superhero.

—Lou Cozolino

Teaching is a dangerous occupation. Teachers are like soldiers, law enforcement officers, and firefighters; when trouble erupts, they show up. Regardless of conditions. They do it because they do it. They are wired and trained to protect.

Education is a habitat for heroes.

We need those who protect and preserve us. That means we desperately need teachers; those who teach, care for, and prepare children for the future. But, because that role is so ambiguous, so hard for society to see and appreciate, we neglect them. They don't wear uniforms, so we don't know to applaud when they walk down airport concourses; we can't ask waitresses to "Bring me the check for that table of teachers."

Remember when we entered a new era of unconventional warfare in the early 1990s? Not only did the old rules of war not apply, but the military had to operate in a totally unmapped terrain. The psychological, cultural, and technological dimensions defied old forms of logic. And that meant that, while military strategists, planners, historians, theorists, and commanders figured out what was going on, our soldiers, sailors, and marines faced new depths of danger and vulnerability. As a result, we lost too many young lives and sent 45% home disabled.[1] For example, Humvees and Bradleys were not designed for roadside IED's (Improvised Explosive Devices). It took fifteen years before the Department of Defense began making them with Mine-Resistant Ambush Protection (MRAP). My nephew Nathan drove a Bradley that was hit with an IED. He was injured and some of his crew died.

Of course, soldiers improvised, as soldiers do. Many, including Nathan, had to buy their own life-saving equipment, like flak jackets and protection from the heat. Soldiers spent $400 and more to simply improve their odds of survival.[2]

The Classroom Battlefield

We saw the same patterns in the teachers on our team. When the rules, and the very environment of teaching, changed, teachers began facing greater risks. Many become casualties on the battlefield. Like soldiers, to survive, they have to improvise. Many teachers spend several hundred dollars of their own money per school year for supplies and equipment. And they do it, not for their own children, but for yours. For mine. That means teachers make up the difference between what we give them and what they need. They pay our debts. Because some get crushed under the load, we lose too many too soon. Too many others remain in the classroom as wounded warriors.

The battle for the hearts and minds of this generation requires well-equipped and conditioned teachers for the new realities in schools. But, that equipping and readiness require more self-management under pressure and self-care after the battle than about new teaching philosophies and methods.

The real issue is support for teachers. We must develop healthy and happy teachers who have the resilience to bounce back with kindness, resolve, and grit. We cannot expect them to care for each child if they are not cared for.

America loves its teachers, we need them to thrive to build our better future. And, we know that teachers are not the problem; we know they are not disengaged. Like our military personnel, they are caught in an outdated and dangerous job. Most do that job as heroically as they can. Teachers are wired to care, and they often care too much. Many suffer, some die because of that intensity of care.

Teaching and the Art of Motorcycle Maintenance

Sometimes it's a little better to travel than to arrive.

—Robert M. Pirsig[3]

Miranda teaches eighth grade math at Freedom Middle School on the southwest edge of the city. On Thursday, she melted down. It all came unraveled for her when two girls tore into each other, gouging, pulling, punching, screaming. Miranda threw herself between them and got tangled in elbows and hips. After so many other classroom brawls, that was it; Miranda was done. She had no more tricks, she was fed up with getting slammed to walls and bruised breaking up fights. And, it was now three years in a row that most of her class will fail the standardized test for math.

She walked into the teachers lounge and lost it, "I'm sick of being afraid of my own students, sick of their threats. Why do I have to listen to their language, their disrespect? But, they're right; if I had a shred of self-respect, I'd get in my car and drive away from here forever." The two other teachers in the lounge wanted to reach out, but her eyes scared them. They quickly left.

That's when Tess walked out of the kitchen.

"Tough day?"

"No different than any other."

Tess walked to the door and stopped. "Look; we may need to talk. Meet me at the red Harley in the parking lot about 3:15. OK?"

"Oh, I don't know."

"You just said if you had any self-respect you'd leave forever. Do you not even have enough to meet me for coffee?"

Miranda saw that her hands were still shaking.

"OK. I'll be there."

Miranda had seen Tess around school but never got to know her. She knew Tess taught one of the three eighth-grade math classes, and that most of her students passed. In fact, Miranda heard that many finish high school and some go to college. She has a reputation for beating the system.

Tess struts into school each morning like some kind of superhero. She wears a black leather bomber jacket, sports several tattoos, and wears her hair in a ponytail that falls to her belt. Miranda had seen kids part like the Red Sea when Tess rumbled in. Then, she had seen some huddle around her 2013 Harley Street Bob. But, no one ever touched the Harley.

Tess is about 50, youthful, fit and feisty, a free spirit, maybe the only one in the faculty. She had something definitely working for her. Even in her burnout, Miranda began to look forward to coffee.

Dying to Teach

When Miranda bumped into Miguel in the hall, she asked, "So, what's up with the biker lady?"

"Tess? She was here for a long time, but she looked old, shot. Her attitude sucked. She always complained about her weight, blood pressure, and no sleep. And then about three years ago she just quit, just walked out the door. No notice, no warning.

"No one knew where she went or what she did but she came back last year and was rehired; we were desperate for teachers. We were shocked that she returned at all; we wondered, what happened to the Tess we knew? Who is this lady? But, no one had the guts to ask."

An hour later, Miranda climbed on the back of Tess's Harley, and they roared off to Fred's Coffee. Miranda had never even seen the place, tucked away in the bend of the river. When the barista delivered their concoctions, they found a table in the corner of the quiet and peaceful courtyard. As Miranda sat down between a weeping willow and koi pond, she suddenly knew she had found a safe place.

Without waiting for small talk, she split open, pouring it all out through anger, tears, and cussing. She felt like her whole life bounded across the table like an unraveling ball of yarn.

When she grew quiet and sipped her latte, Tess spoke very softly.

"Miranda, remember, there is what happens to you and then there is what you tell yourself it means. Right now, these kids are happening to you and there is a voice whispering, 'You're failing your students so give up!'

"You can't control who walks in your class but you can control that voice. And, if you can do that, you can help your kids control their voices, the ones that tell them they are losers. By changing your voice, you can change what happens in your classroom."

The Cowboy Yogi

After refilling their chai teas, they returned to the table.

"Miranda, I went through the same thing. In fact, you have my old classroom," Tess began, while slowly stirring her drink. "After fifteen years, it was killing me, literally. So, I walked out and didn't even say goodbye. I sold my house, bought a Harley, and hit the road for two years. I headed to Rapid City, as far away as I could get and still find a decent coffee shop.

"In Rapid City, I met a rancher, Jimmy, who came to town a few times a week. I needed rent and he needed a hand with the horses. The first day he took me into the corral, those big horses scared me. Jimmy looked at me and said, 'Lady, you are wound so tight you're spooking the horses. And, you were a teacher? Bet you spooked your kids too.'

"Truth is, he was right. I had the same charm with horses I did with students. I knew I was a failure. I even told Jimmy I wasn't cut out for kids or horses.

"And, he said, 'Aw, hell, lady, no need to beat yourself up. Horses read people better than most people do. I think you're facing the three enemies: stress, ego, and fear. If you can conquer them, you can do just about anything.'

"Then, Jimmy asked, 'Why do you ride a motorcycle?'

"I told him I liked the open road, peace of mind, freedom, and control.

"He nodded, as he saddled his horse, 'If you conquer those three enemies, your classroom will feel just like that open road, with the wind blowing your hair behind you.'"

Miranda chuckled, "I'd sure like to feel that in my class."

After sipping her tea, Tess spoke again, "Did you know that almost half of teachers face high stress, every day? And it grinds us down to powder. I never knew that and I certainly didn't take care of myself. But, I sure do now. I eat right, sleep right, and think right; I take care of myself. Look; I don't want to intrude, but you sure need to take care of yourself too, before you flame out."

Miranda listened very carefully before she spoke, "Stress as a villain I understand. But ego? I've never had a big ego. Break that down for me."

Tess grinned, "Of course. you don't have a big ego, Miranda, you're a teacher. I'm not talking about 'big E ego,' but your enemy is the little ego; you let it whisper to you all of the time. We all do. And, it can be pretty harsh."

"Oh, OK, my mind nags at me all of the time, 'You don't have what you need, your kids don't respect you, you're going to die alone, no one will remember you,' that kinda stuff. Is that what you mean?"

"Yes, that's it. The little ego loves to pull you and me down. But, a third villain—fear—drives the other two. Fear makes you second-guess, hesitate, pull back, play it safe. And that ends up stealing your hopes and plans. Those three enemies totally controlled me. They made me suspicious, defeated, afraid, and anxious. Does that sound familiar?

"Miranda, listen; the whole system is designed to trigger all three every day. Stress starts with those standardized tests, it comes down from the superintendent who feels her job is on the line, it comes from parents who worry about their kids, it comes out in our kids when they act out. And over time, caring too much, it catches up and we end up believing what is happening to us is what we deserve. We think we just gotta take it."

"So, how did you break that cycle?"

"I finally realized if fear is the source and stress the trigger, I could at least control the trigger."

Settle Your Glitter

"So, one day while we were moving cattle to another pasture, Jimmy reached into his saddlebag and pulled out a clear rubber ball about the size of a racquetball; it was filled with liquid and glitter. He told me about seeing a video of this school in Dallas called the Momentous Institute. He showed me the video later.

"And in the video, a little girl at the school held up a ball just like Jimmy's to show what happened when stress sent her brain into fight or flight. She shook it and the glitter swirled. She said that's how the amygdala blocks our ability to think clearly. So, holding that ball still, she said her teachers told them to breathe slowly while watching the glitter settle to the bottom. By the time the glitter settles to the bottom, your heart has slowed and your pre-frontal cortex can take back the driver's seat. Jimmy said he figured if it works for a 3-year-old. it would work for twitchy cowboys."

Miranda's eyes brightened, but all she said was, "Oh, wow."

"Miranda, slow intentional breathing slows the heart and a calm heart calms the mind. If you practice this a bit, you will go from calm to refreshed to pumped, even about school. People want to know how I can be so *on* throughout the day. I just take 90 seconds to breathe when I feel stressed. I also do it before I go to bed and again around three in the morning when my body wakes up because it's time to flush it out again. Let me tell you; I used to have a hard time sleeping. I don't anymore."

Pay Attention to What You Pay Attention To

When you live in the shadow of insanity, the appearance of another mind that thinks and talks as yours does is something close to a blessed event.
—Robert Pirsig[4]

Tess helped Miranda know she wasn't the only one struggling with stress, poor quality sleep, and a sense of defeat. And, she wasn't crazy. She also wasn't through talking. So, they moved to a nearby restaurant.

As they dined, Tess remembered something else Jimmy told her, "Whenever you think you know, it's time to get stupid and curious."

"What does that mean?" Miranda asked.

"When we think we know something, that knowledge hardens. It's no longer warm and pliable. It becomes a stuffed trophy animal on the wall, the taxidermy of what was once alive. And that stuffed knowledge kills the thrill and magic of teaching. That's why we teachers just have to remain curious. Our work should display curiosity and adventure, not fear, compliance, and control."

As Tess watched Miranda laugh, she remembered how she learned to laugh again at Jimmy's ranch.

Make Room for Joy and Play

Miranda sipped her coffee and slowly began nodding. "I think I'm starting to see. I thought teaching was the problem, but it really comes down to what I see and don't see."

"I think that's right. But, there's something else. One day, Jimmy said, 'I bet you used to have fun teaching. But, lady, you are way too serious.' I told him I left because teaching because the fun left first, and that's when it started killing me.

"And he said, 'You know; my daddy said, if it ain't fun, you ain't learning. You let that happen to you. But if you keep ridin' that Harley, you'll have fun and you'll learn about yourself, the country, swim in new rivers, eat food you never thought was edible; there's a whole world waiting to be discovered. You will have fun as you do.' Then, he grinned and said, 'See, you already learned how to shoe horses and deliver calves.'

"He helped me to understand if I had curiosity, and wonder, and fun, students would learn and love it. If you and I and other teachers are not having fun, guess what? Those kids know; we can't hide it. But we can't have fun if we're stressed, defeated, and afraid."

"I hear you, but I'm not sure I understand."

"OK, think about someone in your world that, any time she or he walks into the room, regardless of concerns or a present crisis, the mood picks up; and they bring that consistently wherever they go. You also know energy vampires that can walk into a party and kill the joy. You can be both within the same day.

"When I returned to teaching, I decided I would be that person who can make the class feel safe, and then fill it with positive energy and possibilities. Now, I'm still a work in progress; I have bad days. But, now, when I feel those joy-sucking fangs in my skin, I pause, settle my glitter, shift my energy, and then swing back into the dance.

"I've even shared parts of my journey with the kids. They call them 'Tess Tales.' When they see me stressed, they say, 'Hey, Miss Tess, we think you should go settle your glitter.' The laughter alone resets the mood. The students say the same thing with one another, and everyone gets it and knows—they're just having a moment and then we're back at it.

"You have to be ready and stay ready to teach every day. If we don't love and enjoy what we do, we won't be able to love our kids. And, you know so many of them come to class feeling unloved and, worse, unlovable; then they live down to those expectations. We won't be able to absorb their pain and exchange it for a little hope if we get hog-tied by our three enemies."

Running on Empty

A couple days later, Tess and Miranda slipped away again to Fred's Coffee. Tess opened her iPhone notes to a poem Jimmy gave her, as he said, "For the road."

It is unsustainable

to give

and give

and give until you have nothing left.

before you hit empty

you will be offering something

that isn't even real.[5]

As Miranda's eyes burned, Tess took her hand and whispered, "Honey, I can see you are running on empty. You've gone from dying to teach, to dying on the vine. You can't reach those kids if you are TUI (teaching under the influence) of stress, ego, and fear. You're like a car out of alignment, you will pull toward the ditch of negativity.

"I'll just tell you when I returned from the road, I saw my doctor. She froze when she saw me; her mouth fell open. When she weighed me, all she could say was 'wow!' After she took my vitals, she just said, 'Whatever you're doing, don't stop!'

"And I haven't. And you can travel the same path. If you need a guide, call me."

With Tess's help, Miranda started to rebuild her health and resiliency, and reclaim her passion for teaching. She and Tess continued to rumble out of the parking lot together for coffee at Fred's. Miranda found the road back, and so did her students. It took a year to restore her health and learn how to take care of her whole self. At some point, she wasn't sure when; she lost the anxiety that used to start in the parking lot and follow her into her class.

She also found some of Tess's strut.

When school broke for the summer Miranda headed off to Santa Fe, New Mexico. She re-engaged her passion for art and spent time touring the countryside. When school started back in the fall, two Harleys sat in the STAFF parking lot.

Essential Conversations

Science is not a cure for sadness and evaluation is not a pathway to excellence. Relationships defined by trust, openness, and exploration of ideas move teachers, students and schools forward ... and will ultimately build the future of this country.

—Kevin Baird

The Tess and Miranda story touches conversations that could and should bloom in schools all over America. Let's consider some of them:

- *From Fear to Safe*: Tests, grades, ratings, inadequate income, the future, and other monsters create fear. And fear builds stress. But, all the sources of fear remain hidden back in the dark caves. We hear them; we smell them, but we do not disturb them. Creating and maintaining a safe environment represents a pivotal job for administrators and teachers. That must start with designing conversations that bring these topics safely into the light of day.
- *From Fragile to Resilient*: If the real problem with teachers is burnout, not disengagement, then burnout has produced fragility. That means rebuilding resilience is the real challenge. That can only be achieved through a broad-based culture shift. A sound mind requires a sound body, particularly with the new realities and demands of teaching. It also requires educating the heart. The Momentous Institute has built a culture of Social and Emotional Health for both teachers and students. Caregivers need the same kind of care. Some schools are designated as Centers of Excellence. We hope the imagination will inspire some to become Centers of Health.
- *From Reactive to Ready*: Most schools operate out of a deficit mindset. They have been taught to react to problems; they play Whack-a-mole. The deficit starts with children who arrive "not ready to learn." So, what if schools shifted to the upstream strategy, equipping children with early learning and preparing teachers to be emotionally ready to teach?
- *From Isolation to Village*: How can administrators shift from operating as islands of secrecy to developing ecosystems of deep social capital? How can schools invite teachers out of the isolation of their classroom into working as a community of learning? How can teachers create deeper student connections? Lou Cozolino reminds us that, "… close supportive relationships stimulate positive emotions, neuroplasticity, and learning. That's why it pays for teachers to create positive social experiences in the classroom."[6]
- *From Head to WHOLE*: Kintsugi, a Japanese art form, reassembles broken pieces of pottery. The pieces are glued together by golden beads. That's how the artistry of Kintsugi highlights each vessel's

unique pattern of brokenness. The beauty is the pattern and its signature. To accomplish this, a teacher must be free to teach, not driven by tests or bureaucratic efficiencies. Allowing a teacher to be human and touch the life of a student can be a life-changing experience for both. And that life is returned back to the teacher in the fulfillment of their calling. Teachers are naturally gifted to restore the broken pieces in children's lives. Learning is healing.

Every society honors its live conformists and its dead troublemakers.
                        —Marshall McLuhan

Don't Wait for Permission

We have discovered that learning can be a vehicle for healing, and healing opens the door to genuine curiosity. Those who understand that can change the mission, strategy, and tone of education. We hope to speed up that transformation.

We hope to provoke (or drive away) the conformists while releasing the troublemakers to make positive change. Someone told us this book is a treasure trove of new research, stories, ideas, and tools. We hope it is more than that. We want to start new and necessary conversations. Better yet, a mini-revolution. Our philosophy at MindShift is, "Don't wait for permission."

Someone once said, "The best time to plant an oak tree is 25 years ago. The second-best time is today."

We hope our readers will plant their oak tree today.

Wrapping Up

- We know that teaching is dangerous and that the classroom is a battlefield.
- But, we can control our own role, health, happiness, and resilience in the midst of the battle.
- Stress, ego, and fear cripple us.
- But, small steps carry great power to keep us from being crushed. What if, by breathing slowly, sleeping well, eating right, focusing our attention, leading with our curiosity, and having fun, you could avoid the toxicity of teaching?

Practical Reflections

1. Consider the role fear, ego, and stress play in your life. Is there one of the three that drives you most frequently? What helps you (or might help you) to reduce or eliminate them in your daily life?
2. Given the body of research behind the benefits of meditation, would you consider adding meditation or other reflective exercises to your daily life?
3. What do you practice for self-care? Has this book expanded your thinking about other self-care measures?

Notes

1. Traci Taylor, "Almost Half of All Afghanistan and Iraq Veterans Are Disabled." *98.1 The Hawk*, Nov. 8, 2016. 981thehawk.com/almost-half-of-all-afghanistan-and-iraq-war-veterans-are-disabled/
2. *The Christian Science Monitor*, "U.S. Troops Buy Own Gear for Safety, Style in Battle." Mar. 6, 2008. www.csmonitor.com/USA/Military/2008/0306/p03s06-usmi.html
3. Robert M. Pirsig, *Zen and the Art of Motorcycle Maintenance: An Inquiry into Values* (New York: Corgi, 1975).
4. Ibid.
5. Danielle Doby, *I Am Her Tribe* (Kansas City: Andrews McMeel Publishing, 2018).
6. Lou Cozolino, "Nine Things Educators Need to Know About the Brain." Greater Good, Mar. 19, 2013. greatergood.berkeley.edu/article/item/ninethings educatorsneedtoknowaboutthebrain

APPENDIX A
CONTRIBUTORS

I would like to thank our core WHOLE MindShift team. These members participated in our summits, provided ongoing advice, and were invaluable resources. This group of highly diverse experts and educators quickly developed a trusted and safe environment to wrestle with hard issues.

In addition to listing them I have also provided their Clifton Strengthsfinder results. This was an invaluable tool along with our Core-Clarity lens to get to know one another faster and deeper. It allowed us to discover the diverse talents we brought together and to free people to function in areas they naturally enjoy and excel at. We also took time to teach and practice how using this knowledge can improve our engagement, our well-being, and our resilience in life and work.

Lead Contributors

Kevin Baird
MeTEOR Education
kbaird@meteoreducation.com

1. Achiever
2. Learner
3. Positivity
4. Input
5. Activator

Ed Chinn
Cool River Publishing, Inc.
edchinn@me.com

1. Adaptability
2. Intellection
3. Developer
4. Positivity
5. Activator

Marilyn Denison
DLR Group
mdenison@DLRGROUP.com

1. Maximizer
2. Learner
3. Individualization
4. Relator
5. Achiever

John Gasko
UNT Dallas
john.gasko@untdallas.edu

1. Ideation
2. Strategic
3. Learner
4. Intellection
5. Achiever

Michelle Kinder
Michelle Kinder LLC
michelle@michellekinder.com

1. Strategic
2. Achiever
3. Connectedness
4. Intellection
5. Learner

Michael Lagocki
MindShift
michael@michaellagocki.com

1. Strategic
2. Connectedness
3. Ideation
4. Activator
5. Adaptability

Bill Latham
MeTEOR Education
blatham@meteoreducation.com

1. Strategic
2. Ideation
3. Command

4. Communication
5. Belief

Rex Miller
MindShift
rex@gomindshift.com

1. Strategic
2. Learner
3. Achiever
4. Connectedness
5. Relator

Summit Leaders

Dan Beerens
Dan Beerens EducConsulting
danbeerens@gmail.com

1. Connectedness
2. Learner
3. Intellection
4. Ideation
5. Strategic

Remco Bergsma
MiEN Company
rbergsma@miencompany.com

1. Relator
2. Arranger
3. Activator
4. Individualization
5. Ideation

Mara Richards Bim
Cry Havoc Theater
mara@cryhavoctheater.org

1. Strategic
2. Achiever
3. Intellection
4. Ideation
5. Input

Anton Blewett
DLR Group
ablewett@dlrgroup.com

1. Ideation
2. Strategic
3. Learner
4. Activator
5. Command

Karla Crow
Momentous Institute
kcrow@momentousinstitute.org

1. Relator
2. Responsibility
3. Empathy
4. Discipline
5. Developer

Page Dettman
MeTEOR Education
pdettmann@meteoreducation.com

1. Achiever
2. Strategic
3. Learner
4. Ideation
5. Futuristic

Chris Erwin
Carroll Daniel
cerwin@carrolldaniel.com

1. Activator
2. Harmony
3. Arranger
4. Positivity
5. Learner

Rick Ferns
Hamilton Community Schools
rfrens@hamiltonschools.us

1. Adaptability
2. Self-Assurance
3. Arranger
4. Developer
5. Strategic

Lynn Frickey
Researcher, Developer, Education
lfrickey@comcast.net

1. Maximizer
2. Ideation
3. Relator
4. Learner
5. Activator

Mark Hubbard
Paragon Furniture, L.P.
mhubbard@paragoninc.com

1. Achiever
2. Strategic
3. Learner

4. Responsibility
5. Activator

Rachel Hucul
Outdoor Discovery Center
rachel@outdoordiscovery.org

1. Learner
2. Achiever
3. Individualization
4. Discipline
5. Restorative

Michael Justice
MeTEOR Education
mjustice@meteoreducation.com

1. WOO (Winning Others Over)
2. Belief
3. Positivity
4. Communication
5. Includer

Marianna Lavezzo
DLR Group
mlavezzo@dlrgroup.com

1. Strategic
2. Intellection
3. Positivity
4. Futuristic
5. Connectedness

Carla Levenson
DaVinci Schools
clevenson@davincischools.org

1. Learner
2. Responsibility
3. Achiever
4. Arranger
5. Relator

Lisa Miller
MindShift
lmiller1409@yahoo.com

1. Ideation
2. Learner
3. Strategic
4. Input
5. Intellection

Russ Nagel
MeTEOR Education
rnagel@meteoreducation.com

1. Futuristic
2. Learner
3. Input
4. Individualization
5. Achiever

Irene Nigaglioni
In To Architecture
irene@in2arch.com

1. Achiever
2. Learner
3. Maximizer
4. Responsibility
5. Command

John Oberly
Leadership ISD
johno.oberly@gmail.com

1. Strategic
2. Developer
3. Activator
4. Intellection
5. Achiever

Will Richey
Journeyman INK
will@journeymanink.com

1. Adaptability
2. Empathy
3. Positivity
4. Connectedness
5. WOO (Winning Others Over)

Jonathan Stanley
Tarkett
Jonathan.Stanley@tarkett.com

1. Maximizer
2. Individualization
3. Belief
4. Responsibility
5. Arranger

Joe Tankersley
Unique Visions
joe@uniquevisions.net

1. Positivity
2. Context

3. Developer
4. Responsibility
5. Significance

David Tebo
Hamilton Community Schools
dtebo@hamiltonschools.us

1. Futuristic
2. Ideation
3. Strategic
4. Input
5. Relator

David Vroonland
Mesquite Independent
School District
DVroonland@mesquiteisd.org

1. Strategic
2. Futuristic
3. Learner
4. Self-Assurance
5. Activator

Matt Wunder
DaVinci School
mwunder@davincischools.org

1. Futuristic
2. Ideation
3. Connectedness
4. Arranger
5. Belief

Summit Participant or Contributor

Jill Allshouse
MeTEOR Education
jallshouse@meteoreducation.com

1. Futuristic
2. Discipline
3. Intellection
4. Input
5. Positivity

Sean Baum
MeTEOR Education
sbaum@meteoreducation.com

1. Strategic
2. Futuristic
3. Communication
4. Ideation
5. Positivity

Denise Benavides
Independent Education Consultant
denisembenavides1@gmail.com

1. Self-Assurance
2. Maximizer
3. Strategic
4. Input
5. WOO (Winning Others Over)

Jeben Berg
Wild Evidence
mr.jebenberg@gmail.com

1. Strategic
2. Adaptability
3. Ideation
4. Empathy
5. Maximizer

Nancy Board
Global Women 4 Wellbeing
nancy.board@gw4w.org

1. Belief
2. Responsibility
3. Arranger
4. Connectedness
5. Positivity

Tamera Bouman
Be Nice
Tamrajbouman@gmail.com

1. Strategic
2. Intellection
3. Connectedness
4. Belief
5. Developer

Solomon Brezin
seberezin@gmail.com

1. Significance
2. Futuristic
3. Focus
4. Achiever
5. Responsibility

Heather Bryant
Momentous Institute
hbryant@momentousinstitute.org

1. Deliberative
2. Responsibility
3. Input
4. Intellection
5. Learner

Ron Burkhardt
Newmark Knight
rburkhardt@ngkf.com

1. WOO (Winning Others Over)
2. Activator
3. Maximizer
4. Connectedness
5. Communication

Allison Caldwell
Outloud Consulting
allisoncaldwell123@gmail.com

1. Ideation
2. Strategic
3. Learner
4. Intellection
5. Input

Kathy Edwards
Novus Academy
kedwards@thenovusacademy.org

1. Strategic
2. Ideation
3. Command
4. Individualization
5. Self-Assurance

Kemberly Edwards
Mesquite ISD
kedwards@mesquiteisd.org

1. Belief
2. Adaptability
3. Communication
4. Developer
5. Input

Erik Ellefsen
Legacy Christian
epellefsen@gmail.com

1. Maximizer
2. Arranger
3. Context
4. Strategic
5. Self-Assurance

Chris Everett
Engage2Learn
chris@engage2learn.org

1. Futuristic
2. Responsibility
3. Harmony
4. Intellection
5. Restoration

Maureen Fernandez
Momentous Institute
mfernandez@momentousin-
        stitute.org

1. Developer
2. Includer

3. Communication
4. Positivity
5. Adaptability

Tracy Fisher
Coppell ISD
antraasa@gmail.com

1. Maximizer
2. Self-Assurance
3. Strategic
4. Input
5. Futuristic

Candace Fitzpatrick
CoreClarity
cfitzpatrick@coreclarity.net

1. Strategic
2. Learner
3. Connectedness
4. Input
5. WOO (Winning Others Over)

Darius Frasure
Professor, Dallas County
Community College District
dfrasure@assurepress.org

1. Individualization
2. Achiever
3. Command
4. Deliberative
5. Futuristic

Michael Gayles
IGNITE Middle School
mgayles@dallasisd.org

1. Strategic
2. Achiever
3. Futuristic
4. Learner
5. Focus

Sue Ann Highland
MeTEOR Education
shighland@meteoreducation.com

1. Achiever
2. Arranger
3. Individualization
4. Strategic
5. Relator

Brandon Hillman
MeTEOR Education
bhillman@meteoreducation.com

1. Adaptability
2. Strategic
3. Maximizer
4. Communication
5. Achiever

Patrick Horne
MeTEOR Education
phorne@meteoreducation.com

1. Responsibility
2. Achiever
3. Individualization
4. Discipline
5. Learner

Amy Kelton
Shelton School
akelton@shelton.org

1. Input
2. Learner
3. Context
4. Developer
5. Connectedness

M.K. Larson
Hudson Foundation
mkmrhfoundation@aol.com

1. Input
2. Strategic
3. Intellection
4. Achiever
5. Relator

Niki McCuistion
Board Member, CoreClarity
nikimccuistion@gmail.com

1. Input
2. Strategic
3. Learner
4. Intellection
5. Achiever

Jeffrey Moffitt
Outloud Studios
jefferymoffitt14@gmail.com

1. Strategic
2. Ideation
3. Futuristic

4. Learner
5. Activator

Sandy Nobles
The Momentous Institute
snobles@momentousinstitute.org

1. Achiever
2. Arranger
3. Responsibility
4. Self-Assurance
5. Positivity

Alejandro Perez
Journeyman INK
alejandrop@journeymanink.com

1. Strategic
2. Connectedness
3. Relator
4. Learner
5. Positivity

Chelsea Poulin
MeTEOR Education
cpoulin@meteoreducation.com

1. Individualization
2. Achiever
3. Arranger
4. Relator
5. Restorative

Joe Powell
Association of Persons Affected
    by Addiction (APAA)
joep2722@aol.com

1. Maximizer
2. Connectedness
3. Self-Assurance
4. Includer
5. Arranger

Darryl Ratcliff
Ash Studios
daratcliff@gmail.com

1. Input
2. Strategic
3. Learner
4. Arranger
5. Ideation

Delilah Richey
Journeyman Ink LLC
delilah@journeymanink.com

1. Harmony
2. Positivity
3. Connectedness
4. Maximizer
5. Developer

Tina Robertson
The Momentous Institute
trobertson@momentousin-
    stitute.org

1. Connectedness
2. Relator
3. Includer
4. Responsibility
5. Arranger

David Rodriguez
Dr. Gorilla
david@drgorilla.com

1. Connectedness
2. Achiever
3. Input
4. Individualization
5. Relator

David Schmidt
DLR Group
dschmidt@dlrgroup.com

1. Ideation
2. Input
3. Learner
4. Competition
5. Strategic

Tricia Schrotenboer
Black River School
schrotenboert@brpsk12.org

1. Relator
2. Developer
3. Learner
4. Harmony
5. Discipline

Jayne Schutter
ODC Network
jayne@outdoordiscovery.org

1. Includer
2. Responsibility
3. Developer

4. Positivity
5. Belief

John Sumlin
Tarkett
john.sumlin@tarkett.com

1. Achiever
2. WOO (Winning Others Over)
3. Communication
4. Learner
5. Competition

Rhonda Vincent
The Momentous Institute
rvincent@momentousin-
   stitute.org

1. Achiever
2. Learner
3. Harmony
4. Positivity
5. Intellection

Phil Williams
Delos
phil.williams@delos.com

1. Strategic
2. Learner
3. Ideation
4. Input
5. Developer

Scott Wilson
Gratitude & Grace Consulting
wscottwilson@gmail.com

1. Connectedness
2. Positivity
3. Strategic
4. Arranger
5. Restorative

Ellen Wood
Teaching Trust
ewood@teachingtrust.org

1. Learner
2. Input
3. Intellection
4. Responsibility
5. Achiever

Roberto Zuniga
Huckabee
rzuniga@huckabee-inc.com

1. Strategic
2. Ideation
3. Communication
4. Connectedness
5. Learner

APPENDIX B
SLEEP HYGIENE TIPS

In Chapter 14, Rex Miller said he asked his coaching clients some questions on their sleeping habits. Here are some of these questions as part of Rex's more detailed elaboration of proper sleep.

1. **What time do you typically go to bed and wake up?**
   - Don't fool yourself; you need seven to nine hours of sleep.
   - Sleep and time in bed are not the same thing. For example, my sleep efficiency averages 83%. To be at my best, I need 7 hours and 23 minutes of sleep each night. But, that requires sleeping 8–8½ hours of time in bed to achieve my optimum baseline.
   - If you have devices as I do, that measure strain and recovery, you may need more or less sleep time (factors like stress and strain, or catching a power nap can influence the sleep need).

2. **What is your evening routine before bed?**
   Routines vary according to specific people and situations. But alcohol and screen time seem to be prevalent factors for many in those routines. So, we present more detail about managing both in relation to sleep.
   - One beer or glass of wine less than two hours before bed can reduce sleep by 40% and more. Why? The body must work hard to process alcohol. And that extra work raises the body temperature, and that takes us out of the deeper sleep needed for recovery. The best rule says to limit alcoholic intake to two glasses of wine or beer at least two hours before bedtime.
   - The blue light from our screens tells our circadian optic nerve that it is noon. So, we produce cortisol when we should be producing melatonin. It takes about two hours for the hormone shift to take place. When you watch television, play games on your smartphone or pad, or spend time on your computer, your body will not wind down

until two hours later. That's why I've developed a digital sunset; I shift to blue blocker glasses if I am going to be on a screen within two hours before bed. And, I get off all screens one hour before going to bed.

3. **How do you find your optimal sleep rhythm?**

We all have an optimal time to go to bed and to wake up (that's our "chronotype," our optimal cycle for sleep). My optimal bedtime is between 9:15 and 9:45 p.m.. I set my alarm for 6:00 a.m., but I often wake up 20–30 minutes before.

- Experiment by going to bed at different times and discover what works for you. My target was finding the time that I can best go to bed and wake up naturally. I suggest using one of several devices that measure the quality of your sleep (WHOOP, Fitbit, Apple Watch, Oura Ring, Biostrap, etc.). Use one to track your recovery levels until you find that sweet spot.

4. **What gets in the way of prioritizing sleep?**

It may seem crazy to think we now have to be re-educated on something that should be natural. But we do. The biggest challenge is shifting behavior, like enforcing bedtimes or shutting down technology. So, ask yourself what gets in the way. Start with the easy obstacles and work your way up. Lisa and I needed a whole year to adjust and find our compatible rhythms. But once we experienced a few nights in a row of good sleep, we were hooked. We will never go back to our old routines.

5. **How do I learn more?**

These are some of the resources that have helped me the most:

- *Why We Sleep: Unlocking the Power of Sleep and Dreams,* by Matthew Walker.[1]
- *Deep Work: Rules for Focused Success in a Distracted World,* by Cal Newport.[2]
- Sleep monitoring devices, as referenced above.

Note

1. Matthew Walker, *Why We Sleep: Unlocking the Power of Sleep and Dreams* (New York: Simon & Schuster, 2018).
2. Cal Newport, *Deep Work: Rules for Focused Success in a Distracted World* (New York: Grand Central, 2016).

WORKS CITED AND FURTHER READING

ABC News, "Parents Secretly Record Kindergarten Teacher Allegedly Screaming atStudents.abcnews.go.com/US/video/parents-secretly-record-kindergarten-teacher-allegedly-screaming-students-62357460.

Action for Healthy Kids. "Brain Breaks, Instant Recess and Energizers." www.actionforhealthykids.org/tools-for-schools/1252-brain-breaks-instant-recess-and-energizers.

"Activist Critical of Police Undergoes Use of Force Scenarios," FOX 10 Phoenix, youtu.be/yfi3Ndh3n-g.

Allen, Corey. "Stress Contagion Possible amongst Students and Teachers: UBC Study." *UBC News*, Feb. 28, 2017. news.ubc.ca/2016/06/27/ubc-study-finds-stress-contagion-amongst-students-and-teachers/.

Amadeo, Kimberly. "See for Yourself if Obamacare Increased Health Care Costs." *The Balance,* Mar. 12, 2019. www.thebalance.com/causes-of-rising-healthcare-costs-4064878.

Ambrogi, Mark. "Carmel Parents on a Mission to Raise Awareness after Son's Sudden Suicide Shocks Community." *Current Publishing*, Sept. 20, 2018. youarecurrent.com/2018/09/20/carmel-parents-on-a-mission-to-raise-awareness-after-sons-sudden-suicide-shocks-community/.

American Heart Association. "BMI in Children." www.heart.org. www.heart.org/en/healthy-living/healthy-eating/losing-weight/bmi-in-children.

American Institute for Learning and Human Development, "Multiple Intelligences." www.institute4learning.com/resources/articles/multiple-intelligences/.

American Political Science Association. "The President's Physical Fitness Challenge." *Social Policy*: *Essential Primary Sources*, Encyclopedia.com, 2005. www.encyclopedia.com/social-sciences/applied-and-social-sciences-magazines/presidents-physical-fitness-challenge.

"Antifragility." Wikipedia (accessed Dec. 5, 2018). en.wikipedia.org/wiki/Antifragility.

Anwar, Yasmin. "The Sleep-Deprived Brain Can Mistake Friends for Foes." *Berkeley News,* July 27, 2015. news.berkeley.edu/2015/07/14/brain-facial-expressions/.

Anxiety and Depression Association of America, ADAA, "Facts & Statistics." adaa.org/about-adaa/press-room/facts-statistics.

APCH, "Who We Are." A Place Called Home. apch.org/who-we-are/.

Applied Educational Systems, Inc, "What Are 21st Century Skills?" *Digital Curriculum for CTE & Elective Teachers.* www.aeseducation.com/career-readiness/what-are-21st-century-skills.

Ardell, Donald B. *High Level Wellness: An Alternative to Doctors, Drugs, and Disease.* Berkeley, CA: Ten Speed Press, 1986.

Art & Seek, Relics of Violence: Cry Havoc Theater's 'Cenotaph'." youtu.be/s3uehDK51C8.

"Athlete." Wiktionary, en.wiktionary.org/wiki/athlete.

Austin, Nan. "Prescott Junior High PE Program Stars in Documentary." *Modbee,* Modesto Bee, May 27, 2017. www.modbee.com/news/local/education/article153089529.html.

Bahrampour, Tara. "Romanian Orphans Subjected to Deprivation Must Now Deal with Dysfunction." *The Washington Post*, Jan. 30, 2014. www.washingtonpost.com/local/romanian-orphans-subjected-to-deprivation-must-now-deal-with-disfunction/2014/01/30/a9dbea6c-5d13-11e3-be07-006c776266ed_story.html?utm_term=.14f550b47e05.

Bennis, Warren G., and Burt Nanus. *Leaders: The Strategies for Taking Charge.* New York: HarperBusiness, 1997.

BigThoughtChannel, YouTube. youtu.be/OO-um7sSzyM.

"Blended Learning." Wikipedia (accessed June 11, 2019). en.wikipedia.org/wiki/Blended_learning.

"Blue Zone." Wikipedia (accessed May 11, 2019). en.wikipedia.org/wiki/Blue_Zone.

"Blue Zones Challenge for Teachers." *Blue Zones.* www.bluezones.com/services/education/blue-zones-challenge/teachers/.

Brinson, Linda C. "10 Most Stressful Jobs in America." HowStuffWorks, Oct. 12, 2010. money.howstuffworks.com/10-most-stressful-jobs-in-america10.htm.

Brown, David W., et al. "Adverse Childhood Experiences and the Risk of Premature Mortality." *American Journal of Preventive Medicine,* Uvol. 37, no. 5, 2009, pp. 389–396.

Brunson, Krista, et al. "Should Elementary Schools Have Recess? Some Parents Fight for Break." *TODAY,* Jan. 14, 2015. www.today.com/parents/should-elementary-schools-have-recess-some-florida-parents-fight-break-1D80423842.

Buckley, John P., et al. "Standing-Based Office Work Shows Encouraging Signs of Attenuating Post-Prandial Glycaemic Excursion." *Occupational and Environmental Medicine*, vol. 71, no. 2, 2013. www.ncbi.nlm.nih.gov/pubmed/24297826.

Building Green. "We Spend 90% of Our Time Indoors. Says Who?" Building Green blog, Dec. 15, 2016. www.buildinggreen.com/blog/we-spend-90-our-time-indoors-says-who

Bullock Creek Schools, "1/10/18 – Nature Kindergarten Update." www.bcreek.k12.mi.us/?p=15823.

Busteed, Brandon. "Many College Graduates Not Equipped for Workplace Success." Gallup.com, Sept. 23, 2015. www.gallup.com/education/243389/college-graduates-not-equipped-workplace-success.aspx.

Carpenter, Ryan W., and Timothy J. Trull. "Components of Emotion Dysregulation in Borderline Personality Disorder: a Review." *Current Psychiatry Reports*, vol. 15, no. 1, 2013. www.ncbi.nlm.nih.gov/pmc/articles/PMC3973423/.

Casel, "What Is SEL?" casel.org/what-is-sel/.

Centers for Disease Control and Prevention, "About the CDC-Kaiser ACE Study, Violence Prevention, CDC Injury Center." www.cdc.gov/violenceprevention/childabuseandneglect/acestudy/about.html.

Centers for Disease Control and Prevention, "Data and Statistics About ADHD." www.cdc.gov/ncbddd/adhd/data.html.

Centers for Disease Control and Prevention, "Data and Statistics on Children's Mental Health." www.cdc.gov/childrensmentalhealth/data.html.

Centers for Disease Control and Prevention, "Early Childhood Education, Health Impact in 5 Years, Health System Transformation, AD for Policy." www.cdc.gov/policy/hst/hi5.

Centers for Disease Control and Prevention, "Teen Drivers: Get the Facts, Motor Vehicle Safety, CDC Injury Center." www.cdc.gov/motorvehiclesafety/teen_drivers/teendrivers_factsheet.html.

Chetty, Raj, et al. "How Does Your Kindergarten Classroom Affect Your Earnings? Evidence from Project STAR." *NBER*, Sept. 23, 2010. www.nber.org/papers/w16381.

Child Mind Institute. "What's the Tie between Mental Health and Juvenile Justice?" childmind.org/2015-childrens.

Childre, Doc Lew, et al. *Science of the Heart: Exploring the Role of the Heart.* HeartMath Research Center, Boulder Creek, CA: HeartMath Institute, 2001.

Christakis, Nicholas A., and James H. Fowler. "Social Contagion Theory: Examining Dynamic Social Networks and Human Behavior." *Statistics in*

Medicine, vol. 32, 2013, pp, 556–577. www.ncbi.nlm.nih.gov/pmc/articles/
PMC3830455/.

Christian Science Monitor, "U.S. Troops Buy Own Gear for Safety, Style in
Battle." Mar. 6, 2008. www.csmonitor.com/USA/Military/2008/0306/
p03s06-usmi.html.

"Chronotype." Wikipedia (accessed Apr. 3, 2019). en.wikipedia.org/wiki/
Chronotype.

Cohut, Maria. "Serotonin Enhances Learning, Not Just Mood." *Medical News
Today,* June 26, 2018. www.medicalnewstoday.com/articles/322263.php.

College Factual, "University of Illinois at Chicago Loan Debt." Feb. 22, 2019.
www.collegefactual.com/colleges/university-of-illinois-at-chicago/paying-
for-college/student-loan-debt/.

Cowen, Tyler. "Raj Chetty on Teachers, Taxes, Mobility, and How to Answer
Big Questions (Ep. 23)." *Medium*, Conversations with Tyler, Nov. 21, 2018.
medium.com/conversations-with-tyler/raj-chetty-tyler-cowen-inequality-
mobility-american-dream-d5ea7f4742b1.

Cozolino, Lou. "Nine Things Educators Need to Know About the Brain."
Greater Good, Mar. 29, 2013. greatergood.berkeley.edu/article/item/nine_
things_educators_need_to_know_about_the_brain.

Cozolino, Lou. *Attachment-Based Teaching: Creating a Tribal Classroom.* New York:
W.W. Norton Company, 2014.

Darling-Hammond, Linda. "The 74: The Problem with Homework Not Much
Evidence on Whether It Works, Comments," Nov. 8, 2017. www.the74million
.org/article/teacher-turnover-debate-linda-darling-hammond-colleagues-
respond-to-critiques-of-their-latest-study/.

Dea, Allison. "Adolescent Girls and Anxiety." Anxiety and Depression Association of America, ADAA. adaa.org/learn-from-us/from-the-experts/blog-
posts/consumer/adolescent-girls-and-anxiety.

Delisio, Ellen. "Brain Suffers If Sleep Deprived." *Nordic Life Science – the Leading
Nordic Life Science News Service*, Feb. 20, 2015. nordiclifescience.org/brain-
suffers-sleep-deprived/.

Deutschman, Alan. *Change or Die: The Three Keys to Change at Work and in Life.*
New York: HarperCollins, 2008.

Dickler, Jessica. "42% of Americans Have Less than $10,000 Saved and May
Retire Broke." CNBC, Apr. 18, 2018. www.cnbc.com/2018/03/06/42-
percent-of-americans-are-at-risk-of-retiring-broke.html.

Djokovic, Jelena. "Interview – Dr. Jim Loehr: The Psychology of Success."
Sept. 22, 2018. jelenadjokovic.com/dr-jim-loehr-the-psychology-of-
success/.

Doby, Danielle. *I Am Her Tribe.* Kansas: Andrews McMeel Publishing, 2018.

Duffy, Francesca. "Gallup: Student Engagement Drops with Each Grade." *Education Week — Teaching Now*, Jan. 15, 2013. blogs.edweek.org/teachers/teaching_now/2013/01/gallup_student_engagement_drops_with_each_grade.html.

Dunster, Gideon P., et al. "Sleepmore in Seattle: Later School Start Times Are Associated with More Sleep and Better Performance in High School Students." *Science Advances*, vol. 4, no. 12, 2018. advances.sciencemag.org/content/4/12/eaau6200.

"Dysregulation Medical Definition." Merriam-Webster Dictionary. https://www.merriam-webster.com/medical/dysregulation.

Electric Choice, "Schools and School Districts." www.electricchoice.com/business-electricity/schools-and-school-districts/.

"Epigenetics: Fundamentals, History, and Examples." What Is Epigenetics?. www.whatisepigenetics.com/fundamentals/.

"Evidence-Based Design." Wikipedia (accessed June 24, 2019). en.wikipedia.org/wiki/Evidence-based_design.

"Exercise and the Brain: How Fitness Impacts Learning." *Hey Teach!*, Jan. 16, 2018. www.wgu.edu/heyteach/article/exercise-and-brain-how-fitness-impacts-learning1801.html.

Faber, Jay. "Home." Dr Jay Faber, drjayfaber.com/.

Fallows, James M., and Deborah Fallows. *Our Towns: A 100,000-Mile Journey into the Heart of America*. New York: Vintage Books, 2019.

Fensterwald, John. "Half of New Teachers Quit Profession in 5 Years? Not True, New Study Says." *EdSource*, July 16, 2015. edsource.org/2015/half-of-new-teachers-quit-profession-in-5-years-not-true-new-study-says/83054.

Frasure, Darius. "'Partner in Crime' Featuring Darius Frasure." YouTube. youtu.be/VfiAPfy4lpc.

French, Raechel. "Transitions 18 Conference." Innovative Learning Environments & Teacher Change, University of Melbourne, 2018. www.iletc.com.au/melbourne-event/video-transitions18-melbourne/.

"Froebel Gifts." Wikipedia (accessed Apr. 13, 2019). en.wikipedia.org/wiki/Froebel_gifts.

Galloway, Scott. *The Four: The Hidden DNA of Amazon, Apple, Facebook, and Google*. New York: Corgi Books, 2018.

Gallup, Inc. "Gallup Daily: U.S. Employee Engagement." news.gallup.com/poll/180404/gallup-daily-employee-engagement.aspx.

Gallup, Inc. "Make a Difference. Show Students You Care.", Oct. 9, 2014. news.gallup.com/businessjournal/178118/difference-show-students-care.aspx.

Giles, Jim. "Internet Encyclopaedias Go Head to Head." *Nature News*, vol. 438, no. 7070, 2005, pp. 900–901. www.nature.com/articles/438900a.

GoNoodle, "Movement and Mindfulness for Kids." www.gonoodle.com/.

Gorski, Deb. "Tiered Instruction and Intervention in a Response-to-Intervention Model." RTI Action Network. www.rtinetwork.org/essential/tieredinstruction/tiered-instruction-and-intervention-rti-model.

"Got Your ACE Score?" *ACEs Too High*, Feb. 27, 2019. acestoohigh.com/got-your-ace-score/.

Greenberg, M.T., et al. "Teacher Stress and Health." *RWJF*, Jan. 31, 2018. www.rwjf.org/en/library/research/2016/07/teacher-stress-and-health.html.

Gross, Terry. "A Lesson in How Teachers Became 'Resented and Idealized'." NPR, Sept. 2, 2014. www.npr.org/templates/transcript/transcript.php?storyId=345104706.

Hagel, John, and John Seely Brown. *The Power of Pull: How Small Moves, Smartly Made, Can Set Big Things in Motion.* New York: Basic Books, 2012.

Harris, Nadine Burke. *The Deepest Well: Healing the Long-Term Effects of Childhood Adversity.* Boston: Houghton Mifflin Harcourt, 2018.

Harvard Health, "Understanding the Stress Response." May 1, 2018. www.health.harvard.edu/staying-healthy/understanding-the-stress-response.

Heckman, James J. "13% ROI Research Toolkit." *The Heckman Equation*, May 10, 2019. heckmanequation.org/resource/13-roi-toolbox.

Heckman, James J. "Schools, Skills, and Synapses." *Economic Inquiry*, vol. 46, no. 3, 2008, pp. 289–324. www.ncbi.nlm.nih.gov/pmc/articles/PMC2812935/.

Heckman, James J. "Invest in Early Childhood Development: Reduce Deficits, Strengthen the Economy." *The Heckman Equation*, Feb. 15, 2017. heckmanequation.org/resource/invest-in-early-childhood-development-reduce-deficits-strengthen-the-economy/.

Henry J. Kaiser Family Foundation "Generation M2: Media in the Lives of 8- to 18-Year-Olds.". www.kff.org/other/event/generation-m2-media-in-the-lives-of/.

Hess, Abigail. "Here's How Much the Average Student Loan Borrower Owes When They Graduate." CNBC, Feb. 15, 2018. www.cnbc.com/2018/02/15/heres-how-much-the-average-student-loan-borrower-owes-when-they-graduate.html.

"Historical Perspective on Hand Hygiene in Health Care." *WHO Guidelines on Hand Hygiene in Health Care: First Global Patient Safety Challenge Clean Care Is Safer Care*, Jan. 1, 1970. www.ncbi.nlm.nih.gov/books/NBK144018/.

"History of Education in the United States." Wikipedia (accessed May 19, 2019). en.wikipedia.org/wiki/History_of_education_in_the_United_States.

Hobbs, Tawnell D. "Down with Homework, Say U.S. School Districts." *The Wall Street Journal,* Dec.12, 2018. www.wsj.com/articles/no-homework-its-the-new-thing-in-u-s-schools-11544610600.

"Home." First Generation Foundation. www.firstgenerationfoundation.org/.

Horton, Melissa. "What Rate of Return Should I Expect on My 401(k)?" Investopedia, July 6, 2019. www.investopedia.com/ask/answers/041015/what-rate-return-should-i-expect-my-401k.asp.

Hughes, Timothy. "Commentary: Army Strength Begins with Physical Fitness." May 9, 2013. www.army.mil/article/102969/commentary_army_strength_begins_with_physical_fitness.

"Inflation Rate for Electricity between 2008–2019." *Electricity Price History from 2008 through 2019.* www.in2013dollars.com/Electricity/price-inflation/2008-to-2019?amount=100.

Institute for Research on Poverty, YouTube. youtu.be/n-2okB6W4r8.

International WELL Building Institute. "About International WELL Building Institute." www.wellcertified.com/about-iwbi/.

Inter-Pathé, YouTube. www.youtube.com/watch?v=u9L_nDorXbw.

Jaschik, Scott. "Dozens Indicted in Alleged Massive Case of Admissions Fraud." *Inside Higher Ed.,* Mar. 13, 2019. www.insidehighered.com/admissions/article/2019/03/13/dozens-indicted-alleged-massive-case-admissions-fraud.

Javanbakht, Arash, and Linda Saab. "What Happens in the Brain When We Feel Fear." Smithsonian Institution, Oct. 27, 2017. www.smithsonianmag.com/science-nature/what-happens-brain-feel-fear-180966992/.

"Jeff Jernigan, Ph.D., LPC, BCPPC, Director." Stanton Chase. www.stantonchase.com/consultant/jeff-jernigan-phd-lpc-bcppc/.

Jernigan, Finith E. *Big BIM, Little Bim: the Practical Approach to Building Information Modeling: Integrated Practice Done the Right Way!* Limerick: 4Site Press, 2008.

JFK Library, "The Federal Government Takes on Physical Fitness." www.jfklibrary.org/learn/about-jfk/jfk-in-history/physical-fitness.

Joelson, Richard. "Locus of Control." *Psychology Today,* Aug. 2, 2017. www.psychologytoday.com/us/blog/moments-matter/201708/locus-control.

Joshi, Sumedha M. "The Sick Building Syndrome." *Indian Journal of Occupational and Environmental Medicine,* Aug. 2008. www.ncbi.nlm.nih.gov/pmc/articles/PMC2796751/.

Kahn, William. "Psychological Conditions of Personal Engagement and Disengagement at Work." *Academy of Management Journal,* vol. 33, no. 4, 1990. journals.aom.org/doi/abs/10.5465/256287.

Kamal, Rabah, and Cynthia Cox. "How Has U.S. Spending on Healthcare Changed over Time?" Peterson-Kaiser Health System Tracker, Dec. 10, 2018.

www.healthsystemtracker.org/chart-collection/u-s-spending-healthcare-changed-time/#item-health-services-spending-growth-slowed-a-bit-in-recent-quarters_2018.

Karasek, Robert, and Theorell Töres. *Healthy Work: Stress, Productivity, and the Reconstruction of Working Life*. New York: Basic Books, 2010.

Kehoe, Jeff. "What Leaders Can Learn from Jazz." *Harvard Business Review*, Mar. 30, 2015. hbr.org/2012/08/what-leaders-can-learn-from-ja.

Kenney, Caitlin. "What's a Good Kindergarten Teacher Worth?" *NPR,* July 28, 2010. www.npr.org/sections/money/2010/07/28/128819707/the-kindergarten-experiment.

"Kintsugi." Wikipedia (accessed Feb. 18, 2019). en.wikipedia.org/wiki/Kintsugi.

Kolker, Robert. "Cheating Upwards." Sept. 16, 2012. nymag.com/news/features/cheating-2012-9/.

"Kostoryz Elementary." *SchoolDigger*, 2019. www.schooldigger.com/go/TX/schools/1527001065/school.aspx.

Kotler, Steven. "The Method to Their Madness: Flow and the Final Four." *Forbes*, Apr. 4, 2014. www.forbes.com/sites/stevenkotler/2014/04/01/the-method-to-their-madness-the-secret-science-of-the-final-four/#461b37ee7d5a.

Kuhn, John. "Exhaustion of the American Teacher." *The Educators Room*, Dec. 26, 2013. theeducatorsroom.com/the-exhaustion-of-the-american-teacher/.

Kuhn, Thomas S., and Ian Hacking. *The Structure of Scientific Revolution*. Chicago: University of Chicago Press, 2012.

Lakna. "Difference Between Hormones and Neurotransmitters: Definition, Characteristics, Classification, Function." pediaa.com/difference-between-hormones-and-neurotransmitters/.

Lander, Jessica. "Secondary Traumatic Stress for Educators: Understanding and Mitigating the Effects." *KQED,* Oct. 8. 2018. www.kqed.org/mindshift/52281/secondary-traumatic-stress-for-educators-understanding-and-mitigating-the-effects?utm_medium=Email&utm_source=ExactTarget&utm_campaign=20181014MindshiftNewsletterSubscribers&mc_key=00Qi000001frtn9EAA.

LaVito, Angelica. "About 10 Percent of US Children Are Diagnosed with ADHD." CNBC, Aug. 31, 2018. www.cnbc.com/2018/08/31/adhd-diagnosed-in-about-10-percent-of-us-children-study-finds.html.

Lee, Ingrid Fetell. *Joyful: The Surprising Power Of Ordinary Things To Create Extraordinary Happiness*. Boston: Little Brown Spark, 2020.

Lee, Kevan. "The Science of Motivation: Your Brain on Dopamine." I Done-This Blog, Apr. 9. 2019. blog.idonethis.com/the-science-of-motivation-your-brain-on-dopamine/.

Lehrer, Jonah. "The Mirror Neuron Revolution: Explaining What Makes Humans Social." *Scientific American*, July 1, 2008. www.scientificamerican. com/article/the-mirror-neuron-revolut/.

Leshin-Harwood, Dyane. "Scanning: FMR's Sleep Deprived v. Post Partum Depression." *Brainzaps*, Aug. 2, 2008. brainzaps.wordpress.com/2008/08/02/ scanning-fmrs-sleep-deprived-v-post-partum-depression/.

Long, Cindy. "When Physical Education Is Cut, Who Picks Up the Slack?" *NEA Today*, Mar. 28, 2017. neatoday.org/2017/03/28/cuts-to-physical-education/.

Marino, Vivian. "Paul Scialla." *The New York Times*, Aug. 19, 2014. www.nytimes. com/2014/08/20/realestate/commercial/thirty-minute-interview-paul-scialla.html.

Marks, Tracy. "ADHD, Not Just for Kids." markspsychiatry.com/adhd-not-just-for-kids/.

"Martin Seligman." Wikipedia (accessed Mar. 27, 2019). en.wikipedia.org/wiki/Martin_Seligman.

Matos, Alejandra. "1 in 4 U.S. Teachers Are Chronically Absent, Missing More than 10 Days of School." *The Washington Post*, Oct. 26, 2016. www. washingtonpost.com/local/education/1-in-4-us-teachers-are-chronically-absent-missing-more-than-10-days-of-school/2016/10/26/2869925e-9186-11e6-a6a3-d50061aa9fae_story.html?utm_term=.83911df73c41.

McCarty, Rollin. "Science of the Heart: Exploring the Role of the Heart in Human Performance," vol. 2. *HeartMath Institute*, 2015. www.heartmath .org/resources/downloads/science-of-the-heart/.

McCoy, Mary Kate. "Schools Cut Back Physical Education as Childhood Obesity Remains High." Wisconsin Public Radio, Mar. 1, 2018. www.wpr .org/schools-cut-back-physical-education-childhood-obesity-remains-high.

McCray, Vanessa. "As APS Approaches Key Decisions, Superintendent Gets Mid-Year Review." *AJC, The Atlanta Journal-Constitution*, Jan. 16, 2019. www .ajc.com/news/local-education/atlanta-school-board-chairman-reports-superintendent-mid-year-review/BkHpgSjiPGle27e374yHbL/.

McKay, Brett, and Kate McKay. "The History of the Army's PT Test." *The Art of Manliness*, Nov. 29, 2018. www.artofmanliness.com/articles/history-of-the-armys-pt-test/.

Miller, Rex. M. *Millennium Matrix: Reclaiming the Past, Reframing the Future of the Church*. San Francisco: Jossey-Bass, 2004.

Miller, Rex. M. *The Commercial Real Estate Revolution: Nine Transforming Keys to Lowering Costs, Cutting Waste, and Driving Change in a Broken Industry*. Hoboken, NJ: Wiley, 2009.

Miller, Rex M., Mabel Casey, and Mark Konchar. *Change Your Space, Change Your Culture: How Engaging Workspaces Lead to Transformation and Growth.* Hoboken, NJ: Wiley, 2014.

Miller, Rex, M., et al. *Humanizing the Education Machine: How to Create Schools That Turn Disengaged Kids into Inspired Learners.* Hoboken, NJ: John Wiley & Sons, Inc., 2017.

Miller, Rex, M., P. Williams, and M. O'Neill. *The Healthy Workplace Nudge: How Healthy People, Cultures, and Buildings Lead to High Performance.* Hoboken, NJ: John Wiley & Sons, Inc., 2018.

Mochari, Ilan. "Why Half of the S&P 500 Companies Will Be Replaced in the Next Decade." Mar. 23, 2016. www.inc.com/ilan-mochari/innosight-sp-500-new-companies.html.

Momentous School, "Donate." momentousinstitute.org/blog/a-peek-inside-momentous-school.

Muldavin, Scott R. *Value beyond Cost Savings: How to Underwrite Sustainable Properties.* San Rafael, CA: Muldavin Company, 2010.

Najimi, Arash, et al. "Causes of Job Stress in Nurses: A Cross-Sectional Study." *Iranian Journal of Nursing and Midwifery Research*, vol. 17, no. 4, 2012, pp. 301–305. www.ncbi.nlm.nih.gov/pmc/articles/PMC3702151/.

Naperville 203. "Curriculum & Instruction/Physical Education Overview K-12." *Physical Education Overview K-12.* www.naperville203.org/Page/4193.

National Renewable Energy Lab. "Myths About Energy in Schools." NREL, Feb. 2002. www.nrel.gov/docs/fy02osti/31607.pdf.

National Sleep Foundation. "School Start Time & Sleep." www.sleepfoundation.org/articles/school-start-time-and-sleep.

NCES. "Digest of Education Statistics, 2012." nces.ed.gov/programs/digest/d12/tables/dt12_098.asp.

Nerurkar, Aditi. "When Physicians Counsel About Stress: Results of a National Study." *JAMA Internal Medicine*, vol. 173, no. 1, 2013, pp. 76–77. jamanetwork.com/journals/jamainternalmedicine/fullarticle/1392494.

New Buildings Institute, "2019 Zero Energy Schools Watchlist." newbuildings.org/resource/2019-zero-energy-schools-watchlist/.

News, ABC Action. "Parents Accuse Teacher of Bullying." YouTube. www.youtube.com/watch?v=V2uMkMA5UZY.

"Next Jump." YouTube. www.youtube.com/channel/UClxt05oUbYNWQTfhDw5G7qA.

NHTSA, National Highway Traffic Safety Administration. "Traffic Safety Facts 2009 Data." crashstats.nhtsa.dot.gov/Api/Public/ViewPublication/811387.

North Jersey. "Lessons Learned from Columbine, Virginia Tech and Sandy Hook." www.northjersey.com/videos/news/2018/03/02/lessons-learned-columbine-virginia-tech-and-sandy-hook/106975044/.

"No Time for Recess, No Need for Nap." FairTest, fairtest.org/no-time-recess-no-need-nap.

O'Brien, Amanda. "The Power of Walking." *Central Athlete blog.* www.centralathlete.com/blog/the-power-of-walking-1.

O'Connor, Anahad. "The Claim: Heart Attacks Are More Common on Mondays." *The New York Times*, Mar. 14, 2006. www.nytimes.com/2006/03/14/health/14real.html.

The Motivation Factor, Aug. 22, 2017. motivationmovie.com/.

"Overtraining." Wikipedia (accessed Apr. 26, 2019). en.wikipedia.org/wiki/Overtraining.

Pearl, Dr. Robert. "Shame, Scandal Plague Healthcare Providers in 2018." *Forbes,* Dec. 11, 2018. www.forbes.com/sites/robertpearl/2018/12/10/shame-scandal/#247fd55b6807.

Penninx, Brenda, et al. "Effects of Social Support and Personal Coping Resources on Mortality in Older Age: The Longitudinal Aging Study Amsterdam." *American Journal of Epidemiology,* vol. 46, no. 6, 1997, pp. 510–519.

"Perceived Stress Scale." Wikipedia (accessed Jan. 31, 2019). en.wikipedia.org/wiki/Perceived_Stress_Scale.

Pettibone, Jeffrey, et al. "The Role of Dopamine in Motivation and Learning." *NeuroscienceNews*, Nov. 24, 2015. neurosciencenews.com/dopamine-learning-reward-3157/.

Pink, Daniel H. *Drive.* New York: Penguin, 2009.

Pirsig, Robert M. *Zen and the Art of Motorcycle Maintenance: An Inquiry into Values.* New York: Corgi, 1975.

"Prefrontal Cortex." Wikipedia (accessed Mar. 14, 2019). en.wikipedia.org/wiki/Prefrontal_cortex.

Pressman, Sarah D., et al. "Is the Emotion-Health Connection a 'First-World Problem'?" *Psychological Science*, vol. 24, no. 4, 2013. www.ncbi.nlm.nih.gov/pubmed/23443305.

Provasnik, Stephen, and Scott Dorfman. "Findings from the Condition of Education 2005: Mobility in the Teacher Workforce." *The Condition of Education – Closer Look 2005 – Mobility in the Teacher Workforce – How Many New Teachers Are Hired in a Year?*, Aug. 18, 2005. nces.ed.gov/programs/coe/analysis/2005-sa02.asp (accessed 3 Nov. 2018).

Public Intelligence. "(U//FOUO) Massachusetts Fusion Center School Shootings Analysis 1992–2012," Sept. 27, 2013. publicintelligence.net/ma-school-shootings/.

Publicolor. "About Publicolor, New York." www.publicolor.org/about.

Publicolor. "Results." www.publicolor.org/statistics.

Putnam, Robert D. *Bowling Alone: The Collapse and Revival of American Community.* New York: Simon & Schuster, 2000.

Putnam, Robert D. *Our Kids: The American Dream in Crisis.* New York: Simon & Schuster, 2016.

Rado, Diane, and Marissa Page. "With Daily Physical Education No Longer the Law, Schools Revising PE Plans." *Chicago Tribune, May* 23, 2019. www.chicagotribune.com/news/breaking/ct-met-illinois-physical-education-20171215-story.html.

Rahal, Anu, et al. "Oxidative Stress, Prooxidants, and Antioxidants: the Interplay." *BioMed Research International*, online. www.ncbi.nlm.nih.gov/pmc/articles/PMC3920909/.

Raz, Guy. "Why Would You Share a Secret with a Stranger?" NPR, Jan. 23, 2015. www.npr.org/templates/transcript/transcript.php?storyId=377506467.

"Re:Work – The Five Keys to a Successful Google Team." Google. rework.withgoogle.com/blog/five-keys-to-a-successful-google-team/.

Reed, Ryan. "John Oliver: Olivia Jade Jokes Are Fair Game After 'Weird' College Admissions Scandal." *Rolling Stone,* Mar. 18, 2019. www.rollingstone.com/tv/tv-news/john-oliver-lori-loughlin-college-admissions-scandal-809511/.

Reeves, Richard V., and Eleanor Krause. "Raj Chetty in 14 Charts: Big Findings on Opportunity and Mobility We Should All Know." Brookings blog, Jan. 11, 2018. www.brookings.edu/blog/social-mobility-memos/2018/01/11/raj-chetty-in-14-charts-big-findings-on-opportunity-and-mobility-we-should-know/.

"Regenerative Design." Wikipedia (accessed Apr. 17, 2019). en.wikipedia.org/wiki/Regenerative_design.

Reilly, Katie. "Is Recess Important for Kids? Here's What the Research Says." *Time*, Oct. 23, 2017. time.com/4982061/recess-benefits-research-debate/.

Reilly, Katie. "Exactly How Teachers Came to Be So Underpaid in America." *Time*, Sept. 13, 2018. time.com/longform/teaching-in-america/.

Robinson, Ken. "Do Schools Kill Creativity?" TED, 2006. www.ted.com/talks/ken_robinson_says_schools_kill_creativity?language=en.

Rose, Andy. "Teacher Describes How He Stopped Shooting." *CNN,* Feb. 24, 2010. www.cnn.com/2010/CRIME/02/24/colorado.school.shooting.benke/index.html.

Rossen, Jake. "This 1960s High School Gym Class Would Ruin You." *Mental Floss*, Apr. 13, 2015. mentalfloss.com/article/62991/1960s-high-school-gym-class-would-ruin-you.

Samuel, Leah. "US Life Expectancy Shortens for First Time in Decades." *STAT*, Dec. 8, 2016. www.statnews.com/2016/12/08/life-expectancy-shorten-american/.

Santos, Danny F. "15 Famous Ideas That Were Invented in Dreams." Theclever, Apr. 25, 2017. www.theclever.com/15-famous-ideas-that-were-invented-in-dreams/.

Schaal, Dennis, et al. "Airbnb's Latest Investment Values It as Much as Hilton and Hyatt Combined." *Skift*, Sept. 23, 2016. skift.com/2016/09/23/airbnbs-latest-investment-values-it-as-much-as-hilton-and-hyatt-combined/.

Schuler, Timothy. "Green Building & Design: A Chat with Rachel Gutter." U.S. Green Building Council, June 28, 2013. www.usgbc.org/articles/green-building-design-chat-rachel-gutter.

Scott, Andrew. YouTube. www.youtube.com/watch?v=a3ONM_6fkRs.

Shah, Parth, et al. "The 'Swiss Army Knife' of Health: A Good Night's Sleep." NPR, Nov. 14, 2017. www.npr.org/2017/11/13/563831137/the-swiss-army-knife-of-health-a-good-nights-sleep.

Shrestha, Alice, et al. "Protective Effects of Psychological Strengths Against Psychiatric Disorders Among Soldiers." *Military Medicine*, vol. 183, no. 1, 2018, pp. 386–395. academic.oup.com/milmed/article/183/suppl_1/386/4959978.

"Sick Building Syndrome." Wikipedia (accessed June 10, 2019). en.wikipedia.org/wiki/Sick_building_syndrome.

"Sleep-Deprived Brains Alternate between Normal Activity and 'Power Failure'.". www.labspaces.net/view_news_comments.php?newsID=5988.

Spotlights. "The Condition of Education, 2013," Spotlights – The Status of Rural Education – Indicator, May, 2013. nces.ed.gov/programs/coe/indicator_tla.asp.

Sraders, Anne. "What Is Middle Class, Really? Income and Range in 2019." *TheStreet,* Jan. 21, 2019. www.thestreet.com/personal-finance/what-is-middle-class-14833259.

Starromand, Richard. "About *Delos®*." delos.com/company/about.

"Start School Later Movement." Wikipedia (accessed May 29, 2019). en.wikipedia.org/wiki/Start_School_Later_movement.

Stauffer, Rainesford. "The Business of Standardized Testing." Huffingon Post, Apr. 28, 2017. www.huffpost.com/entry/the-business-of-standardi_b_9785988.

"Stephen Ritz, Founder of the Green Bronx Machine: His Story." YouTube/www.youtube.com/watch?v=9Dt0odlFzmQ.

Stevens, Jane Ellen. "Nearly 35 Million U.S. Children Have Experienced One or More Types of Childhood Trauma." *ACEs Too High*. acestoohigh. com/2013/05/13/nearly-35-million-u-s-children-have-experienced-one-or-more-types-of-childhood-trauma/.

Stewart, Nicole. "What Is Oral Fixation?" YouTube. youtu.be/QE5P14Xv86I.

Stibich, Mark. "Top 10 Causes of Death for Ages 15 to 24." Verywell Health (accessed June 18, 2019). www.verywellhealth.com/top-causes-of-death-for-ages-15-24-2223960.

Storrs, Carina. "Is Life Expectancy Reduced by a Traumatic Childhood?" *Scientific American*, Oct. 7, 2009. www.scientificamerican.com/article/childhood-adverse-event-life-expectancy-abuse-mortality/.

Stoughton, Seth. "How Police Training Contributes to Avoidable Deaths." *The Atlantic*, Dec. 12, 2014. www.theatlantic.com/national/archive/2014/12/police-gun-shooting-training-ferguson/383681/.

Strauss, Valerie. "Why It's a Big Problem That so Many Teachers Quit — and What to Do about It." *The Washington Post*, Nov. 27, 2017. www. washingtonpost.com/news/answer-sheet/wp/2017/11/27/why-its-a-big-problem-that-so-many-teachers-quit-and-what-to-do-about-it/?noredirect=on&utm_term=.f329eecb76c8. Accessed 3 Nov. 2018.

Sunstein, Cass R., and Richard H. Thaler. *Nudge: Improving Decisions about Health, Wealth and Happiness*. New York: Penguin, 2012.

Taylor, Traci. "Almost Half of All Afghanistan and Iraq Veterans Are Disabled." *98.1 The Hawk*, Nov. 8, 2016. 981thehawk.com/almost-half-of-all-afghanistan-and-iraq-war-veterans-are-disabled/.

"The Motivation Factor — Physical Education in Schools in 1960's - #JFKChallenge." YouTube. youtu.be/fISgKl8dB3M.

"The NCES Fast Facts Tool Provides Quick Answers to Many Education Questions (National Center for Education Statistics)." nces.ed.gov/fastfacts/display.asp?id=94.

"The Social Wolf." *Living with Wolves*. www.livingwithwolves.org/about-wolves/social-wolf/.

"Theory of Multiple Intelligences." Wikipedia (accessed June 8, 2019). en .wikipedia.org/wiki/Theory_of_multiple_intelligences.

Todd, Sarah, "The Astonishing Power of Stoneman Douglas Students, in Their Own Words." *Quartz*, Feb. 21, 2018. qz.com/1212712/florida-shooting-stoneman-douglas-student-quotes-after-the-high-school-attack/.

Tran, Khai. "Why Holland Michigan Is Becoming a Hotbed for Small Businesses." *Forbes*, May 7, 2019. www.forbes.com/sites/khaitran/2019/05/07/why-holland-michigan-is-becoming-a-hotbed-for-small-businesses/#654147305a72.

UChicago Consortium on School Research. "Organizing Schools for Improvement." consortium.uchicago.edu/publications/organizing-schools-improvement-lessons-chicago.

UChicago Consortium on School Research. "The Essential Supports for School Improvement." consortium.uchicago.edu/publications/essential-supports-school-improvement.

UNT Dallas. "The Innovative Dr. Gasko Does It Again with Launch of Dallas Teachers Speak." *News*, Oct. 17, 2018. news.untdallas.edu/innovative-dr-gasko-does-it-again-launch-dallas-teachers-speak.

UNT Dallas. YouTube. www.youtube.com/watch?v=XqG07z4yflQ.

Ulrich, Roger S., et al. "A Review of the Research Literature on Evidence-Based Healthcare Design." *HERD: Health Environments Research & Design Journal*, vol. 1, no. 3, 2008, pp. 61–125.

U.S. Green Building Council, "Number of LEED-Certified Schools Hits 2,000." www.usgbc.org/articles/number-leedcertified-schools-hits-2000.

Van der Kolk, Bessel. *The Body Keeps the Score: Brain, Mind and Body in the Healing of Trauma*. New York: Penguin Books, 2015.

VanderWeele, Tyler J. "Sensitivity Analysis for Contagion Effects in Social Networks." *Sociological Methods & Research,* vol, 40, no. 2, 2011, pp.240–255. www.ncbi.nlm.nih.gov/pmc/articles/PMC4288024/.

Vedantan, Shankar. "Too Little, Too Much: How Poverty and Wealth Affect Our Minds." NPR, Oct. 4, 2018. www.npr.org/templates/transcript/transcript.php?storyId=651468312.

Vo, Lam Thuy. "How Much Does the Government Spend to Send a Kid to Public School?" NPR, June 21, 2012. www.npr.org/sections/money/2012/06/21/155515613/how-much-does-the-government-spend-to-send-a-kid-to-school.

Wagner, James. "Justin Verlander: The Astros' Ace and Sleep Guru." *New York Times*, July 9. 2019. www-nytimes-com.cdn.ampproject.org/c/s/www.nytimes.com/2019/07/09/sports/baseball/justin-verlander-all-star-sleep.amp.html.

Wagner, Joel. "Teacher Burnout: A Sad Story." *So You Want to Teach?*, June 30. 2010. www.soyouwanttoteach.com/teacher-burnout-a-sad-story/.

Wahlstrom, Kyla. "Later Start Time for Teens Improves Grades, Mood, and Safety." www.kappanonline.org/later-start-time-for-teens/.

Walker, Matthew P. *Why We Sleep: Unlocking the Power of Sleep and Dreams*. New York: Simon & Schuster, 2018.

Walker, Tim. "How Many Teachers Are Highly-Stressed? Maybe More Than People Think." *NEA Today*, July 30, 2018. neatoday.org/2018/05/11/study-high-teacher-stress-levels/.

Wallman, Brittany. "What's Being Done to Stop Another School Shooting?" *Sun Sentinel*, Dec. 6, 2018. www.sun-sentinel.com/local/broward/parkland/florida-school-shooting/fl-ne-viz-school-safety-20181206-story.html.

Walsh, Fergus. "How Lack of Sleep Affects the Brain." BBC News, June 26, 2017. www.bbc.com/news/health-40036667.

Wargo, Eric. "How Many Seconds to a First Impression?" Association for Psychological Science. www.psychologicalscience.org/observer/how-many-seconds-to-a-first-impression.

Waxman, Olivia B. "Adam Walsh Murder: The Missing Child Who Changed America." *Time*, Aug. 10, 2016. time.com/4437205/adam-walsh-murder/.

Weigel, Margaret. "Head Start Impact: Department of Health and Human Services Report." *Journalist's Resource*, Aug. 11, 2011. journalistsresource.org/studies/society/education/head-start-study/.

Weller, Chris. "Schools around the US Are Finally Pushing Back Their Start Times – and It's Working." *Business Insider*, Sept. 4, 2017. www.businessinsider.com/school-start-times-are-finally-getting-pushed-back-2017-8.

"What Is an Amygdala Hijack?" *GoStrengths!*. gostrengths.com/what-is-an-amygdala-hijack/.

"Wicked Problem." Wikipedia (accessed Nov. 3, 2018). en.wikipedia.org/wiki/Wicked_problem.

Williams, Jasmine K. "Publicolor Teaches Students the Power of Hue." *New York Amsterdam News: The New Black View*, July 11, 2013. amsterdamnews.com/news/2013/jul/11/publicolor-teaches-students-power-hue/.

Woodruff, Emily. "Study: Deep Sleep Is Required to 'Clean' the Brain, Prevent Alzheimer's." *Being Patient*, Feb. 27, 2019. www.beingpatient.com/deep-sleep-brain/.

World Vision. "Our Work." www.worldvision.org/our-work.

"Wraparound Basics or What Is Wraparound: An Introduction." nwi.pdx.edu/wraparound-basics/.

Wu, Katherine. "Love, Actually: The Science behind Lust, Attraction, and Companionship." *Science in the News*, Feb. 14, 2017. sitn.hms.harvard.edu/flash/2017/love-actually-science-behind-lust-attraction-companionship/.

Zengul, Ferhat D., and Stephen J. O'Connor. "A Review of Evidence Based Design in Healthcare from Resource-Based Perspective – Semantic Scholar." *Journal of Management Policy and Practice*, vol. 14, no. 2, 2013, pp. 19–36.

A GUIDE FOR ADMINISTRATORS, TEACHERS, PARENTS, AND COMMUNITY LEADERS

REX MILLER
BILL LATHAM · BRIAN CAHILL

humanizing
— THE —
EDUCATION
MACHINE

HOW TO CREATE SCHOOLS THAT TURN
DISENGAGED KIDS INTO
INSPIRED LEARNERS

WILEY

INDEX

A

Accountability
    definition of, 233
    how an ownership culture
        works in a culture
        of, 232–233
    No Child Left Behind Schools
        test mandate for, 188–189
    replacing it with a sense of
        ownership, 233
ACEs (adverse childhood
    experiences)
    DaVerse Lounge helping to
        rewrite stories of, 73–76
    emotional dysregulation as
        result of, 143
    Jamel and Jamie's story as
        children with, 142–143, 144
    long-term impact of, 38–39
Addiction, 96
ADHD
    how adequate sleep cuts down
        on diagnosis of, 173
    Standing desks study findings
        on performance by students
        with, 184–187
    See also Learning disabilities
Adolescents. See Students

Ahab and white whale, 16
Airbnb, 228
*Alice's Adventures in
    Wonderland, 105*
Amazon, 228
Amen Clinics, 44, 143
Amen, Daniel, 44
American Dream, 88–89, 155
Amygdala hijack
    description of an, 26–28, 245
    techniques to prevent and
        recover from, 31
Anterior cingulate, 45
Aphorisms, 46
Apple, 77, 233
Apple Genius bar model, 171
Ardell Wellness Stress Test, 109
Ariely, Daniel, 217
Asperger's Syndrome, 43–44
Atlanta Public Schools
    (APS), 73, 77
Attention
    benefits of 90/20 work
        pattern for, 188
    benefits of taking physical breaks
        to improve, 187–189
    James's story on obesity
        and, 182–183

Attention *(continued)*
  Little Hawks preschool
    (Holland, Michigan), 190
  N.E.A.T. (Non-Exercise
    Activity Thermogenesis) to
    improve, 189–190, 199
  pay attention to what you
    pay, 245–246
  Sally's story on, 186
Austin ISD, 73
Autism spectrum, 43
Autonomic nervous system (ANA)
  description of the, 25
  heart rate variability (HRV)
    measurement of the, 96–99,
    100, 147–149
  teachers are also subject to
    their, 108

B
Backer, Tom, 85
Bain School of Arts and Language
  (Wisconsin), 188
Baird, Kevin, 30, 217, 248
Baker, Vaughn, 117–119, 122, 123
Balboa, Rocky, 76–77
Ballistic Missile Defense
  System, 27, 28
Banks County School System
  (Georgia) shooting [August
  2012], 116
Barrett, Frank, 226, 227
Basal ganglia, 45
Beerens, Dan, 156
Behaviors
  contagion effect of emotional
    deregulation, 110, 144–145

educating the heart-brain
    connection to, 147–149
  immediate positive feedback
    reinforces, 218–219
  Jamel and Jamie's experience
    with deregulated,
    142–143, 144
  leadership strategies for
    producing positive, 219
  See also School safety
Benavides, Denise, 3
Benden, Mark, 184–185,
    186, 189, 198
Benke, David, 118, 119
Bereens, Dan, 3
Biblical aphorisms, 46
Bim, Mara Richards,
    124–125
Biostrap, 100
Black River charter school
    (Michigan), 158
Blessen, Karen, 69, 70, 127
Blue Zones Challenge for Teachers
    strategy, 204
Blue Zones program (Fort
    Worth), 190
Blue Zones study (National
    Geographic), 189–190, 204
Bodies
  how secrets can create war zones
    in our, 34–35
  how sleep-deprivation
    affects, 171–173
  James's story on obesity,
    182–184
  Michelle's experience with
    chronic disease, 42–45, 47

teacher training on emotional
and body-based work, 40–41
See also Brain
Bono, 113
Book Barn Raising
(MindShift), 50–51, 52
Boyle, Deborah, 14
Brady, Tom, 95, 97, 98
Brain
central nervous system (CNS)
and, 86, 108, 111, 143–144
central nervous system (CNS)
and the, 86
chaos in the brain build chaos
through community,
143–144
"Default Mode Network"
(DMN) and cycle of
rumination, 44, 45
how movement provides increased
blood flow to the, 186–187
how sleep-deprivation affects
the body and the, 171–173
improved learning through
getting more sleep for
the, 173–180
"mindlessness" and negative
thinking patterns of, 173
nudging your, 215–216
nutrition, diet, and, 184
parasympathetic nervous system
(PNS) and the, 25, 28, 97,
127, 145, 147
positive effects of physical
education for the, 201
risk of the sleep–
deprived, 177–178

sympathetic nervous system
(SNS), 25, 28, 44, 97, 112, 145
See also Bodies
Brain fatigue, 96
Brain scans
of healthy brains and brains with
ADHD, 44–45
showing chronic stress, trauma,
and abuse impact, 143
showing "ring of fire," 143
SPECT, 44–45, 143
Brand stories, 78
Bregman, Alex, 95
Brontë, Charlotte, 142
Brown, John Seely, 227
Brown, Jon, 158
Buddha, 194
Built environment
changing North Rowan High
School, 210–212
Design-Bid-Build (DBB) tradi-
tionally used in, 138
how the community is impacted
by, 222–223
LEED Certification for
commercial, 132, 136
May Clinic Children's
Center, 212–213
Publicolor approach
to, 213–215
"Safety Culture" of, 127
twenty-first-century project
approach to, 138–139
See also Construction;
Environment; Gardens;
School construction/
design; Spaces

Bulldog Tech, 191
Burke Harris, Nadine, 38–39
Burnout
    conditions leading to, 150
    non-caring due to teacher,
        14
    relational fractures from chronic
        stress and, 21
    See also Stress
Buzzispace, 211

C
Cab companies, 228
Canyon View High School, 110,
    119–121, 218, 219
Career and Technology Center
    (CTE), 104
Caregiver's dilemma, 17–18
Caring
    educating the heart for,
        150
    heart-to-heart communication
        results in, 153–154
    teacher disengagement due to
        non-caring instead of, 14
    teacher-student relationship
        with non-caring vs., 14
Carpenter, Margaret, 188
Carpenter, Ryan W., 143
Carroll Daniel Construction,
    122
Carstarphen, Meria ("Dr. C"),
    73
Cat hair contagion
    Dringenberg's experiment on
        rat learning and fear of,
        24–25

finding solutions for students
    with, 25–26
mandatory testing requirement
    as school, 189
Michelle's "Default Mode
    Network" (DMN) as her, 45
C.A.V.E. (Consistently, Virtually,
    Against, Everything)
    dwellers, 20–21
Center for Green Schools, 132
Centers for Disease
    Control (CDC), 87
Centers of Excellence, 249
Centers of Health, 249
Central nervous system (CNS)
    abuse and trauma create chaos
        in the, 143
    controls child's capacity for
        learning, 86
    education's neglect of the
        learning role of, 144
    remembering that teachers
        are also subject to their,
        108
    should be considered a driver of
        healthy schools, 111
CF Stinson textiles, 211
*Change Your Space, Change Your
    Culture* (Miller), 210
Character Strong, 104
Charlie (long-time colleague),
    47
Chetty, Raj, 87–89
Chiarchiaro, Peter, 7
Chicken Fat record, 200
Chick-fil-A franchise
    model, 233–234

Child abuse and neglect
ACEs (adverse childhood experiences) or, 38–39, 73–76, 142–143, 144
ACE study on ACE assessment and findings, 39
DaVerse Lounge helping to rewrite ACE stories, 73–76
emotional dysregulation as result of, 143
trauma is now a classroom norm, 40–41
Childhood Development Institute (CDI)
childhood window focus of, 86
deep design approach taken by, 83–84
Early Learning Center (CDI), 82–83
origins and early development of, 80–82
reaching out to parents, 110
Childhood obesity
increasing rate of, 198
James's story on, 182–183
TIME Magazine's article (2017) on, 184
Childre, Doc, 147
Children
ACEs (adverse childhood experiences) of, 38–39
Mayo Clinic's use of Evidence Based Design (EBD) for, 212–213
providing strategies for overcoming amygdala hijack, 31
See also Students

Chinn, Carl, 117–119
CHOICE high school, 234–235
Choices
how nudging can influence our, 215–216
how we make our, 216–217
the six pillars to effective nudges toward, 218–219
Christakis, Nicholas, 144–145, 187
A Christmas Story performance (Holland High School), 157–158
Chronic disease
association between obesity and, 196–198
Blue Zones study identifying communities with less, 189–190, 204
Cleveland Clinic's approach to reducing employee, 194–196
"living younger" approach to managing, 195
Michelle Miller's story on managing her, 42–45, 47, 142, 153
type two diabetes, 183
Years of Life Lost (YLL), 39
See also Health
Circadian rhythm shift, 174
CivicLab (Indiana), 161
Classroom battlefield, 239–240
Classroom management
the conventional response-to-intervention approach to, 146
educating the heart-brain connection approach to, 147–149

Classroom management *(continued)*
    greeting ritual role in, 149
    seen through CNS-augmented
        reality glasses, 145–146
Classrooms
    beginning and ending
        rituals, 104
    exploring ways to improve
        teaching math, 169–171
    the hidden costs of maximizing
        time in, 188–189
    mirror the behavior of least
        regulated students, 144–145
    negative contagion effect
        on, 110, 144–145
    90/20 work pattern for taking
        breaks as optimal for, 188
    positive network effects in, 187
Cleveland Clinic, 194–196, 206
CliftonStrengths Assessment, 73
Clinton (Ohio), 155, 156
Colin (ninth-grade student),
    50, 51, 60
Collaborative Social Emotional
    Learning (CASEL) model, 104
Collins, Jim, 13
Columbus Coalition–Building
    Process, 163
The Columbus renewal story
    (Indiana), 161–163
Communication
    hard conversations on school
        safety, 124–127
    how caring comes from
        heart-to-heart, 153–154
    Miranda and Tess's story on
        essential conversations,
        240–249

"Mr. Rogers" formula on,
    154–155
stress conversation project,
    54–60
Communities
    Blue Zones study (National
        Geographic) identifying
        healthy, 189–190, 204
    the Columbus story of
        renewal, 161–163
    "Dunbar's number" for personal
        relationships within, 159
    educating the heart for
        caring, 150
    every school is embedded
        within an existing, 238
    how built environment impact
        surrounding, 222–223
    renewal of Holland
        (Michigan), 156–158
    resiliency and renewal features
        of, 155–156
    resiliency requires a caring, 154
    revillaging your, 159–165
    RISE community garden for
        the, 219–221
    the Roots (coffee shop), 153
    scalable simplicity for renewal
        of, 154–155, 158–159
    social capital within our,
        154–155, 158–159
    social ROI for investing in
        disadvantaged children, 86
    "town squares" heart of,
        156
Compliance system
    ownership vs., 227–228,
        230–232

transition to ownership
from, 235–236
Conflict
James's T-shirt story on,
29–30
Kindergarten student's fear of
her teacher, 28, 29
our new social context
driving, 28–29
Construction
Design-Bid-Build (DBB)
traditionally used in, 138
LEED Certification for
commercial, 132, 136
"Safety Culture" of,
127
twenty-first-century project
approach, 138–139
See also Built environment;
School construction/design
Contagion effect, 110, 144–145
Coppell, Texas, ISD, 135–136
Cortisol, 18, 100
Cosgrove, Toby, 203
Council of Youth Fitness
(1956), 199, 200, 201–202
Cowboy Yogi, 243–244
Cozolino, Lou, 13, 21, 238, 249
Crowley School District, 190
Cry Havoc Theater Company
(Dallas), 124, 127
Culture
avoidance of failure is a
fear-based, 232
how ownership culture works in
accountability, 232–233
New Jump's experience with
rebuilding their, 6–7

ownership vs. compliance,
227–228, 230–232
See also School culture
Culture circles, 104
Cummins Diesel, 161

D
Dallas ISD schools, 69, 71
Dallas Teachers Speak exhibition,
69–71
Daniel, Britt, 121, 122
Dan (math teacher),
169–171
Dass, Ram, 153, 159
Davidson, Harley, 78
DaVinci School, 191
Davis, Brian, 157
Davis, Miles, 225
Dead Poets Society (film), 3
Decision making
how nudges influence,
215–216, 218–219
how we make our
choices, 216–217
Deep sleep (slow wave sleep or
SWS), 172, 176–177
*Deep Work: Rules for Focused
Success in a Distracted World*
(Newport), 188
Deer Creek Middle School
(Littleton, Colorado), 118
Default mastery, 16–17
"Default Mode Network"
(DMN), 44, 45
Delos, 214–215
Dementia, 47
Denison, Marilyn, 4, 135–136
Dettmann, Page, 149

Diet and nutrition, 43,
    45, 182–184
Disadvantaged children
    ACEs (adverse childhood
        experiences), 38–39, 73–76,
        142–143, 144
    importance of invest-
        ing in, 85–87
    social ROI for investing in, 86
    WHOLE Project for healing
        broken and, 105–107
Discovery High School
    (Washington), 218
Distributive Leadership
    Model, 231
District 203 (Illinois), 204–205
Dominquez, Assistant Principal, 38
Door Dash, 228
Dopamine, 18, 68, 96
Dreams (REM sleep), 177
Dringenberg, Hans, 24
Dunbar, Robin, 159
"Dunbar's number," 159
Dweck, Carol, 175–176

E
Early childhood education
    earnings gains ROI of
        investing in, 87
    importance of investing
        in, 85–87
    as linchpin to American
        Dream, 88–89, 155
    Momentous Institute's focus
        on, 86, 89–90
Early Learning Center
    (CDI), 82–83

Education
    current system designed "against
        learning," 62
    as gathering place for heroes,
        3–4, 238
    importance of investing in
        disadvantaged children,
        85–87
    "neurological duplication
        process" of, 16
    ownership model of, 230–231
    physical education (PE),
        199–206
    See also Learning
Education system
    demands outstripping capacity
        of the, 104–105
    need to adapt to modern
        needs, 108
    setting up teachers to fail,
        94
Ego
    TUI (teaching under the
        influence) of, 248
    as your enemy, 244
Eisenhower, Dwight, 199
Emerging Teacher Institute
    (UNTD), 71–72
Emily's story, 56, 57–59
Emja, Susan, 38
Emotional dysregulation
    of both Jamel and
        Jamie, 142, 143, 144
    the contagion effect
        of, 110, 144–145
    description and causes of,
        143

Emotional pain
  how secrets create, 34–35
  postcard experiment on sending
    out secrets and, 35
  the power of releasing
    secrets and, 35
  of teachers who absorb pain of
    students' trauma, 36–41
Emotional resilience, 150
Emotional safety
  building a foundation of, 150
  watching out for others',
    150–151
Emotional self-regulation
  coherence and incoherence
    impact, 149–150
  educating the heart-brain
    connection for, 147–149
  imparting as part of school
    culture, 164
Emotional spaces
  process of stepping into,
    126–127
  process when walking into
    potentially traumatic, 127
Emotions
  coherence and incoherence
    impacting, 149–150
  "dysregulated," 142, 143,
    144–145
  educating the heart-brain con-
    nection to, 147–149
  See also Fear
Employees
  C.A.V.E. (Consistently, Virtually,
    Against, Everything)
    dwellers, 20

Cleveland Clinic's approach to
    increasing health of, 194–196
  moving from engagement to
    disengagement, 20–21
Endorphins, 96
Enos, the space chimp
    (scrapbook), 11–12
Environment
  Green Bronx Machine, 221–222
  RISE community garden,
    219–221
  See also Built environment
Environmental Protection Agency
    (EPA), 203
Erwin, Chris, 116, 118, 123, 129
Evidence Based Design
    (EBD), 212–213
Evidence Based Medicine
    (EBM), 212

F
Faber, John ("Jay"), 44–45, 143
Faith-Based Security Network,
    117
Fallows, Deborah, 155–156
Fallows, James, 122, 155–156
Fear
  amygdala hijack resulting
    in, 26–28
  avoidance of failure is
    based on, 232
  cat hair contagion metaphor
    for, 24–26, 45, 189
  Dringenberg's experiment on
    rat learning and, 24–25
  fight, flight, Freeze, reactions
    to, 25, 245

Fear *(continued)*
  moving to feeling safe
    instead of, 249
  murder of 6-year-old Adam
    Walsh creating, 201
  as real villain against school
    safety, 129
  sense of ownership replaces
    accountability, 233
  story of Kindergarten girl full of,
    28, 29
  students' sense of fear
    increased by "hardening"
    schools, 26, 30
  students with fear of failure, 20
  Tess's story on overcoming
    her, 243–244
  TUI (teaching under the
    influence) of, 248
  See also Emotions; Fight-or-
    flight trigger
Federer, Roger, 97
Feedback culture, 219
Feedback reinforcement, 218–219
Field hospitals metaphor, 106–108,
  110–112, 113
Fight, flight, Freeze, reactions,
  25, 245
Fight-or-flight trigger
  description of the, 32
  schools have their own, 32
  See also Fear
The Five Dysfunctions of a Team
  (Lencioni), 164
Five essentials, 111
Forbes healthcare industry article
  (2018), 194

401K enrollment nudge, 216
Francis, Pope, 107–108
Franklin, Ben, 46
Frasure, Darius, 73
Freedom Middle School, 240–241
Frickey, Lynn, 3
Froebel Gifts blocks, 113

G
Gadsden School District
  (Alabama), 188
Gainesville (Georgia) community
  ethos, 122
Gallup
  APS' partnership with, 73
  fifth–twelfth grade students
    engagement survey, 19
  findings on importance of
    teachers, 12
  teacher disengagement
    surveys, 5–6, 12, 17
  Teacher Wellbeing Index
    (2018), 9
Gandhi, Mahatma, 127
Gardens
  Green Bronx Machine,
    221–222
  RISE community
    garden, 219–221
  See also Built environment
Gasko, John
  on changing mental health
    framework to building
    wholeness, 110
  on "Default Mode Network"
    (DMN) and cycle of
    rumination, 44, 45

on education's neglect of CNS
role in learning, 144

equating washing our hands to
providing emotional support
to teachers, 46

his concern for teachers,
71

introduction to, 3

on number of students exposed
to trauma, 26

process of re-centering and
reactivating PNS, 127

on schools serving as field
hospitals, 106–108, 113

on Singapore schools'
PULSE and Living Room
spaces, 111–112

on teachers as "human shields," 36

on teacher training to handle
classroom stress, 40–41

TIME Magazine cover story
(September 2018) con-
cerns by, 69

Georgia Gwinnett College, 121

Gibson, William, 161

"Glitter" (settle your) practice, 31,
90, 245, 246, 247

Golden, Arthur, 24

"Golden gut" leaders, 225–226

GoNoodle.com, 203

Goodbye, Mr. Chips (film), 3

Google
psychological safety
research by, 164

revenue of, 6

system that franchises schools
discussion with, 233

Graham, Tessa, 81–82, 84

Green Bronx Machine, 221–222

Green movement, 132

Green Standards/Wells Fargo, 211

Greenville (South Carolina), 156

Greeting rituals, 149

"Grit" research, 176

H

Habits
"Settle Your Glitter," 31, 90,
245, 246, 247

simple aphorisms on developing good, 46

Hadid, Zaha, 131

Hagel, John, 227

Haleigh (student), 50, 51, 60, 175

"Hall of the Future" (Momentous
Institute), 68

Hamilton District Christian
School (Ontario), 155

Hamilton District Schools
(Michigan), 158

Hamilton High School
(Holland, Michigan)
"Book Barn Raising" gathering
at, 51

Emily's story as student
of, 56, 57–59

sleep survey of students
at, 175–176

stress conversation project
at, 54–60

Hard conversations on school
safety, 124–127

Harden schools, 26, 30

Haworth, G.W., 157

Haworth, Inc., 156, 157

Haworth, Matthew, 156, 158

Head Start programs, 87

Healing through learning, 250

Health
  Cleveland Clinic's commitment
    to employee, 194–196, 206
  making schools into
    Centers of, 249
  mental, 109–110
  obesity and childhood obesity as
    threat to, 182–184, 196–198
  physical fitness for, 203–205
  See also Chronic disease; Physical
    education (PE)

Healthcare crisis
  Forbes article (2018) on the, 194
  reducing Cleveland Clinic's
    chronic disease of employees,
    194–196

Healthy buildings concept,
  132–133

The Healthy Workplace Nudge
  (Miller), 188

HeartMath Institute, 147

Heart rate variability (HRV)
  the heart-brain connection
    to, 147–149
  HRV studies on stressed-out vs.
    calm teachers, 147–148
  measuring either resiliency or
    stress, 96–99, 100, 149

Heckman, James J., 80, 85,
  86, 87, 88

Heifetz, Ronald A., 158

Henry J. Kaiser Family
  Foundation, 186

Hero's Journey, 61–62

Hess, Jack, 161

High Tech High (San
  Diego), 30, 119

Hinckson, Erica, 183

Holland Christian High School
  (Michigan), 158

Holland District Schools
  (Michigan), 158

Holland High School
  (Michigan), 157–158

Holland (Michigan), 156

Holland Summit (MindShift)
  Book Barn Raising during
    the, 50–51, 52
  Jos Tankersley's storytelling
    presentation, 52–53
  storytelling project during the,
    54
  stress conversation project
    during, 54–60
  student stress survey taken
    during the, 54–57

Holmes-Winn, Kristin, 99

The Hope Circuit
  (Seligman), 109–110

Hormone thermostat, 18–19

Hospitals
  Mayo Children's Center
    design, 212–213
  usual environment
    found in, 212

Hucul, Rachel, 3

Hu, Dr., 42

Humanizing the Education Machine
  (Latham, Cahill, and
  Miller), 14, 20

Humphreys, Robert, 43
Hypoglycemia, 183

I
IED (Improvised Explosive
    Devices), 239
Inclusiveness teaching, 104
Inflammation
    optic neuritis, 42, 44
    removing foods that con-
        tribute to, 45
    Wall Diet to reduce, 43
"Inside the box" approach, 232
Interface flooring, 211
International Association of
    Functional Neurology, 43
International WELL Building
    Institute (IWBI), 133–134
Isabel (tutored student), 59

J
Jamel and Jamie's story,
    142–143, 144
James, Lebron, 97
James's obesity story, 182–183
James's T-shirt conflict story,
    29–30
Jan (first-grade teacher), 142, 144
Jekyll, Gertrude, 219
Jernigan, Jeff, 9, 149, 150
Jess's culture story, 7
Jimmy (rancher), 243–244, 246, 247
Jobs, Steve, 77
Joel, Billy, 172
Joe's culture story, 7–8
Jovi, La Justicera comic
    (UNTD), 71–72, 127

K
Kahneman, Daniel, 215, 217
Kaiser Family Foundation, 186
Kastrounis, Chantel Renea, 136
Kennedy, John F., 200, 201, 204
Kim, Charlie, 6, 7, 8
Kindergarten student's fear
    story, 28, 29
Kinder, Michelle, 3, 24, 89
Kinney, Taryn, 135, 136, 137
Kintsugi (Japanese art form),
    105–106, 249–250
Korean War, 199
Kostoryz School, 191
Kuhn, Thomas S., 103

L
Lander, Jessica, 26
La Sierra High School
    (California), 200
Latham, Bill, 13, 14–16, 18, 20, 99
Lawson, Cara, 125–126
Leader in Me, 104
Leaders
    "golden gut" of, 225–226
    "inside the box" approach by,
        232
    learning to improvise, 226–227
    managing emotional journey of
        their organizations, 235–236
    need for bold physical
        fitness, 203
    PUSH vs. PULL model followed
        by, 227–228
    strategies for producing positive
        behaviors, 219
    Walkthroughs by, 230–231, 233

Leadership model
  compliance versus ownership,
    227–228, 230–232
  distributive, 231
Learning
  central nervous system (CNS)
    controls capacity for
    structured, 86
  economic development lens of
    early, 86–87
  education system designed
    "against," 62
  experiment on rats and fear
    impact on, 24–25
  Gutenberg-era vs. natural
    ecosystem of, 20
  healing power of, 249–250
  healthy school buildings ROL
    (return on learning), 132
  iatrogenic nature of, 63
  "iterative" process of, 62
  natural ecosystem, 19–20
  PBL (project-based learning),
    11–12, 13, 14
  rats play as part of their, 24
  sleep as silver bullet for
    student, 173–180
  social and emotional learning
    (SEL), 40, 69
  students who are not ready
    for, 104, 105, 144, 249
  See also Education
Learning disabilities
  national percentage of students
    struggling with, 187
  stress and stigma often lead to, 39
  See also ADHD

"The Learning Flywheel,"
    13, 18
LEED Certification, 132, 136
Lee Elementary (Texas), 135–138,
    159–160, 218, 219
Lee, Ingrid Fetell, 209
Legionnaire's disease, 131
Lencioni, Patrick, 164
Les Misérables, 58
Little Hawks preschool (Holland,
    Michigan), 158, 190
Living Room space (Singapore
    schools), 46, 111–112
"Living younger" patient care,
    195
Lockhart, Laura, 103–105
"Loco parentis," 121–122
Loehr, Jim, 14
Loncar, Sue, 125–126
Lowe, Mrs., 57–60
Low, Juliette, 38
Low resting heart rate (RHR),
    98
Luke 6:40, 11
Luke (student), 50, 51, 60, 175
Lyft, 228

M
Mahtomedi School District
    (Minnesota), 178
Maltese, Joan, 80–81, 82, 84
Martial arts mastery, 14–16
M*A*S*H (TV show), 107–108
Massachusetts Fusion Study, 118
Mastery, 14–17
Maternal mortality rates
    (mid–1880s), 46

Math class
   Apple Genius bar model set up in, 171
   asking students if they like math, 169–170
   Dan's experiments to improve, 170–171
   online students, 171
Mayo Clinic
   Children's Center of, 212–213
   Resilient Mind Program of, 173
McKeown, Les, 225
McLuhan, Marshall, 211, 250
Media Center (Richard J. Lee Elementary), 218
"Megachurches," 160
Memoirs of a Geisha (Golden), 24
Mental health, 109–110
Mental resilience, 150
Messenger, Meghan, 6
MeTEOR, 100
Mike (coaching client), 225, 226
Mike (first-grade volunteer), 142–143, 144
Miller, J. Irvin, 161, 162
Miller, Lisa, 42, 44, 45, 142, 153
Miller, Michelle, 42–45, 47, 142, 153
Miller, Nathan, 45
Mind-Body Initiative (Mayo Clinic), 96
Mindful breathing, 31
Mindfulness training, 104
"Mindlessness," 173

MindShift
   "Don't wait for permission" philosophy at, 250
   Holland Summit and Book Barn Raising, 50–57
   HRV sensors research engaged in by, 100
   Kintsugi art as metaphor of the WHOLE Project, 105–107, 249–250
   stories and information collected by, 52–54
   team members sharing their struggles, 47
   telling the story of heroic teachers, 3–4
   using technology to measure workplace stress, 95, 96
Mine-Resistant Ambush Protection (MRAP), 239
Miranda and Tess's story, 240–249
Momentous Institute (Dallas)
   creating engaging experiences for their students, 191
   culture of Social and Emotional Health at, 240
   early childhood education focus of, 86, 89–90
   "Hall of the Future" in, 68
   helping students to imagine their future, 68–69
   imparting self-regulation as part of culture, 164
   reaching out to parents, 110
   scalable simplicity discussion at, 154
   staircase of growth at, 90

teaching students how to
de-escalate tension, 31
video on settling the glitter,
245
Moore, Diana, 189
"More Than Half of Kids May Be
Obese by 35" article (2017)
[*Time Magazine*], 184
The Motivation Factor
(documentary), 200
Movement (body), 186–187
Mr. Holland's Opus (film), 3
"Mr. Rogers" formula, 154–155
"Muck farming" (Holland,
Michigan), 51
Multiple sclerosis (MS), 42, 47
Myers, Joseph, 159

N
Nathan, Tyler, 45
National Center for Biotechnology
Information (NCBI), 39
National Center for Education
Statistics, 209
National Geographic's Blue Zones
study, 189–190, 204
National Institute of Neurological
Disorders and Stroke,
43
National Institutes of Health's school
start time study, 178–179
National Renewable Energy
Laboratory (Colorado), 137
National University for Health
Sciences, 43
A Nation at Risk report, 201

Natural ecosystem of
learning, 19–20
N.E.A.T. (Non-Exercise Activity
Thermogenesis), 189–190,
199
Neighborhood Partners in
Action, 84
Netflix, 228
New Holland Brewery, 157
New Jump, 6–7
Newport, Cal, 188
Next Jump leadership academy
(New York City, 2018), 6
90/20 work pattern, 188
Nobles, Sandy, 89
No Child Left Behind Schools test
requirements, 188–189
Non-English-speaking families,
107
Non-Exercise Activity
Thermogenesis
(N.E.A.T.), 189–190, 199
Norms of behavior, 219
North Korean People's Army
(NKPA), 199
North Park Elementary (San
Bernardino), 122
North Rowan High School
(North Carolina),
210–212
Not ready to learn, 104,
105, 144, 249
Nowlin, Principal, 120
NPR poll, 108
Nudges
being nudged toward over-
eating, 215

description of a, 216
the six pillars to effective, 218–219
Nutrition and diet, 43, 45, 182–184

O
Obesity
  association between chronic
    disease and, 196–198
  childhood, 182–184, 198
O'Brien, Amanda, 189, 190
OFS Furniture, 211
Online math students, 171
Optic neuritis, 42, 44
Orange County Classroom
    Teachers Association, 189
Ortiz, Mrs. ("Mrs.
    O"), 183–184, 187
Oura rings, 100
*Our Kids: The American Dream in
    Crisis* (Putnam), 28–29, 155
Our Towns (Fallows and
    Fallows), 155–156
Outdoor Discovery Center's
    "Little Hawks Program"
    (Michigan), 19–20
"Outside the box" approach,
    232
"Over-training syndrome," 96
Ownership
  Chick-fil-A franchise model
    of, 233–234
  compliance vs., 227–228,
    230–232
  ownership model of educa-
    tion, 230–231
  point of excellence creating
    ecosystem of, 234–235

requirements for transition from
    compliance to, 235–236
Oxytocin, 18

P
Parasympathetic nervous
    system (PNS)
  helps body to recover from
    stress, 25, 97
  how it decelerates the
    heart rate, 147
  imagine a teacher who can
    "see," 145
  process of re-centering and
    reactivating, 127
  society reflects the tension
    between SNS and, 28
  See also Brain
Parents
  school's "loco parentis"
    responsibility to act in place
    of, 121–122
  schools that reach out to, 110–112
Passion
  Emily's story on finding
    her, 57–59
  for learning and collaborate
    growth of passion, 57, 59
Passion code, 58
"The Passion Code" (Colin,
    Haleigh, and Luke), 51–52
Paying attention. *See* Attention
PBL (project-based learning),
    11–12, 13, 14
Perceived Stress Scale, 109
PERMA study, 149
Physical breaks, 187–189

Physical education (PE)
  Council of Youth Fitness
    era (1956) and, 199,
    200, 201–202
  District 203 (Illinois) approach
    to, 204–205
  perfect storm for
    decline of, 201
  positive effects of, 201
  as strategic initiative to national
    security, 199–201
  why it is more important than
    ever, 202–203
  See also Health
Physical fitness
  Blue Zones Challenge for
    Teachers strategy, 204
  GoNoodle.com resources to
    help with, 203
  need for bold leadership
    for, 203
  reimagining physical education
    for lifelong, 204–205
Physical resilience, 150
The Piano Man (song),
  172
Pink, Daniel, 187–188
Pirsig, Robert M., 240, 245
A Place Called Home (APCH)
  [Los Angeles], 219, 221
Pluse space (Singapore
  schools), 46, 111–112
Post-Traumatic Strengths
  Syndrome, 149
Post-Traumatic Stress
  Syndrome (PTSD)
  Charlie's struggle with, 47

soldiers and sailors remaining in
    battle mode due to, 5
  study on active duty soldiers
    with PERMA vs., 149
  See also Stress
Preczewski, Stas, 121, 123
Prefrontal cortex, 31
Prescott Junior High
  (California), 200, 203
Priestly vocation, 107–108
Prince, Ed, 157
Privilege, 104
Professional sports
  Alex Bregman's home runs due
    to improved sleep habits,
    95
  comparing strain of teaching to
    level of, 99–101
  the Tom Brady effect of restored
    vitality, 98–99
Psychological safety
  amygdala hijack due to
    threats to, 26–28
  cat hair contagion metaphor for
    loss of, 24–26, 45, 189
  hardening our schools erodes
    student sense of, 26, 30
  importance of providing,
    164
Publicolor, 213–215
PULL model of leadership,
  227–228
Purpose Built Schools Atlanta,
  110
PUSH model of leadership,
  227–228
Putnam, Robert, 28–29, 155, 156

Q

Quality of Life Years (QALY), 198
Questions
to ask about schools and
teachers, 113
asking students if they like
math, 169–170
leading to different lines of
inquiry, 114
Sleep Audit, 179–180

R

Rapid–eye–movement (REM), 177
Rats
Dringenberg's experiment on fear
impact on learning of, 24–25
play as part of their learning, 24
Real Age assessment, 195
Reality
lessons about life through expo-
sure to, 20
Outdoor Discovery Center's
"Little Hawks Program"
exposure to, 19–20
Recess, 187–189
Recovery SNS response, 25
The Red Queen (_Alice's Adventures
in Wonderland_), 105
Reed (coaching client), 225–226
Reilly, Katie, 67
Relational cleansing, 47
Renaissance Festival (Waxahachie,
Texas), 45
Resiliency
building martial arts, 15
Dweck's study on
"grit" and, 176

four different types of, 150
heart rate variability (HRV) as
sign of, 96–99, 100, 149
improving sleeping patterns to
improve, 98–99
mental health framework on
building, 110
Miranda and Tess's story on
rebuilding, 240–249
moving from being fragile
to, 249
Our Towns identifying
communities with renewal
features and, 155–156
physical, 150
requires a caring community,
154
self-management and energy
utilization to sustain, 149–150
Resilient Mind Program (Mayo
Clinic), 173
Returns on learning (ROL), 132
Revillaging
Columbus (Indiana), 161–163
description of and steps
in, 159–161
Revillaging steps
1. secure stakeholder
engagement, 161–162
2. discover the what, why, how,
and who, 162–163
3. trust the process, 163
4. build safety, 164
5. impart self-regulation, 164
Richard J. Lee Elementary
(Texas), 135–138, 159–160,
218, 219

Richey, Will, 126–127
Rideshare, 228
RISE community garden,
    219–221
RISE School, 191, 219
Ritz, Stephen, 221–222
Riverside Military
    Academy, 121–122
Robert's culture story, 8
Robertson, Tina, 89
Robinson, Ken, 20
Roizen, Michael, 194–195,
    196, 197, 203
Roots (coffee shop), 153
Rosenstock, Larry, 30, 119
Rumination cycle, 44
Running on empty, 247–248
Russell, John, 78

S
"Safety Culture," 127–129
Safety. *See* School safety
Sally's story, 186
San Bernardino (California),
    156
Sandy Hook Elementary School
    shooting, 124–127
Sarasota Middle School
    (Florida), 149, 191, 218
Scalable simplicity, 154–155,
    158–159
"Scapegoat Brand," 76
Schmidt, David, 119–120
School 55 (Bronx), 221–222
School administrators
    providing support to teachers,
        36–41, 46, 100–101, 240

understanding how new teach-
    ers feel overwhelmed,
    37–38
School construction/design
    changes in the twenty-first-
        century project approach
        to, 138–139
    importance of a well-
        designed, 209–210
    importance of well-designed
        environment, 209–210
    Lee Elementary (Texas) example
        of WELL Building, 135–138,
        159–160
    moving from Green to WELL
        buildings, 132–133
    North Rowan High School
        (North Carolina), 210–212
    things you can begin to do
        now to shift to WELL
        Buildings, 139
    WELL Building strategies
        for, 133–135
    See also Built environment;
        Construction
School culture
    building a "Safety Culture" as
        part of, 127–129
    creating hostile climate for
        learning drives, 19
    imparting self-regulation as part
        of the, 164
    implications of New Jump's
        experience with culture
        for, 6–7
    Momentous Institute's Social
        and Emotional Health, 240

real-time feedback culture, 219
See also Culture
Schools
    building a foundation around
        five essentials, 111
    Council of Youth Fitness
        (1956), 199, 200
    creating hostile climate for
        learning drives, 19
    current broken state of, 30
    demanding that students wake
        up too early, 176
    embedded within an existing
        community, 238
    extending their care
        efforts, 109–110
    fight-or-flight trigger of, 32
    "loco parentis" responsibility
        of, 121–122
    making them Centers of
        Health, 249
    National Institutes of Health's
        start time study on,
        178–179
    proposed Chick-fil-A franchise
        model for, 233–234
    providing opportunities for con-
        necting with reality, 19–21
    questions to ask about,
        113–114
    restorative space design of
        Singapore, 46, 110–112
    revillaging your, 159–165
    serving as field hospitals,
        106–108, 110–112, 113
    students' chaos becomes our
        chaos, 143–144

    students' sense of fear increased
        by "hardening," 26, 30
School safety
    building a "Safety Culture"
        for, 127–129
    common traps when developing
        sensible plan for, 123
    fear as the real villain of, 129
    having hard conversations
        about, 124–127
    High Tech High's strategy
        for, 119
    moving to feeling fear to
        feeling safe, 249
    psychological, 24–28, 30, 164
    school shootings, 116
    strategies taken by three
        different schools, 119–122
    "The Walking School Bus"
        program (Crowley School
        District) for, 190
    "wicked problems" era
        of, 116–117
    See also Behaviors
School shootings
    Banks County School System
        (Georgia), 116
    Deer Creek Middle School
        (Littleton, Colorado), 118
    fear as the real villain of, 129
    having hard conversations
        about, 124–127
    myths about, 117–119
    Sandy Hook, 124–127
Schulman, John, 16
Schuman, Ruth Lande, 213
Schwartz, David B., 212

Scott, Andrew, 177
Secrets
  creating war zones in our bodies
    and minds, 34–35
  postcard experiment on
    sending, 35
  the power of releasing, 35
  teachers who absorb pain of
    students' trauma and, 36–41
Self-care, 8, 244
Seligman, Martin, 109–110
Semmelweis, Ignaz, 46
"Settle Your Glitter" practice, 31,
  90, 245, 246, 247
Shape of the Nation report
  (2016), 189
Shuman, Ruth Lande, 213
Sick buildings, 131–132
Singapore schools' space design,
  46
Sleep Audit, 179–180
Sleeping patterns
  Alex Bregman's home runs
    increase due to improved,
    95
  circadian rhythm shift, 174
  Dan's experiments to improve
    math teaching, 170–171
  National Institutes of Health's
    start time study findings,
    178–179
  power of sleep and
    dreams, 173–174
  rapid–eye–movement
    (REM), 177
  restoring vitality by
    improving, 98–99

sleep as silver bullet for student
  learning, 173–180
Sleep Audit, 179–180
sleep-deprived brain and
  risk, 177–178
slow wave sleep (SWS) or deep
  sleep, 172, 176–177
students forced to wake up too
  early, 176
student sleep survey findings
  on, 175–176
Slow wave sleep
  (SWS), 172, 176–177
Smith, Angela, 73
Social and emotional learning
  (SEL), 40, 69
Social capital
  building community, 155
  the Columbus story on rebuild-
    ing, 161–163
  moving from isolation to village
    and, 249
  revillaging to rebuild and
    restore, 161–165
  scalable simplicity to
    build, 154–155, 158–159
  when a community loses,
    155
Social emotional literary
  (SEL), 104
Society
  postcard experiment revealing
    emotional pain of our, 35
  reflecting tension between SNS
    and PNS, 28
Sood, Amit, 96, 173
South Korea, 199

Spaces
  emotional, 126–127
  Living Room space (Singapore
    schools), 46, 111–112
  outdoor garden, 219–222
  Pulse space (Singapore
    schools), 46, 111–112
  See also Built environment
Spangler, Angela, 133–135
SPECT brain scans, 44–45, 143
Spiritual resilience, 150
Sraders, Anne, 95
Stand and Deliver (film), 3
Standing desks study (Texas A&M
  University), 184–187
Stanley, Edward, 182
Stanley, Jonathan, 213
Stavoe, Mrs., 11–12, 13, 14
Stories
  Atlanta Public Schools
    (APS), 73, 77
  brand, 78
  collected by MindShift,
    52–54
  Dallas Teachers Speak exhibi-
    tion, 69–71
  DaVerse Lounge helping to
    rewrite ACE, 73–76
  Hero's Journey, 61–62
  Jovi, La Justicera comic
    (UNTD) on teacher super-
    hero, 71–72, 127
  keys to telling, 53–54
  told by *TIME Magazine* cover
    story (September 2018), 67,
    68, 69, 76
Storytelling keys, 53–54

Strain levels
  comparing professional sports to
    teaching, 99–101
  "team dashboard" to
    monitor, 99
  WHOOP wrist strap to measure,
    97–100
Strategos International, 117
Stress
  consequences of teacher, 9–10
  Emily's story on, 56, 57–59
  Gallup's Teacher Wellbeing
    Index (2018), 9
  heart rate variability (HRV)
    measuring resiliency vs.,
    96–99, 100, 149
  John Gasko on training teachers
    to handle classroom, 40–41
  of living in an unpleasant envi-
    ronment, 211
  MindShift's Holland Summit
    student survey on, 54–57
  negative teacher–student rela-
    tionship triggering, 18–19
  relational fractures from
    chronic, 21
  setting up teachers for
    additional, 109
  TUI (teaching under the
    influence) of, 248
  See also Burnout; Post-Traumatic
    Stress Syndrome (PTSD)
Stress assessments
  Ardell Wellness Stress Test, 109
  on Dr. Seligman's Authentic
    Happiness website, 110
  Perceived Stress Scale, 109

Stress conversations
  Hamilton High School student
    project on, 54–60
  steps in designing a, 60–61
  student survey findings on,
    55
Student disengagement
  Gallup's fifth–twelfth grade
    student survey on, 19
  negative teacher–student rela-
    tionship triggering, 18–19
  process of mastering, 16–17
  taking ownership of learning
    marking the spot of, 17–18
Students
  fear of failure destroying creative
    capacities of, 20
  Gallup's fifth–twelfth grade
    student survey on engage-
    ment of, 19
  importance of investing in dis-
    advantaged, 85–87
  living with cat hair conta-
    gion, 25–26, 45
  MindShift's Holland Summit
    survey on stress of, 54–57
  need for more sleep during
    adolescence by, 174
  providing opportunities for con-
    necting with reality, 19–21
  providing strategies for over-
    coming amygdala hijack, 31
  sleep as silver bullet for learning,
    173–180
  social ROI for investing in, 86
  their chaos becomes our
    chaos, 143–144

who are not ready to learn, 104,
    105, 144, 249
  See also Children
Student Services for Keller
    (Texas) ISD, 103
Students with disabilities
  ADHD, 173, 184–187
  national percentage of, 187
Suicide
  Chris Erwin on his schools'
    response to student, 129
  losing students to, 117
  studies on in-school vio-
    lence of, 122
  Sue Loncar on her daughter's,
    125–126
Summer Design Studio
    Program, 213–214
Suprachiasmatic nucleus, 174
Sustainability
  changes in the twenty-first-
    century project approach
    to, 138–139
  Lee Elementary (Texas) example
    of WELL Building, 135–138,
    159–160
  moving from Green to WELL
    buildings, 132–133
  things you can begin to do
    now to shift to WELL
    Buildings, 139
  WELL Building strategies
    for, 133–135
Suzanne Tick Design, 213
Sympathetic nervous system (SNS)
  how increased demands impact
    the teachers', 112

how it affects the heart rate, 145
Michelle's story on experiencing
   chronic stress of, 44
response to stress by the, 25, 97
society reflects the tension
   between PNS and, 28

T

Tahoma High School
   (Washington), 218
Tankersley, Joe, 53, 56, 61, 62
Tarkett, 213–214
Teacher absence category, 21
Teacher athletes
   comparing strain of professional
      sports to strain on, 99–101
   heart rate variability (HRV)
      of, 96–99, 100
   "over-training syndrome," 96
   providing quality of care to
      our, 93–96
Teacher disengagement
   caregiver's dilemma and, 17–18
   at center of school performance
      debate, 5–6
   Gallup surveys on, 5–6, 12, 17
   teachers at risk for, 108–109
   TIME Magazine cover story
      (September 2018) photos
      showing, 67, 68, 69, 76
   when caring becomes non-
      caring, 14
Teacher physicians, 112–113
Teacher round tables, 104
Teachers
   Blue Zones Challenge for
      Teachers strategy, 204

C.A.V.E. (Consistently, Virtually,
   Against, Everything)
   dwellers, 20–21
Dallas Teachers Speak exhibition
   reclaiming the narrative,
   69–71
education system setting them
   up to fail, 94
feeling overwhelmed, 37–38
as heroes, 3–4, 238
HRV studies on stressed-out vs.
   calm, 147–148
Jovi, La Justicera comic (UNTD)
   on superhero, 71–72
"the Learning Flywheel" experience with excellent, 13, 18
Mrs. Stavoe example of the
   permanent influence
   of, 11–12, 13, 14
questions to ask about, 113–114
at risk, 108–109
scalable simplicity at work
   for, 154–155
"Scapegoat Brand" of, 76
story of Kindergarten girl afraid
   of her, 28, 29
Teacher support
   equating washing our hands to
      creating, 46
   John Gasko on training to handle
      classroom stress, 40–41
   Miranda and Tess's story
      on, 240–249
   need for emotional hygiene,
      36–41
   need for self-care as part
      of, 8, 244

Teacher support *(continued)*
  need to provide emotional,
    38–39, 100–101, 240
Teacher–student relationships
  consequences of a caring/
    non-caring, 14
  flywheel experience and
    healthy, 18
  survival triggers stimulated by
    negative, 18–19
Teaching
  the art of motorcycle mainte-
    nance and, 240–241
  as a dangerous occupation, 238
  "dying" to, 242–243
  make room for joy and play as
    part of, 246–247
  math, 169–171
  Miranda and Tess's story on
    essential conversations
    about, 240–249
  running on empty, 247–248
  "Settle Your Glitter" practice, 31,
    90, 245, 246, 247
Tebo, Dave, 51, 54, 60, 175
Tess and Miranda's story,
    240–249
"Tess Tales," 247
Test scores
  No Child Left Behind Schools
    test mandate on, 188–189
  physical education's decline and
    focus on, 201
Texas A&M University's standing
    desks study, 184–187
Thalamus, 45
Thaler, Richard, 216
38th Parallel (Korea), 199

Thoreau, Henry David, 3
Threat assessment protocols, 104
TIME Magazine
  childhood obesity article
    (2017), 184
  cover story on teachers
    (September 2018), 67,
    68, 69, 76
"Town squares," 156
Trauma informed care, 104
Trull, Timothy J., 143
Trust the process, 163
TUI (teaching under the
    influence), 248
Tutoring Center (Emily's story),
    59
Tversky, Amos, 217
29 Pieces, 69
Type two diabetes, 183

U
Uber, 228
Ultradian rhythms, 188
Unconventional warfare, 239
University of North Texas at
    Dallas (UNTD)
  Dringenberg's cat hair conta-
    gion experiment, 24–25
  Emerging Teacher
    Institute of, 71–72
  School of Education, 26
University of North Texas at Dallas
    (UNTD) Summit, 71
Up the Down Staircase (film), 3

V
Valley Nonprofit Resources, 85
Van der Kolk, Bessel, 34, 41

Verlander, Justin, 95, 96, 97
Vincent, Rhonda, 89, 154
Violence. *See* School shootings
Vo, Lam Thuy, 95
Vroonland, David, 3, 229–231, 232, 233–236
VUCA (volatile, uncertain, complex, ambiguous) world, 13

W
Wagner, Joel, 93
Walker, Matthew, 169, 173, 174, 176, 179
"The Walking School Bus" program (Crowley School District), 190
Walkthroughs, 230–231, 233
Wall Diet, 43
Walmart, 6
Walsh, Adam, 201
Warren, Frank, 35
Washing hands habit, 46, 47
WELL Building certification, 133–135
WELL Buildings
  changes in the twenty-first-century project approach to, 138–139

Lee Elementary (Texas) example of, 135–138, 159–160
moving from Green to, 132–133
strategies for schools, 133–135
things you can begin to do now to shift to, 139
visiting Delos (founder of WELL Building Standard), 214–215
When: The Scientific Secrets to Perfect Timing (Pink), 187–188
Wholeness (Kintsugi), 105–106, 249–250
WHOLE Project (MindShift), 105–107
WHOOP wrist strap, 97–100
Why We Sleep (Walker), 173
"Wicked problems" era, 116–117
Williams, Meredith, 210–212
Williams, Phil, 42
Williams, Wynell, 188
W.L. Gore, 159
Workplace health and well-being, 47
World Vision, 30–31

Y
Years of Life Lost (YLL), 39